BOUNDLESS

BOUNDLESS

NATIVE AMERICAN ABUNDANCE IN ART AND LITERATURE

Lisa A. Crossman and Heid E. Erdrich, editors

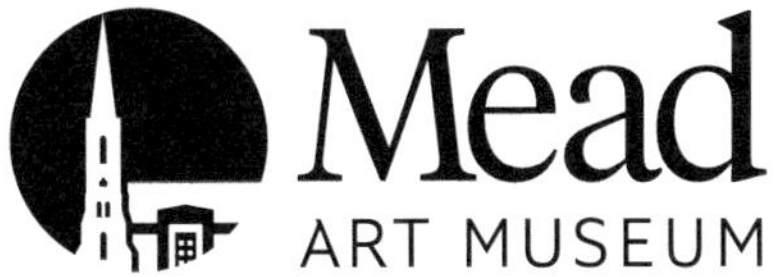

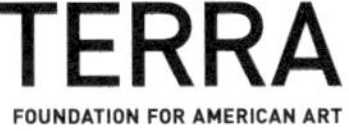

Amherst
College
Press

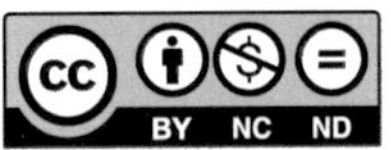

The complete manuscript of this work was subjected to a partly closed ("single-anonymous") review process. For more information, visit https://acpress.amherst.edu/peerreview/.

Published in the United States of America by Amherst College Press
Manufactured in the United States of America

Library of Congress Control Number: 2024941016

DOI: https://doi.org/10.3998/mpub.14513702

ISBN 978-1-943208-83-8 (paper)
ISBN 978-1-943208-84-5 (open access)

Dedication

Boundless acknowledges the Native American people of the Northeast region who have endured and resisted centuries of the genocidal consequences of colonialism starting with European diseases that spread through the hemisphere, and in that aftermath colonial occupation, removal, and displacement.

Northeast culture groups referenced in writing or represented in art in the exhibitions in the Mead Art Museum's galleries included: Brothertown, Mahican, Mohawk, Mohegan, Montauk, Munsee, Narragansett, Niantic, Nipmuc, Onondaga, Penobscot, Seneca, Shinnecock, Wabanaki, Wampanoag, and others. These artists and writers whose work *Boundless* centers are from the present as well as the past, and their creativity ensures that Indigenous people will persist into the future of the Northeast.

Table of Contents

List of Figures

Acknowledgments

Boundless would not have been made possible without the vision and hard work of its guest curator, Heid E. Erdrich. Since 2021, Erdrich has been building an exhibition that embraces its name: BOUNDLESS.

The vast nature of *Boundless*, and its rootedness in relationships and interconnectedness between *all* things, has meant that the list of individuals to thank for their involvement with this project is long and still growing. Furthermore, *Boundless* in its entirety includes not only a two-part exhibition, the main iteration of which was installed across nearly the entire expanse of the Mead, but also a publication, a new Amherst College course and course modules, and a website to share college student research, an audio tour, and a curriculum for grades 3+. We are grateful to each person who invested time, ongoing or brief, including all the artists and authors whose contributions make up the exhibitions and this publication. The list below recognizes individuals and organizations that most directly contributed to the creation of *Boundless*.

Boundless was developed in dialogue with an advisory committee that includes members from the Nipmuc, Wampanoag, Shinnecock, and Mohegan, as well as other communities, and with the support of staff from the Mead Art Museum, Amherst College Archives and Special Collections, the Five Colleges, and Native students. Special thanks to our advisory committee members: Jaime Arsenault, Jacquelyn Cabarrubia ’25, Brandon Castle, Lisa Crossman, Amanda Herman, Elizabeth James-Perry, Mike Kelly, Ellie Kerns ’24, Courtney M. Leonard, Aaron Miller, Emily Potter-Ndiaye, Rachel Beth Sayet, Kimberly Toney, and Kiara Vigil.

As the project spanned collections, we’d like to thank all the staff at the Mead Art Museum and Archives and Special Collections, as well as key Amherst College faculty and Five Colleges staff. In addition to the individuals who worked directly on the *Boundless* project, we must also thank those involved with the formation of Amherst College’s Collection of Native American Literature, which inspired and has remained foundational to the project. Our gratitude extends to Pablo Eisenberg for his assembling of a collection of nearly 1,500 books written by Native American writers, which forms the basis of the collection, and to Younghee Kim-Wait (Class of 1982) for her generous donation that enabled the purchase of Eisenberg's collection in 2013. The collection continues to grow, as explored in Mike Kelly's essay in this publication.

A core group composed of Mike Kelly, Brandon Castle, Kiara Vigil, Emily Potter-Ndiaye, and Lisa Crossman were involved in the early stages of the project's development, and remained central to its evolution. Thanks particularly to the following individuals who shared their expertise, talent, and time: Arts at Amherst Initiative (and coordinators of Bailey Brown House), Chef Melissa Baehr of Indigenous Deliciousness and the team that assisted her in catering the opening reception for the first iteration of the *Boundless* exhibition (Krysia Lycette Villon of Chiqui's Kitchen, Jonathan Baehr, and Monica Weeks), Maghan Baptiste, Lisa Brooks, Bea Cusin, Angela D'Souza, Olivia Feal, Stephen Fisher, Martin Garnar, Carolyn Gennari, Rebecca Henning, Hawk and Lisa Henries, Mila Hruba, Maida Ives and her team at Book & Plow, Justin Lee and his design team, Charlotte Murtishaw, Victoria Nardone, Pyramid Communications, Siddhartha Shah, Genevieve Simermeyer, Mary Strunk, Nicholas Taupier, John Thornbury, Maria Timina, and Chief Cheryll Toney Holley. Without their commitment and efforts, this project would not have been realized. We also thank the students in the Native and Indigenous Students Association at Amherst College, as well as Rhonda Anderson of Ohketeau Cultural Center, David Brule, Chris Couch, and Sandra Matthews.

An important goal of the exhibition was to involve students in all aspects of the project, as part of the advisory committee and research team. The exhibition was supported by academic-year curatorial and research interns: Jacquelyn Cabarrubia '25, Catherine Charnoky '24, Cameron Findlay '23 (Smith College), and Ziji Zhou '25. The Mead summer 2023 curatorial and education interns Isabella Fuster-Crichfield '26, Samuel Nkengla '26, and Max Valdez '24 also worked on projects that supported educational materials and label captions for *Boundless*. The students in Kiara Vigil's fall 2023 course at Amherst College, Indigenous Art and Books: A Boundless Approach to Image and Text, developed resources for the website that extend the project with creativity and connections. We thank these students, Charlotte Abrams '27, Jack Betts '23, Jacquelyn Cabarrubia '25, Courtney Hall '27, Arlo Harrison (Smith College), Mone Kawano '25, Nora Lowe '26, Yasemin Özden, Ellie Stolzoff '27, Adela Thompson Page '26, and Francelia Walsh-Despeignes '24.

Thanks to individuals and institutions that supported loans to the exhibition: Kohar Avakian, Justin Beatty, Brent Michael Davids, Philip J. Deloria, Jeremy Dennis, Historic Deerfield, Sky Hopinka and Broadway Gallery, Elizabeth James-Perry, Jonathan James-Perry, Mount Holyoke College Museum of Art, Smith College Museum of Art, University Museum of Contemporary Art at UMass Amherst, Brittney Peauwe Wunnepog Walley, and the Worcester Historical Museum (including former curator Shelley Cathcart).

This exhibition is made possible through financial assistance from the Terra Foundation for American Art and Five Colleges/NAIS Mellon. The digital curriculum initiative was underwritten in part by Mass Humanities' Expand Massachusetts Stories grant program, which receives support from the Massachusetts Cultural Council. The Native Arts and Cultures Foundation supported an inaugural artist residency as part of *Boundless*.

Tábūtní, kutâputush, pidamaya, nt'oyaxsn, miigwech, thanks!

GROUNDING

1

CURATORIAL STATEMENT

Heid E. Erdrich

The etymology of the word Muhheakunnuk [Mahican], according to the original signifying, is great waters or sea, which are constantly in motion, either flowing or ebbing.

—Hendrick Aupaumut (Mahican), ca.1790[1]

Water actively names the original peoples of what we now call Southern New England. Although English translations vary, the Nipmuc are described as People of the Freshwater; the word Pequot is said to mean the People of the Swamp or People of Shallow Water, the Niantic as People of the Long-Necked Waters because their lands are near a bay; the Narragansett are People of the Point or of the Salt Pond; Shinnecock can be translated to People of the Stony Shore; a meaning for Montauk is given as People of the Sea Coast; the Wampanoag call themselves People of the Morning Light or, like the Wabanaki, People of the Dawnland, meaning the east coast where the sun emerges over the sea.

Water never chooses one path but moves in multiple directions, broadening as it goes. Rivers flowing south find their level at the sea and in that way touch dawn and the setting sun. As I worked on *Boundless*, I felt my way of knowing work like water. I followed the wellspring I found in Amherst College's Collection of Native American Literature, art from the Mead, and work by Native American artists creating today.

Boundless came together organically, elementally, and that element is water. I was carried by words, titles, images, people, voices, histories. I listened to Native people from Massachusetts tell water stories. I considered how water worked into tribal identities: a place of freshwater, a place of moving water, a place of stony shores—all of these are at once a location and the name of its people. Each tribal name is filled with an image, a place, a relationship, a story.

NOTE

1 Bernd C. Peyer, ed., *American Indian Nonfiction: An Anthology of Writings, 1760s–1930s* (Norman: University of Oklahoma Press, 2007), 63.

GROUNDING: EDITORS' NOTES ON THE *BOUNDLESS* PROJECT

> The first string of wampum beads were read,
> "We sent you this to open your eyes."
> The second string is read,
> "That you may see a great way."
> Then the third string is read,
> "That your ears may be opened to hear and fix your hearts
> that you may have a right understanding to what I am going to tell you."
>
> —Sopiel "Selmore" Soctomah, Wampum Keeper for the Passamaquoddy, 1805[1]

The words above greeted visitors entering the *Boundless* exhibitions. The first iteration was a nearly museum-wide installation that filled the Mead Art Museum at Amherst College from August 29, 2023 to January 7, 2024. A second smaller iteration of *Boundless* took place February 27 to July 7, 2024. The words of Soctomah appeared on the glass doors to the galleries and were meant to prepare visitors to read within an art exhibition, as well as comprehend with their other senses, open their hearts, and understand a "great way" of being, told on many levels. The exhibitions and this publication center on telling in books and art produced between 1663 and the present. The project foregrounds ties between Indigenous artistic and literary traditions, incorporating a wide range of materials from Amherst College's Collection of Native American Literature and the Mead. Books and art formed the core of the exhibitions and were joined by key works of art on loan from artists and other institutional and private collections. In these pages, you will find reflections on the process of making *Boundless* along with texts by artists and authors participating in *Boundless*, and documentation and interpretation about the ideas, scope, and content of the exhibitions.

PLACE AND PROCESS

The *Boundless* project is grounded in the importance of place—and human relationship to place. Throughout the project, water describes the curatorial methodology and a connection to the Northeastern region of North America. *Boundless* moves across generations and geographies and expands conversations about kinship, presence, resistance, and history through its flow. The exhibition, the publication, and the collections have evolved over the past few years, alongside the individuals working on the project. The editors and *Boundless* collaborators endeavor to expand on the work of *Boundless* in years to come.

Boundless began with a grant application in 2020 to the Terra Foundation for American Art's initiative to reimagine permanent collections, which outlined a particular interest in art created before 1980. The Mead Art Museum opened in 1950. Amherst College, founded in 1821, began collecting art in the 1850s, in part through the travels of Christian missionaries that sometimes also resulted in the plundering of works like the Assyrian reliefs—now embedded in the walls of the Mead's Kunian Gallery and made part of *Boundless*. The "American" collection of art at the Mead also took shape around gifts from alumni, most initially coming from just a few collectors. Eighteenth- and nineteenth-century portraiture by artists like Thomas Sully, Hudson River School landscape paintings by artists like Thomas Cole, and works by twentieth-century artists from "The Eight," including George Bellows, have often been used by Mead staff to explain the history and highlights of the collection. Among the six thousand or so objects by artists working within what is now the United States, less than half a percent of these works were by Native American artists.

One of the goals of *Boundless* was to intentionally address the limited number of contemporary works by Indigenous artists in the collection, including work by Native artists based in the Northeast, and to do so in relation to Amherst College's Collection of Native American Literature. At the Frost Library, Mike Kelly and staff in Archives and Special Collections have been actively working with professors Lisa Brooks and Kiara Vigil to expand the Kim-Wait/Eisenberg Collection of Native American Literature, delivered to the College in 2013. Efforts to expand Native American and Indigenous studies (NAIS) across the Five Colleges[2] has also been actively underway, reflected, for example, in the NAIS Mellon grant and added efforts to expand curricular ties that were in progress at the Mead in 2020. Thus, *Boundless* sought to build from the abundance of material in the Archives and Special Collections and the work of Indigenous artists and authors in the region. Select works by non-Native artists, including historical portraiture and landscape painting, are interwoven in the exhibitions to provide another context and Indigenous reinterpretation. More on the process of creating *Boundless* and reflections by staff members about our learnings and unlearnings can be found in the Afterword.

PEOPLE

Boundless was developed in dialogue with an advisory committee that includes members from the Nipmuc, Wampanoag, Shinnecock, and Mohegan nations, among other communities, and with the support of Native students and staff from the Five Colleges, Mead Art Museum, and Amherst College Archives and Special Collections—all of whom are thanked by name at the start of this book. Lisa Crossman, Director of Curatorial Affairs at the Mead, in collaboration with Emily Potter-Ndiaye, the Mead's Dwight and Kirsten Poler & Andrew W. Mellon Head of Education and Curator of Academic Programs, and with guidance and support from Kiara Vigil (Dakota from the Sisseton-Wahpeton Oyate), Associate Professor of American Studies and Dean of New Students, and Mike Kelly, Head of Archives and Special Collections, developed the project's initial framework. Brandon Castle (enrolled member of the Ketchikan Indian Community and descendant of the Tsimshian Peoples), Project Coordinator, Mapping Native Intellectual Networks of the Northeast, joined the project in 2021 with the start of his position at Amherst College.

The exhibitions were researched and organized by writer and independent curator Heid E. Erdrich, who is Ojibwe. Erdrich began work on the project in 2021, establishing the advisory committee with support from the project's core team and serving as the guiding force for all aspects of the project. The online curriculum developed alongside the exhibition was written by Genevieve Simermeyer (Osage) and overseen by the Mead's then manager of experiential learning and K–12 programs, Olivia Feal, with design work by Carolyn Gennari.

PUBLICATION

This publication, like the exhibitions, reflects an expanding network of connections, relationships, and what we have learned collectively. The publication includes contributions by artists and authors whose work was included in the exhibitions, essays that reflect the breadth of knowledge and learnings of the advisory committee members (and one of the student curatorial interns), curatorial notes, and poems by Indigenous writers with ties to the Five Colleges area. The selection of contributions was guided by the vision of *Boundless*, which was rooted in place and Native presence in the Northeast. The exhibitions were temporary and the publication offers an experience of the exhibition—a document, a reflection on the process of creating the exhibition, and a resource for continued engagement with the Collection of Native American Literature and the Mead Art Museum's collections, as well as with the artists, writers, and scholars whose words and images are included in this compilation.

This publication includes works from a variety of sources and in a diverse array of styles and formats as chosen by the authors. Most of the essays, poems, and stories have never been published in print before, but a few were previously published in limited formats such as blogs, or are reprints of works now in the public domain. We have retained the styles of previously published works. We respected the forms submission to this publication took, whether in an academic format or a creative response. The editors preserved each author's chosen method of adding footnotes, use of terminology, and other aspects of style. Occasionally an author uses the term "Indian" in a historical context or a framework of familiarity within a Native culture. However, in their own writing, the editors determined to use the terms Native, Native American, and Indigenous—often interchangeably, except where a specific Native American nation is referenced. We the editors expect such diverse approaches will not interfere with the reader's enjoyment of the diversity of the primarily Indigenous intellectual output related to *Boundless*.

These contributions reflect the vision of *Boundless*, which is not only to celebrate the historical and contemporary work in Amherst College and Five Colleges collections but also to build relationships with living Indigenous artists, scholars, and writers, particularly those now living in the Northeast or diaspora communities rooted in the region. The publication is a celebration of the abundance of Native American art and literature that was shaped by relationships.

PRESENTATIONS 2023 AND 2024

The first iteration of *Boundless* was installed in the Mead from August 2023 to January 2024. From February to July 2024, a second iteration of *Boundless* presented art and literature that once again sprang from the works of Northeast Native artists and writers, but it expanded to include global Indigenous artists. We presented paintings, narratives, photographs, poetry, weavings, and carvings, alongside prints and work in other media.

In 2024 *Boundless* featured texts in Indigenous languages of the Haudenosaunee, Cherokee, and Diné that demonstrated the long publishing histories of those cultures that continue today with momentum toward the future suggested by children's books using Indigenous languages. Copies of *Thanksgiving Address*, translated from Mohawk into several global languages, suggested a cosmopolitan view of Indigeneity and Mohawk values as meaningful to the world. Composed of both historic books and contemporary art, the second exhibition opened a space to consider

Native American artists and writers of the Northeast alongside art and writings by Indigenous peoples from the Southwest and Northern California Coast, Mexico, Peru, Brazil, as well as Australia. Indigenous kinship is expansive and knows no bounds.

In both iterations, rather than creating a land acknowledgment, Erdrich used a large wall space near the entrance to include a series of questions that asked visitors to reflect on the notion of place. This "Acknowledgment of Place" served as Erdrich's invitation to deepen the notion of the common practice of institutional land acknowledgment by asking visitors to actively participate in an acknowledgment of place and consider Indigenous peoples' history, presence, and future as related to place. For an Indigenous audience, considering these questions might allow for a moment of reclamation and relationship. For those who are not Indigenous, Erdrich hopes these visitors will center themselves and become receptive to what they will read and encounter. Readers of this publication can ask themselves the same questions as stated below and take a moment to center themselves in place before reading on:

> Where are you now?
> What was the earth like below this building four hundred years ago?
> What will this place be like in the future?
> Who has been here before you?

> When I began curating *Boundless*, I traveled from Minnesota to Amherst. I found myself in a new place, so I followed Ojibwe protocols for entering another culture group's homeland. In curating the exhibition, I was enacting a kind of foraging or gathering as I selected from the published histories and works by current artists of their cultures. I explained to the Indigenous people I met here that I had come to work on *Boundless*, and I asked permission to gather on their grounds. I brought gifts with me and offered them. I did so because that is what we do and because place—not only land, but water and all the living beings in relationship with it—matters.

We invite readers of this publication to reflect on Erdrich's words from the *Boundless* exhibitions and to enact their own acknowledgment of place wherever they are: In the spirit of acknowledgment, I ask you to take a moment to consider how place matters to you.

—The Editors

NOTES

1 Sopiel "Selmore" Soctomah, "Wampum Reading," in *Dawnland Voices: An Anthology of Indigenous Writing from New England*, ed. Siobhan Senier (Lincoln: University of Nebraska Press, 2014), 163.

2 The Five College Consortium is composed of Amherst College, Hampshire College, Mount Holyoke College, Smith College, and the University of Massachusetts Amherst.

HEPSIBETH BOWMAN/CROSMAN HEMENWAY

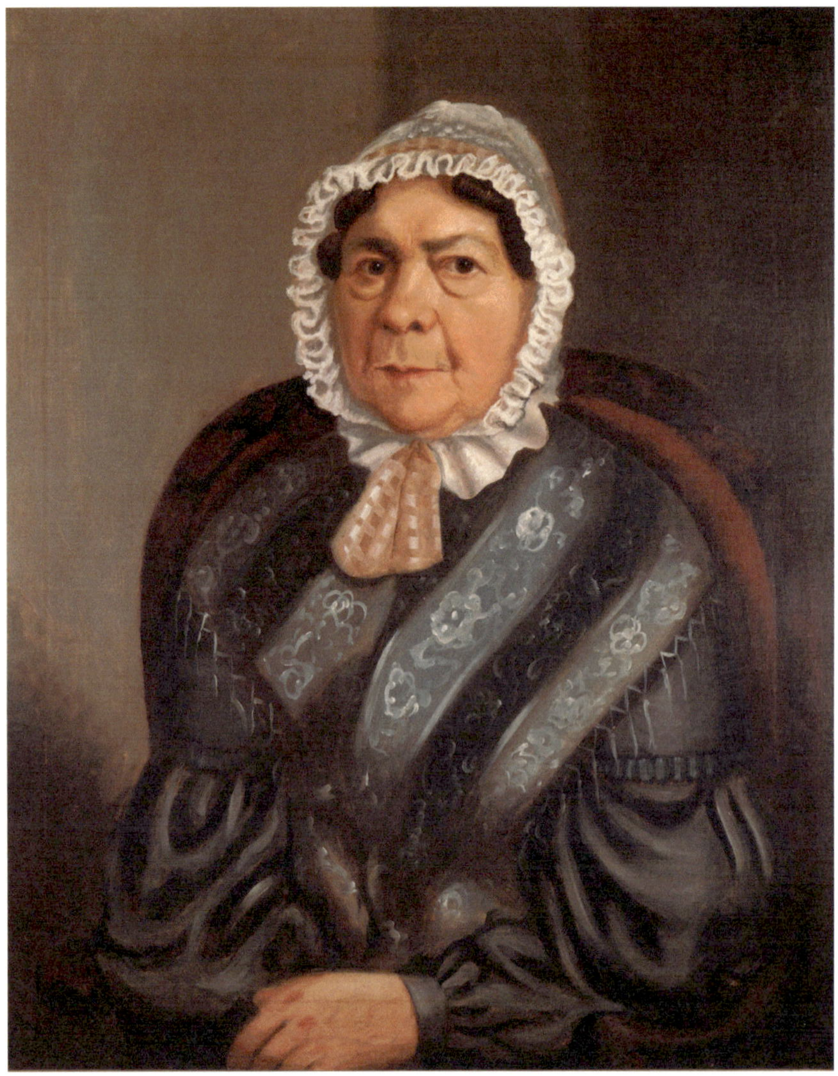

Figure 1: Unidentified artist, *Hepsibeth Bowman/Crosman Hemenway*, ca.1840s. Oil on canvas. From the collection of Worcester Historical Museum, Worcester, Massachusetts, gift of Frederick F. Hopkins.

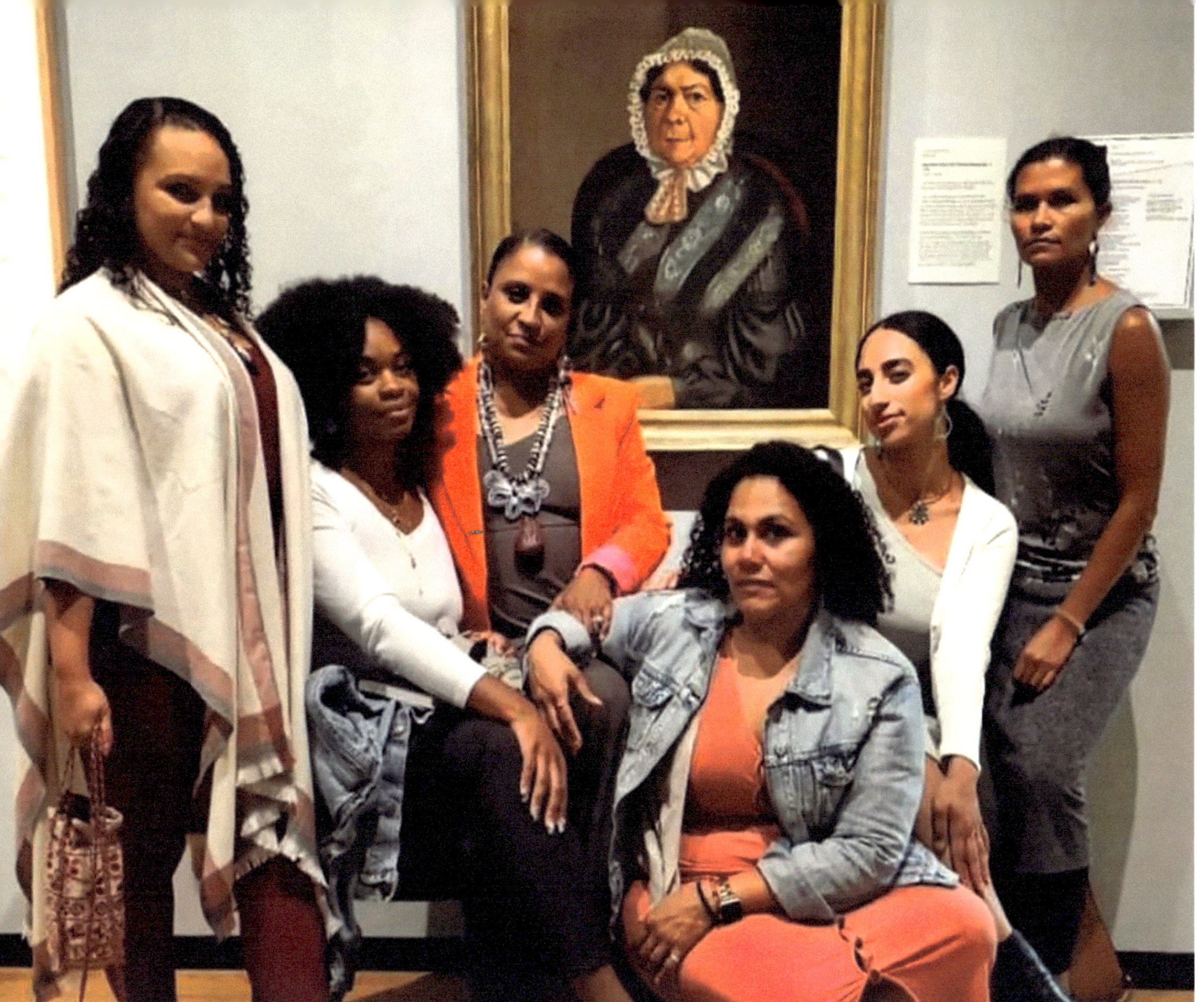

Figure 2: Group portrait at *Boundless* opening reception at the Mead Art Museum, September 14, 2023. Left to right: Brittney Peauwe Wunnepog Walley, Nia Holley, Tracy Ramos, Kimberly Toney, Kohar Avakian, Sierra Henries. Portrait on the wall of Hepsibeth Hemenway. Photography credit: Jonathan Ruf.

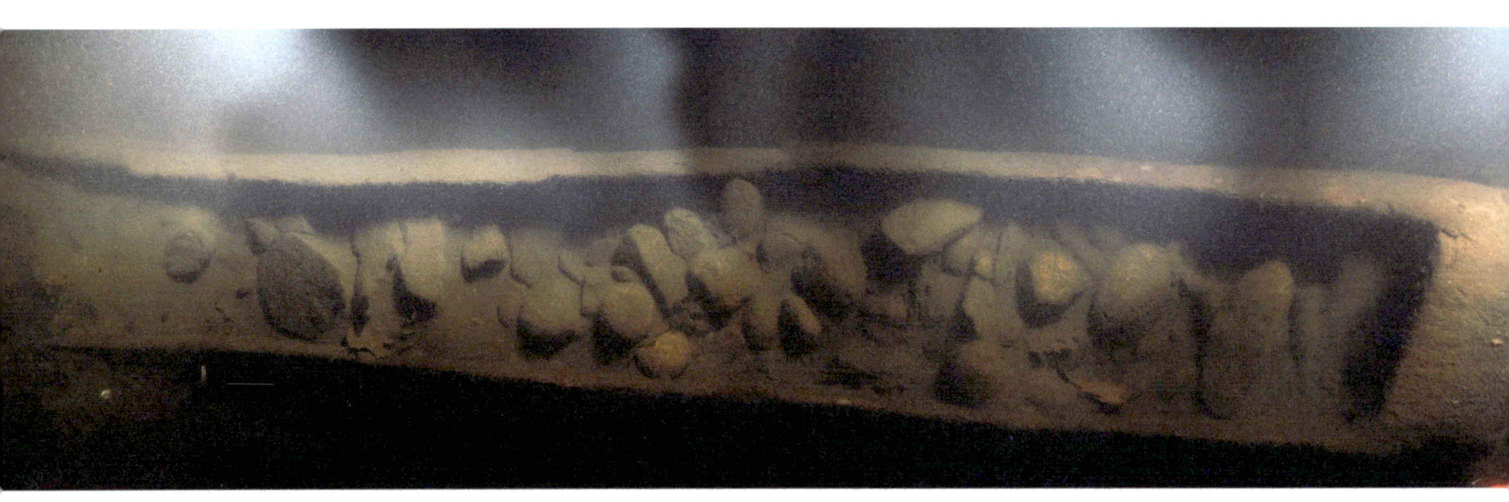

Figure 3: Michael Prange, *Underwater Photograph of In Situ Mishoon, Lake Quinsigamond*, 2008. Courtesy of Project Mishoon.

INTRODUCTION TO THE EXHIBITIONS

Kohar Avakian

Kohar Avakian is a doctoral candidate at Yale University. She is Nipmuc, Black, Armenian.

Manitoo oo, Manitoo oo, wame masugkenuk Manitoo oo
Taubotne kuttabotomish newutche yeu kesukok wunnegin
Nuppeantam newutche paomooonk nesausuk tashe pometuonk

One by one, the Nipmuc men, women, and children whispered into the vastness of Quinsigamond's waters, each placing a stone deep in the basin of the mishoon until it was abounding with prayers. A sweet cloud of sage intermingled with the unrelenting morning fog. Holding hands, they formed an impenetrable circle around the dugout canoe as if it were a newborn child learning to swim. For seven days, through the sacred alchemy of fire and wood, they tirelessly cut the branches and carved out the heart of a white pine tree, as they envisioned and enabled a boundless future on the lake for the next seven generations. Cascading toward the Khetetuk (Blackstone) River, down to Narragansett Bay, into the Atlantic, and along the concentric circles of kinfolk embedded therein, Quinsigamond's humble four-mile body of water connected land, people, and sea.

Neenawun tabuttantameooonk newutche touohkomuk wunnegin
Neenawun tabuttantamooonk newutche kepenemooonk wunne
Nuppeantam asekesukokish newutche wame ninnimmissinouck

Growing louder and speaking in unison, as if to summon God herself, their voices rippled toward the sun and greeted a symphony of spectating trees, aglow in the russet shadows of the autumn light. They thanked the Creator for the beautiful forests and the bountiful harvest, as they asked for protection during the cold season. It was time to sink the canoes. They would be retrieved after the thaw, an ancient act of continuity and preservation that ensured their survival. Winter was coming, and it was going to be a long one. One by one, their hands grasped the vessel's wooden edge, as they released it together, watching it disappear into the water's invisible depths, where it still remains.

What can we learn from the enduring presence of an Indigenous canoe older than the United States, anchored to the bottom of a lake in Massachusetts today (Figure 3) How does a seventeenth-century Nipmuc mishoon at the heart of Lake Quinsigamond in Worcester, Massachusetts relate to *Boundless*, Indigenous art and literature exhibitions at the Mead Art Museum at Amherst College? Where does it belong? The most tangible point of connection speaks to each show's physical inclusion of canoe paddles, handcrafted by Aquinnah Wampanoag artist Jonathan James-Perry (Figure 6). My second answer highlights the expansive imagination of Heid E. Erdrich, Ojibwe guest curator and writer, and Lisa Crossman, the Mead's Director of Curatorial Affairs. Guided by the analogy of a meandering canoe journey, their reciprocal and collaborative approach to museum work exposes and empowers the region's boundless constellation of relationships, intertribal alliances, and diasporic kinship networks including (but not limited to) those between Nipmuc, Wampanoag, Narragansett, Mahican, Mohegan, Pequot, Abenaki, Mohawk, Ho-Chunk, and Dakota artists and writers—rippling north, south, east, and west of Massachusetts and the Kwinitekw (Connecticut) River Valley.

Another crystal-clear connection between *Boundless* and the Nipmuc mishoon is the abundance of Nipmuc artists, writers, and relatives represented in *Boundless*, across time and space. Showcasing the importance of bark work in Eastern Woodlands material culture, Sierra Henries alchemizes wood into intricately hand-carved birch bark designs through pyrography (writing with fire) (Figure 9).[1] Challenging monolithic notions of culture as static, Brittney Walley weaves time-warping baskets (Figure 28) that incorporate historical and contemporary imagery, like seventeenth-century patterns and QR codes, to unsettle colonial myths of linear temporality, in her words.[2] Other Nipmucs serve on the *Boundless* advisory committee, along with Wampanoag, Shinnecock, Mohegan, and other communities, including Kimberly Toney, Inaugural Coordinating Curator for Native American and Indigenous Collections at Brown University. Toney researches and curates a digital project that contextualizes pictographs made by Northeastern Woodlands ancestors on colonial period land deeds, petitions, and documents.[3] At *Boundless*, in a circle of proud Nipmuc women, we posed with a portrait of our ancestor, Hepsibeth Hemenway (Figures 1 and 2). Together, we recreated a new family photograph and enjoyed chef Melissa Baehr's reimagined version of Auntie Hepsibeth's cherished wedding cake from the prime of her baking career in Worcester. The cake was remade from scratch with Nipmuc corn by Melissa Baehr (Anishinaabe Ojibwe), chef and owner of Indigenous Deliciousness. Alongside these artists and ancestors, the Nipmuc mishoon remains a constant living presence, an insistent reminder that Nipmucs—and all Indigenous peoples—belong in the past, present, *and* future.

Rather than reinforcing a linear notion of time or designating one spatial center of gravity over another, *Boundless* calls us to reject the divisive hold of settler boundaries imposed between us, toward a transnational and diasporic framework of Indigeneity and a deeper understanding of our shared histories. Through a collaboration between Amherst's Mead Art Museum and the Collection of Native American Literature, the exhibition brings together a mosaic of genres, cultures, methodologies, and forms, from the seventeenth-century *Mamusse Wunneetupanatamwe Up-Biblum God* (1663) (Figure 7), the first Bible translated into an Indigenous North American language by the expert hand of Nipmuc scholar Wawaus (also known as James Printer)[4] of Harvard Indian College, to a plethora of eighteenth- to twenty-first-century texts, illustrations, paintings, prints, paddles, photographs, plates, cookbooks, and *much* more (notably, a Babylonian cuneiform inscription from 2400 BCE and Assyrian reliefs from 859 BCE).

It is no small feat nor mere happenstance that the ancestral traces of Indigenous peoples worldwide—from Assyria in West Asia to Nipmuc country in North America—now greet each other, face-to-face. *Boundless* places participants in the midst of a global network of Indigenous artists and writers. The list includes Jeremy Dennis (Shinnecock), Elizabeth James-Perry (Aquinnah Wampanoag), Courtney M. Leonard (Shinnecock), Andrea Carlson (Anishinaabe), Mary Sully (Yankton Dakota), Ella Cara Deloria (Dakota), Jaune Quick-to-See Smith (Salish/Kootenai), Joy Harjo (Creek/Mvskoke), Dyani White Hawk (Lakota), N. Scott Momaday (Kiowa), Fritz Scholder (Luiseño), Cara Romero (Chemehuevi), Diane Burns (Anishinaabe/Chemehuevi), and many more. Taken together, these poets, painters, photographers, printmakers, activists, and authors disrupt a one-dimensional understanding of "texts" and underscore the multiplicity of ways in which narratives can be recorded, remembered, and told. What emerges within this kaleidoscopic arrangement is a long, continuous, and international history of Indigenous print and material culture across centuries, proving that there is nothing rare or uncommon about it.

In the spirit of *Boundless*, the Nipmuc mishoon refuses a singular definition of an archive, pushes us to reconsider the meaning of "rare," and challenges us to question the boundaries of "American" art. How does an object, or a person, *become* rare, after all? In the words of Erdrich, "Native people creating art and writing has gone on for centuries, across cultures and other boundaries....We Native American authors and artists are often treated as if we are anomalies, outsiders to the art and publishing world, but in fact there are many remarkable connections."[5] In other words, there is nothing unusual about Indigenous people writing or creating art; we have been *made* rare through the relentless engine of genocide, settler colonialism, historical revisionism, and persistent myths of Indigenous extinction that write us out of existence.

Like the submerged Nipmuc canoe, it would be too simplistic to call the artistic contributions included in *Boundless* inanimate "objects" alone. Rather, the featured creations and their makers are *living* vessels of time that carry and transport history within them; stone by stone, these vessels accrue meaning, gathering the powerful potential to make political waves. In the words of Hiʻilei Julia Kawehipuaakahaopulani Hobart (Kanaka Maoli), "animacy has emerged as a potent point of resistance that contends with Western colonialism's effects on land and knowledge formations."[6] Animacy refutes the colonial notion of *terra nullius*, "a historical fiction" that imagines Indigenous land "as an empty space without Native peoples or Native worlds to contend with."[7] Instead, the Indigenous creations, both within and outside of *Boundless,* are relatives whose collective presence is empowered by the land, imbued with the expansive kinship networks and social entanglements encompassed within the Indigenous Northeast today, between our interconnected lands, peoples, and waterways.

And yet, these answers barely scratch the surface of the water. It seems natural to draw connections between a seventeenth-century Nipmuc mishoon and Indigenous art exhibitions at a college museum in Massachusetts. Some initial reactions may even be: "Well, why isn't the Nipmuc canoe in a museum yet?" The answer is a lot more complicated than it appears. Perhaps we are asking the wrong questions. A better question is this: What can the bounded journey of a submerged seventeenth-century Nipmuc canoe teach us?

In 2001, I was too young to remember the day that Mike Brauer, a white recreational diver from Connecticut, encountered a Nipmuc mishoon older than the United States in my hometown of Worcester, Massachusetts. Between 2000 and 2001, three mishoonash (plural) were found, nestled in the boundless waters of Lake Quinsigamond. Although the oldest dated canoe (mishoon #1) appears to have remained still for nearly four hundred years, its journey through time was neither stagnant nor linear. Its existence is nothing short of a seemingly impossible miracle. For centuries, the mishoon remained untouched, where our Nipmuc ancestors left it—that is, until the time-collapsing "discovery" landed on the internet.[8]

Coinciding with the Nipmuc people's long, fracturing, and impossible fight for federal recognition, the monumental unearthing of mishoon #1 was first uncovered on eBay by Cheryl WatchingCrow Stedtler, Nipmuc tribal member and future director of Project Mishoon. Brauer, the diver who first encountered the mishoon, nearly auctioned off the location of the centuries-old canoe on New Year's Eve, coincidentally my birthday. Luckily, Stedtler was right on time.[9]

The mishoonash remain safeguarded in Lake Quinsigamond under the tribal sovereignty of the Nipmuc people, thanks to Stedtler's timely intervention and decades of dedication to cultural preservation, education, and repatriation, alongside Cheryll Toney Holley (*sonskq* of the Hassanamisco Nipmuc Band, historian, and genealogist), Rae Gould (Executive Director of Brown University's Native American and Indigenous Studies Initiative), and many more unnamed ancestors and community members who ensure our survival today.[10] The mishoonash and the lake's multitude of unmoved Nipmuc artifacts are protected in collaboration with the Massachusetts Board of Underwater Archaeological Resources. The fate of their future rests in the hands of the Nipmuc people, who must collectively decide what to do. If decolonization is not a metaphor, what must we make out of the physical wreckage of colonialism, which stubbornly remains embedded on our present landscape?

Today, Lake Quinsigamond is practically unrecognizable, due to decades of deforestation, industrialization, human contamination (namely, a six-million-gallon sewage spill in February 2022),[11] and the erection of an amusement park/shopping plaza named "The White City" (uncoincidentally named after the World's Columbian Exposition of 1893 in Chicago, celebrating Columbus's arrival). Like the circuitous journey of each creation in *Boundless,* the submerged mishoonash have endured a lot. Carbon-14 testing dated mishoon #1 back to the approximate timeframe of 1640 CE to 1680 CE, which coincides with the nation's first anticolonial intertribal resistance movement, commonly referred to as "King Philip's War," and locally remembered by many names.[12] What can we see and unsee by finding relationality between those whose lives, creations, and histories have been named "unarchivable," "unrecognizable," and "unrepairable"? As we remember our living connections maintained by the land, our waterways, and our kinship networks, we must also not forget the "unarchivable" presences all around us, hidden in plain sight.[13]

As you embark on a journey through *Boundless*, I offer the additional analogy of a submerged Nipmuc canoe, filled with heavy stones, unshakeable amidst a sprawling network of colonial detritus. While many Americans celebrate King Philip's War as a successful and necessary effort to secure land for the foundation of the nation (or forget about it altogether), the event is commemorated by Nipmuc people as a time of immeasurable mourning and earth-shattering loss. We are still mourning our dead. Now home to a wastewater treatment plant, Deer Island in Boston Harbor is a centuries-old site of settler occupation and Indigenous genocide.[14] Today, in the frigid waters of the Atlantic, Nipmucs, Wampanoags, and other Algonquian peoples commemorate our losses in a grueling annual paddle between the Charles River and Deer Island.

In June 2024, a historic gathering of the Nipmuc/k bands met to create a new mishoon on Lake Quinsigamond, "the heart of our homeland," in Stedtler's words. Alongside the community's helping hands, Troy Phillips (Hassanamisco Nipmuc and member of the Massachusetts Commission on Indian Affairs) created the mishoon through ancestral intuition and instinct—an expression of his expert artistry and craftsmanship. With a simple blueprint of the mishoon, he generated a plan to create an exact replica of the seventeenth-century canoe. According to Phillips, "To be able to do it right where our ancestors were, that's the important part. Freely. I haven't been on this land ever. Not one Nipmuc has property here on this waterway. This was our main waterway." For the first time in centuries, Quinsigamond witnessed her original stewards paddle, sing songs, share stories, and honor our ancestors once more.[15] Although the United States has failed to recognize the Nipmuc nation and American history books have repeatedly deemed us extinct, the mishoonash remain a testament to the ancient existence and inherent sovereignty of the Nipmuc people, immersed deep beneath the surface at the heart of the lake—stubborn, unmoving, and abounding with prayers.[16]

Learn more about Project Mishoon and give back today: http://projectmishoon.homestead.com/Index.html.

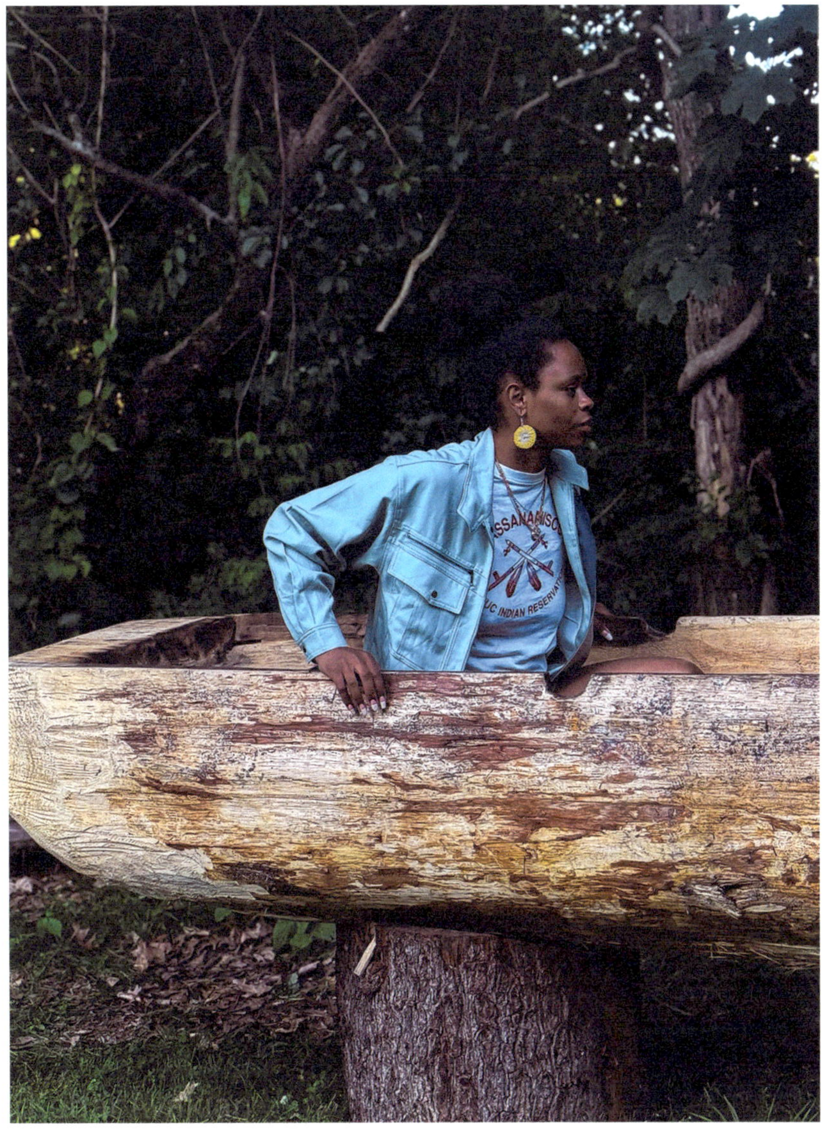

Figure 4: Kohar Avakian, “Rematriation,” digital photograph of Nia Holley in a newly made replica of the 17th-century mishoon of Lake Quinsigamond, Strawberry Moon on Hassanamesit Reservation, June 2024.

NOTES

1 "Beauty Out of Bark," Cultural Survival, September 15, 2023, https://www.culturalsurvival.org/publications/cultural-survival-quarterly/beauty-out-bark.

2 Walley will participate in the exhibition *Restor(y)ing Indigenous Collections* at the Mystic Seaport Museum in Stonington, Connecticut; this is a companion to the gallery exhibit *Entwined: Freedom, Sovereignty, and the Sea* (April 20, 2024–Spring 2026. https://mysticseaport.org/exhibit/entwined-freedom-sovereignty-and-the-sea/).

3 Jennifer Braga, "Kimberly Toney Inaugural Coordinating Curator for Native American and Indigenous Collections," Brown University Library News, March 24, 2022, https://library.brown.edu/create/libnews/kimberly-toney.

4 Christine DeLucia, *Memory Lands: King Philip's War and the Place of Violence in the Northeast* (New Haven: Yale University Press, 2019), 83; Lisa Brooks, *Our Beloved Kin: A New History of King Philip's War* (New Haven: Yale University Press, 2018), 86.

5 Ethan Neuschwander '25, "Indigenous Art Exhibit 'Boundless' to Open Fall 2023," *The Amherst Student*, April 20, 2022, https://amherststudent.com/article/indigenous-art-exhibit-boundless-to-open-fall-2023.

6 Hiʻilei Julia Kawehipuaakahaopulani Hobart, "At Home on the Mauna: Ecological Violence and Fantasies of Terra Nullius on Maunakea's Summit," *Native American and Indigenous Studies* 6, no. 2, (Fall 2019): 30, https://doi.org/10.1353/nai.2019.a755891.

7 Hobart, "At Home on the Mauna," 45.

8 Bob Datz, "Nipmuc Mystery below Quinsigamond," *Worcester Telegram & Gazette*, May 20, 2012, https://www.telegram.com/story/news/local/north/2012/05/20/nipmuc-mystery-below-quinsigamond/49607326007.

9 Cheryl WatchingCrow Stedtler, "Project Mishoon," (stand-alone presentations delivered virtually on Zoom for community members for Project Mishoon), November 7, 2022 and November 2, 2023.

10 Cheryll Toney Holley, https://cherylltoneyholley.com. In her website, Gould talks about their historical preservation, repatriation, and genealogical work, respectively (https://www.achp.gov/initiatives/d-rae-gould).

11 Kiernan Dunlop, "Worcester Fined for 6M gallon sewage discharge into Lake Quinsigamond," *MassLive*, December 9, 2022, https://www.masslive.com/worcester/2022/12/worcester-fined-for-6m-gallon-sewage-discharge-into-lake-quinsigamond.html.

12 Stedtler, "Project Mishoon"; Brooks, *Our Beloved Kin*, 7.

13 Achille Mbembe, "The Power of the Archive and Its Limits," in *Refiguring the Archive*, ed. Carolyn Hamilton, Verne Harris, Jane Taylor, Michele Pickover, Graeme Reid, and Razia Saleh (Cape Town: David Philip Publishers, 2002), 20.

14 DeLucia, *Memory Lands*, 97.

15 The Lake Quinsigamond paddle and mishoon burning took place June 1–9, 2024 (https://spectrumnews1.com/ma/worcester/news/2024/06/04/-project-mishoon--brings-hassanamisco-nipmuc-band-back-to-its-roots).

16 Kohar Avakian, "An Inter/Racial Love History," in *We Are All Armenian: Voices From the Diaspora*, ed. Aram Mrjoian (Austin: University of Texas Press, 2023), 49.

JONATHAN JAMES-PERRY: *PADDLE 1—WHERE WE COME FROM* AND *PADDLE 2—WHERE WE ARE*

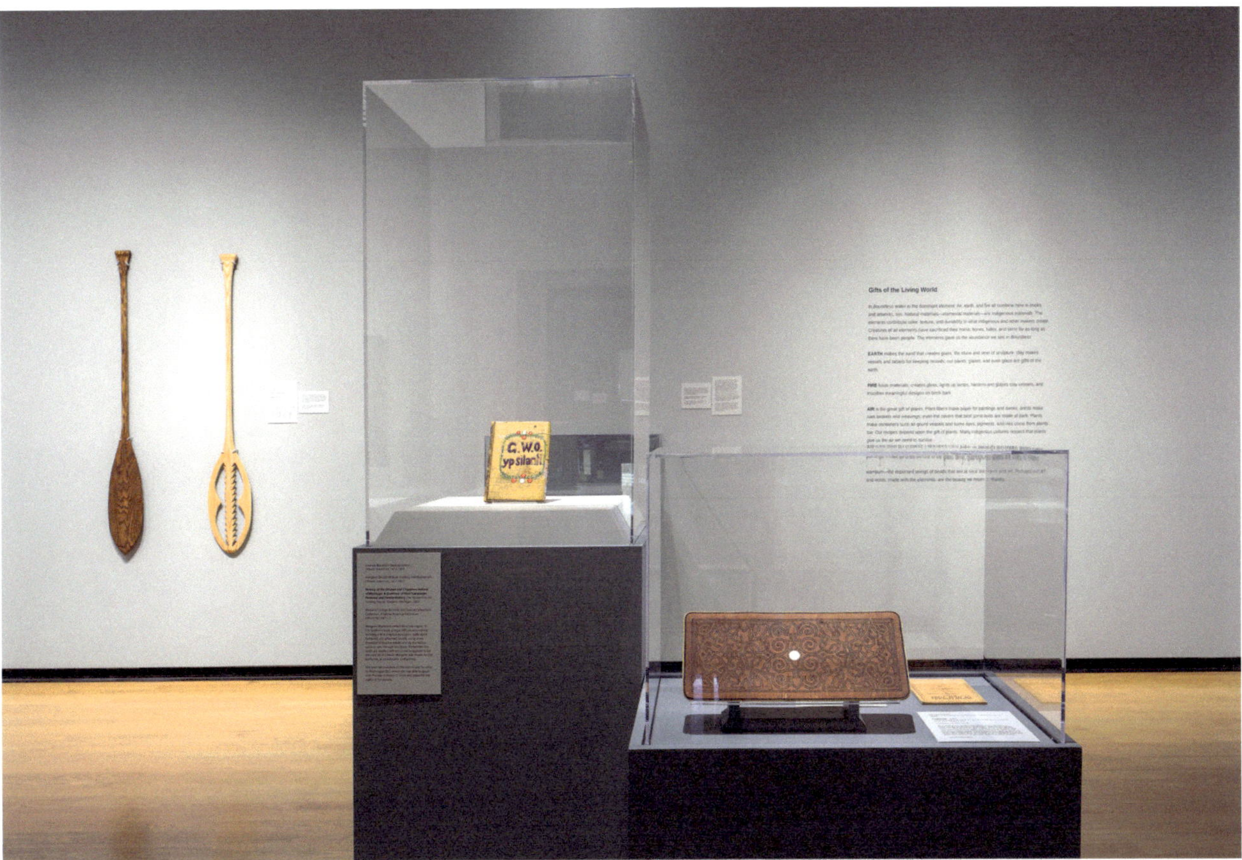

Figure 5: Installation image of *Boundless*, featuring the following works, from left to right: Jonathan James-Perry's *Paddle 1—Where We Come From*, 2023, stain of black walnut and red ochre; and *Paddle 2—Where We Are*, 2023, white ash; Andrew Blackbird (Makadebinesi) (Odawa) and birch bark binding with porcupine quill decoration by Margaret Boyd (Odawa), *History of the Ottawa and Chippewa Indians of Michigan: A Grammar of Their Language/Personal and Family History*, 1887; Sierra Henries's *Pathways*, 2023, freehand pyrography on winter birch bark, scallop shell, braided sinew. Image credit: Stephen Petegorsky.

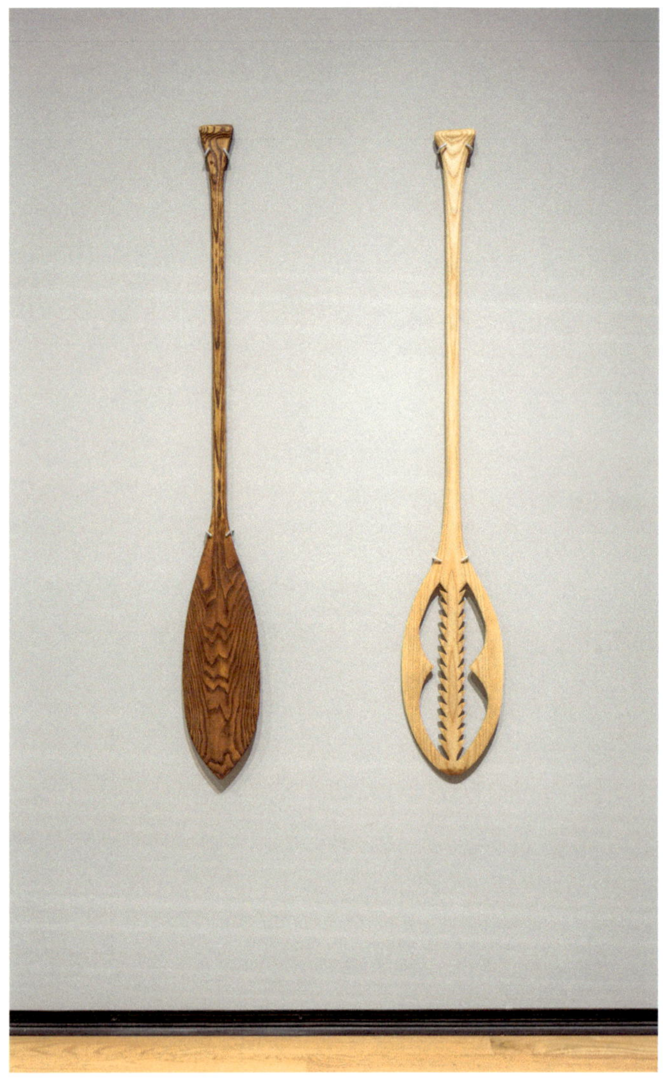

Figure 6: Jonathan James-Perry (Aquinnah Wampanoag), *Paddle 1—Where We Come From*, 2023 (left), white ash, stain of black walnut and red ocher; *Paddle 2—Where We Are*, 2023 (right), white ash. Image credit: Stephen Petegorsky.

Both paddles are carved from a single tree. James-Perry selected ash to draw attention to the deaths of many of these trees caused by the emerald ash borer beetle—an invasive species. The stained paddle is functional and was created using pre-1600s tools. The unstained paddle has a design cut through its blade. The non-functional paddle symbolizes the resiliency of Native people but also the effort of survival.

James-Perry has made nearly fifty dugout canoes to date. He has been making them since he was a teenager and now is recognized as a teacher of this skill. He is grounded in the traditions of his oceangoing ancestors. He considers designs by examining raw materials closely, then draws his images from the grain, hues, and patina of wood, stone, and copper.

James-Perry is a direct descendant of the prominent Cuffe family of Westport, and Martha's Vineyard, Massachusetts. His relative, the notable Captain Paul Cuffe (1759–1817), was an abolitionist, businessman, and one of the most successful people of color in the United States.[1]

Jonathan and his sister, Elizabeth James-Perry, sometimes collaborate on artwork, research, and exhibitions.

—Jonathan James-Perry, in conversation with Lisa A. Crossman

NOTE

1 "About," Jonathan James-Perry, 2021, https://www.jonathanjamesperry.com/about.

POTAWATOMI SONG

Now we all move, we're moving with this earth,
The earth is moving along, the water is moving along,
the grass is moving, the trees are moving,
The whole earth is moving
So we all move along with the earth, keeping time with the earth.[1]

"Potawatomi Song," in *Drink the Winds, Let the Waters Flow Free*, ed. Sharon Day and Pat Panagoulias, illustrated by Jaune Quick-to-See Smith (Minneapolis: Johnson Institute, 1983).

A WATER WAY OF KNOWING

2

BOUNDLESS: A WATER WAY OF KNOWING

Heid E. Erdrich

At the invitation of Amherst College, I accepted the role of guest curator for this project because it seemed like a way to forward my personal and professional mission to expand conversations around the history, presence, and resistance of the original people of this continent through presentation of our art and writing. The work of foregrounding Indigenous art, abundance, and creativity is essential to the health of Native Americans, the audience I think of first. With input from Native artists of the region, the exhibition developed a focus on works by Northeast Native American writers and artists active from the late eighteenth century to the present. Other currents within the show reveal relationship and kinship. *Boundless* enlarged to consider creative legacies and connections between artists and writers that could be displayed in image and text, including images that contain text. The exhibition expanded its scope as it grew into its second iteration, which included work by Indigenous artists beyond the U.S. borders.

In the midst of a global pandemic, I began my contribution from Minnesota. As I started this work, my assignment was to find Native American–authored texts in the Collection of Native American Literature to present along with select art objects from the Mead Art Museum. Working with Amherst College through online catalogs and digital collections, I experienced a flood of words, titles, images, people, voices, and histories. The pull of place grabbed me when, eventually, I visited areas near the college. I considered many Indigenous cultural names for themselves and how water worked into tribal people's identities. Like many Indigenous people elsewhere on Turtle Island, Native Americans in the Northeast came to exist as peoples known in relation to the waters of their homelands. In this watery way, *Boundless* came together as evidence of my immersion and delight in considering thousands of images, artworks, and texts in Amherst's collections.

As an Ojibwe woman writer (enrolled in the Turtle Mountain Band of Chippewa), my perspective is contained in the title for *Boundless*, which I chose because I found relationships between authors and artists that seemed as abundant as waters flowing to the sea.[1] The image came to me of a stone tossed from a canoe and the ripples that enlarge and expand from that one point of contact. I am a poet, and many of my projects start with an image, so I have learned to pay attention when one comes. As I turned to metaphor as a central organizing image for the exhibition, water led me to consider the notion of place more than just land, a spot in a landscape, or a space. Place includes water, sky, and more. Place to Indigenous people often means the living world of the area, the materials, plants, animals, and foods shared by artists, authors, and Indigenous and all peoples of the region. Place is a relationship.

I became determined to present artists and authors in relationship—sometimes kinship, sometimes through bonds of friendship or mentorship—as an important way to interpret the two collections from my distinct perspective. We Native American authors and artists are often treated as if we are anomalies, outsiders to the art and publishing world, but in fact we hold many and remarkable connections to those traditions. Native people were creating art long ago (and still are); storytelling, writing, and publishing have gone on for centuries. This kind of movement of images and ideas crosses cultures and other boundaries.

Because I had known the Kwinitekw (Connecticut) River flowing south when I lived two hours north decades ago, and I had known the waters of Nantucket when I lived on the island, I centered myself in that knowing. My first visit to Amherst took place after my family and I had visited New Hampshire. We drove south along the Kwinitekw (the long river, the long tidal river) and an image came to me of all the rivers moving through Massachusetts and Connecticut toward the Long Island Sound and to the sea. I thought of Indigenous people who traveled south on the great rivers, the Kwinitekw and the Usi-a-di-en-uk (Housatonic River). I thought of how the sea touched the islands and the coasts. I realized that I was already immersing myself in the region as I took the water way from river to shore. I had personal experience of the area, but I was out of my territory. And I couldn't fully engage in the Native community whose territories are near Amherst because we began our work in the uncertainty and required social isolation of the COVID era. I knew I needed help from people of the tribes nearby and, by luck and kindness, I found opportunities to acknowledge Indigenous folks in the community in a way that felt right, that was culturally appropriate, and that allowed me to give gifts, listen, and develop relationships not just for me, but for Amherst College. I researched to learn more about Native American professionals in the field of libraries, galleries, and museums who were Indigenous or worked closely with Native nations. I asked the help of people who knew the area, the region, and literature and art by Indigenous makers being created today. I could not have and would not have engaged in the work without Nipmuc, Wampanoag, and other members of Northeast tribes guiding me.

In conceptualizing the project plan, Mead Director of Curatorial Affairs Lisa Crossman had built-in support from the larger community in the form of an advisory group that we would select together and that would convene regularly. From nearly the beginning, the advisory group of artists and educators encouraged me to form the show around Indigenous people of the Northeast. A few advisory members I selected knew the collections at Amherst College and one, Kimberly Toney, knew the history of Native American publication from the earliest works printed to contemporary authors. With the help of advisors, I began to sense how the exhibitions could take shape. Many people supported my vision and enriched the exhibitions with their contributions. But all mistakes are mine.

In 2021, supported by Lisa Crossman and other wonderful Amherst College staff and student researchers, I came to understand the project *Boundless* would reveal the seemingly endless connections between Indigenous art and writing. From Minnesota, I continued to pore over the online catalogs for both the literary collection and the museum. I continued learning about the tribe closest to Amherst and, through Indigenous organization websites and events, I sought contemporary Nipmuc artists as well as artists from other tribes of the Northeast to participate in *Boundless*. Important to my grounding in the art of the area were the Ohketeau Cultural Center and Nolumbeka Honoring Northeastern Tribal Heritage Project, the anthology *Dawnland Voices* edited by Siobahn Senier, as well as the social media postings of individual artists.

I worked with Mead and Archives and Special Collections staff and student researchers to get a more detailed sense of each book, map, musical score, dictionary, Bible, portrait, landscape, photograph, sculpture, textile, and household item in their collections. Because I couldn't be in the museum except for a few brief visits, I tried to imagine myself in the galleries. The vision continued that I was being carried by currents toward an understanding of how all that I saw is related. This is no doubt a particularly Ojibwe urge because our central lesson is the concept of all things being in relation. When we greet people we often use the phrase *indinaawmaaganidog*, meaning "all my relations." For Ojibwe and other Indigenous cultures, the phrase and the concept extends to all living beings and some that other cultures classify as not living, such as stone. I was seeking relatives more than seeking themes for the exhibitions.

At the same time, I often thought of critic, poet, and novelist Gerald Vizenor's (Ojibwe) notion of *transmotion* and his continued expansion of the term: "The discussion of transmotion, a spirited and visionary sense of natural motion, has evolved in my critical studies as an original aesthetic theory to interpret and compare the modes, distinctions, situations, and the traces of motion in sacred objects, stories, art, and literature."[2] I find Vizenor's a useful term for the sense of activity and ongoingness in Indigenous literature, art, and life. While researching for *Boundless* and reading in the Collection of Native American Literature, I realized I was selecting works that engage transmotion, and that my approach to the exhibitions' organization also enacted transmotion. I wanted the exhibitions to move somehow or to suggest the movement I found in the shared intellectual traditions of art and writing that flowed across cultures and generations, and within families and circles of friends and colleagues.

A few years after I began the research that would result in *Boundless*, I found myself listening to Kenzie Allen, an Oneida scholar, present on Indigenous ways of research for creative writing.[3] She focused on the theory of the *dérive*, not as strictly defined by Guy Debord as part of the Situationists' post-Marxist philosophy of the mid-twentieth century, but as it is applied today. She defined *dérive* as movement in a landscape with no particular purpose except to follow the arising flow and draw from place to place or object to object. Instantly Kenzie's talk made me recognize two things—the importance of my attention to images of rivers I encountered in the Mead's art collection and my own watery method of constructing *Boundless*.

I understood then why I persisted in my meandering direction. This is the water's direction, a general flowing south, spreading out to sea and broadening as it goes. It is the lesson in so many tribal names—we are related to place and influenced by its movements. I also realized that, like water, I was seeking connection and had found it in a relational manner.

Boundless is composed of works that reveal relationality based on family, tribal, cultural, or collegial connections. The materials from the living world, such as bark, gourds, clay, pigments, horn, ivory, food, and plants, are components of items both of Indigenous creative expression and of the domestic life of European/American colonizers. The food and plants we all share and the ways our languages interact—all these directed the organization of *Boundless*. Boundless connections drew me to certain artworks in the Mead's collections and focused my selections from the Frost Library. My faith in my meanderings, my enactment of transmotion, this organic direction moved me toward works from Mahican, Nipmuc, Shinnecock, and Wampanoag artists creating today. Including these works brought the exhibitions to a fullness I so wanted to suggest with *Boundless*.

The ways *Boundless* could have been put together are many, but as I gathered the art and books included in the exhibitions, it was always going to move like water. The ripples of connection I felt between each object that I looked at in the Mead catalog, each book I researched from the Collection of Native American Literature, each Native artist we visited, each conversation with an advisor—all revealed connections that sprang from place, kinship, culture, and the living world, the boundless abundance from which all art and books are created.

NOTES

1 I first thought I would call the exhibition “Unbound” but was uncomfortable with the pun. My sister Louise Erdrich suggested I use another form of the word, and I decided on “Boundless.”

2 Gerald Vizenor, “The Unmissable: Transmotion in Native Stories and Literature,” *Transmotion* 1, no. 1 (2015): 63, https://doi.org/10.22024/UniKent/03/tm.143.

3 Kenzie Allen, “Geolocation and Geocollaborative: Poetry of Place,” presentation, Indigenous Nations’ Poets (In-Na-Po) Retreat, Door County, Wisconsin, April 24, 2023.

TO COMPOSE THE SHEETS, AND CORRECT THE PRESS, WITH UNDERSTANDING

Kimberly Toney

Kimberly Toney (Hassanamisco Band of Nipmuc) is the inaugural Coordinating Curator for Native American and Indigenous Collections at the John Carter Brown Library and the John Hay Library at Brown University

The first Bible printed in British North America is in the language of my ancestors. It is related to me, and I am related to it, not because of the verses or parables or Christian teachings it espouses, but because it carries the translation of an oral language into a printed form. The raised impressions left behind by the hand-pressed type on the pages of the Bible, printed in the seventeenth century, offer a tangible, tactile connection to my ancestors. The words on the page connect me to a time of dispossession of language, land, and culture. These words ask me to remember and awaken a language, and the sounds and the meaning of these written symbols that represent my ancestors' speech.

The project of printing and disseminating a Bible printed in the Algonquian language (dialects of which were—and are—spoken by Native peoples across the eastern region of Turtle Island) began as a way for English colonizers to Christianize, assimilate, and subjugate the Native inhabitants of the Northeast. The decades-long task of translating the Bible into the heretofore oral language of the original peoples of this place was a monumental undertaking. European settlers believed that the best way to dispossess Native peoples of their culture (to therefore make them more English, and purportedly more "civilized") was to convert Natives to Christianity. By translating several English-language Christian and missionary texts into various dialects of the Algonquian language, Native peoples could study Christian teachings, receive the word of God in their own language, and therefore convert.[1]

And so, the thousands of pages of the Bible, New and Old Testaments included, were translated. Over a thousand copies were printed and the books then disseminated across the Northeast and beyond.[2]

Previous histories and even the printed work itself would have us believe that European settlers accomplished this task all by themselves, aided only by divine providence. This major linguistic endeavor, however, was achieved because of the work of Nipmuc, Wampanoag, Pequot, and other Natives who wrote, spoke, interpreted, and performed multilateral translations across English and the various dialects of the Algonquian language they spoke. Because of this work, the Algonquian Bible, heretofore also referred to as *Up-Biblum God*, and other Algonquian-language missionary texts captured the language of Eastern Woodlands peoples on paper.[3] Still, there is so much that these printed works fail to tell us about the lives of these translators and interpreters.

Though the intention was to dispossess Natives of this language through forced assimilation into English culture, today the Bible itself represents the survivance of a people through the visibility, existence, and persistence of our language in printed texts produced through the second half of the seventeenth century.

WAWAUS, SON OF NAOAS, BORN OF HASSANAMESIT

The first printing press, brought in 1638 to the place that has come to be called the United States, found its home in Massachusett territory, placed inside the first structure built of brick on the campus of Harvard, the Indian College. A small number of Massachusett, Nipmuc, and Wampanoag students attended the college between 1655 and 1670. From 1670 until the building was torn down in 1690, the Indian College functioned solely as a space for printing. Before, during, and after the existence of the Indian College turned printing office, Wawaus, a Nipmuc man who would come to be known as James the Printer or James Printer, worked the press.[4]

Before his time at the printing press, Wawaus spent the beginning and end of his life at Hassanamesit, a Nipmuc village in the place renamed by white settlers as "Grafton, Massachusetts." Whether willingly or not, Wawaus was placed in an English household at a young age, and there he learned the English language. Wawaus continued his education at the Indian College at Harvard and apprenticed as a printer there. Like others across our communities at this time, Wawaus soon became known by his English name, James Printer.

Much of what we know, or can know, about Wawaus lives in the spaces between primary sources and historical context. We know that the missionary project in the Northeast valued Wawaus's command of both written and spoken English. John Eliot, a white settler who pushed hard for the forced assimilation and subjugation of Native peoples in the Northeast through missionary work, wrote a letter to Robert Boyle, then Governor of the Society for the Propagation of the Gospel in New England, in 1682, praising Wawaus's work. "We have but one man [Printer] that is able to compose the sheets, and correct the press, with understanding."[5] Wawaus was unique—the "one man"—as he played a major role in the creation of the corpus of Algonquian-language texts printed at the press in the Indian College between about 1655 and 1710.

What we do not or cannot know about Wawaus is what we are called to think about here. Did Wawaus understand the need to capture his language on paper for the ways it could save us today? Did he believe in the missionary project, or did he see something else happening? What do the printed materials he worked to produce ask of us to remember?

THREE SHEETS

The three printed sheets from *Up-Biblum God* included in the *Boundless* exhibitions come from a copy of the first edition of the whole Bible, printed in 1663. The sheets were accessioned by the Frost Library in 2014 to complement the existing collection of Native American Literature in special collections there. The three fragment sheets contain consecutive passages from the Old Testament Book of Numbers, chapter 12, verse 3 through chapter 16, verse 43 (Figure 7). These three sheets represent but a fraction of the labor Wawaus performed in helping to set type, ink it, and pull the press to produce the sheets for the Old and New Testament translations of the Bible. As fragments themselves, the sheets ask us to fill in the blanks.

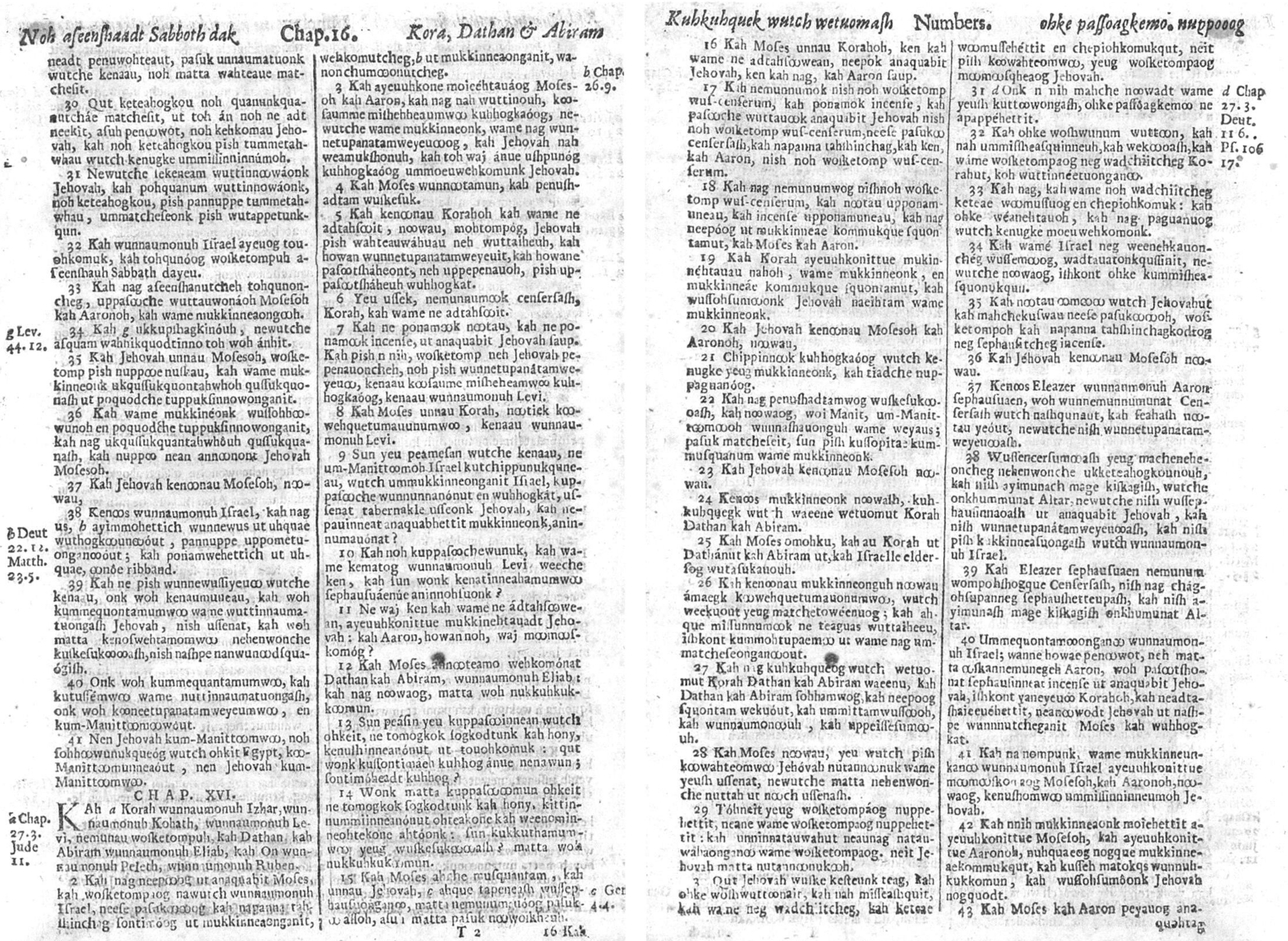

Figure 7: Published by John Eliot. Translated by Job Nesuton (Massachusett), Joel Iacoomes (Wampanoag), and Caleb Cheeshateaumuck (Wampanoag). Printed by Samuel Green, Marmaduke Johnson, and Wawaus/ James Printer (Nipmuc). Fragment of *Mamusse Wunneetupanatamwe Up-Biblum God*, Cambridge, Mass., 1663. Amherst College Archives and Special Collections, Collection of Native American Literature. BS345. A2 E4 1663.

The process of handpress printing is tedious and time-consuming. The task of producing a printed book began not with the press itself, but with a manuscript—words written by hand that are to become text through the labor of casting a single piece of type to form each word on a composing stick. Each line of text then becomes a block, a unit of text that is the sum of its parts, parts set by hand, character by character. A tedious task, to be sure.

Once a block of text or single page is completed and the form laid on the bed of the printing press, it is inked. A thin layer of black ink covers the type. Paper is prepared and eventually laid on top. The layers of metal type, ink, packing, paper, and frame are rolled together underneath the press, and an impression is made. Rolled back out from under the press, the sheet is officially printed. It is removed from the press, and a new blank sheet of paper is added to perform the task again.

Printers work as a team—setting type, inking blocks, loading and unloading sheets, pulling the press—in the hopes of producing 100 or so impressions an hour, several hundred impressions per day. When enough copies of a single sheet are printed (perhaps 1,500 impressions or more), printers and apprentices clean the press entirely, break down the text block, and start over again from the manuscript to produce page two of a text.[6] It is monotonous work.

The printing press has taken on its own mythology as one of the greatest inventions of our time. In the western, dominant view, the press was central to the ways that knowledge was shared. Its invention allowed for many copies of many books, pamphlets, posters, and art to be printed and shared with a literate public. This way of sharing knowledge was not a part of Wawaus's culture. How strange it must have been then for Wawaus to find himself at the press, in a brick-built building, away from home, translating a foreign language.

In the tedium, did Wawaus reflect upon what was happening around him? Did he remember Hassanamesit before it became a Praying Town, appropriated by settlers as a place to congregate and Christianize Nipmuc people? Did he learn, from his indentured time living with English families or at the Indian College, that his culture was in danger of being lost? When he left his work at the press in the 1670s to fight against colonizers in King Philip's War, did he care more about the teachings of the Bible, or the letters printed on the page that made up the Algonquian-language words and sounds he had heard his whole life?

MEHQUANUMAONK (MEMORY)

Across the twenty or so generations since Wawaus labored at the printing press, what do his Nipmuc relations remember of him? How can we hold the many realities and circumstances of his life to be true all at once? At the very least, here and now, we can accept these three sheets from the Algonquian Bible as a call to reflection and remembrance. They serve to remind us that Native people—not just Wawaus but others—were deeply involved in the processes of translating English into Nipmuc, Wampanoag, Narragansett, and other dialects of Algonquian. Because of this work, we can connect our own oral histories and traditions to the words preserved in print form.

Like Wawaus, Nipmuc people today express ourselves through print and print culture. We write, tell, and publish stories. We make art on paper. We share knowledge in our ways. We use these methods to reclaim our traditions and culture. For those of us engaged in language reclamation work, we look back to the printed texts that captured our languages and use these resources to connect to all the ways we communicate with and understand the world around us. We use the words on printed sheets to help us learn, over and over again, to see all our relations, and remember them with new understanding.

NOTES

1 John Eliot, Thomas Thorowgood, and Richard Baxter, *The Eliot Tracts: With Letters from John Eliot to Thomas Thorowgood and Richard Baxter*, ed. Michael Clark (Westport, Conn.: Praeger Publishers, 2003).

2 James Constantine Pilling and Wilberforce Eames, *Bibliography of the Algonquian Languages* (Washington, D.C.: Smithsonian Institution, Bureau of Ethnology, U.S. Government Printing Office, 1891); Isaiah Thomas, *The History of Printing in America: With a Biography of Printers, and an Account of Newspapers* (Worcester, Mass., 1810).

3 Kimberly Toney, *From English to Algonquian: Early New England Translations*, online exhibition for the American Antiquarian Society, March 2016, https://collections.americanantiquarian.org/EnglishtoAlgonquian/.

4 Lisa Brooks, *Our Beloved Kin: A New History of King Philip's War* (New Haven, Conn.: Yale University Press, 2018), see chapter 2; Peabody Museum of Archaeology and Ethnology, "Digging Veritas—The Indian College," https://peabody.harvard.edu/galleries/digging-veritas-indian-college.

5 George Parker Winship, *The Cambridge Press, 1638–1692: A Reexamination of the Evidence Concerning the Bay Psalm Book and the Eliot Indian Bible, as well as Other Contemporary Books and People* (Philadelphia: University of Pennsylvania Press, 1945), 351–352.

6 Lawrence Counselman Wroth, *The Colonial Printer* (Portland, Maine: Southworth-Anthoensen Press, 1938).

ANDREW BLACKBIRD (MAKADEBINESI) AND MARGARET BOYD: *HISTORY OF THE OTTAWA AND CHIPPEWA INDIANS OF MICHIGAN*

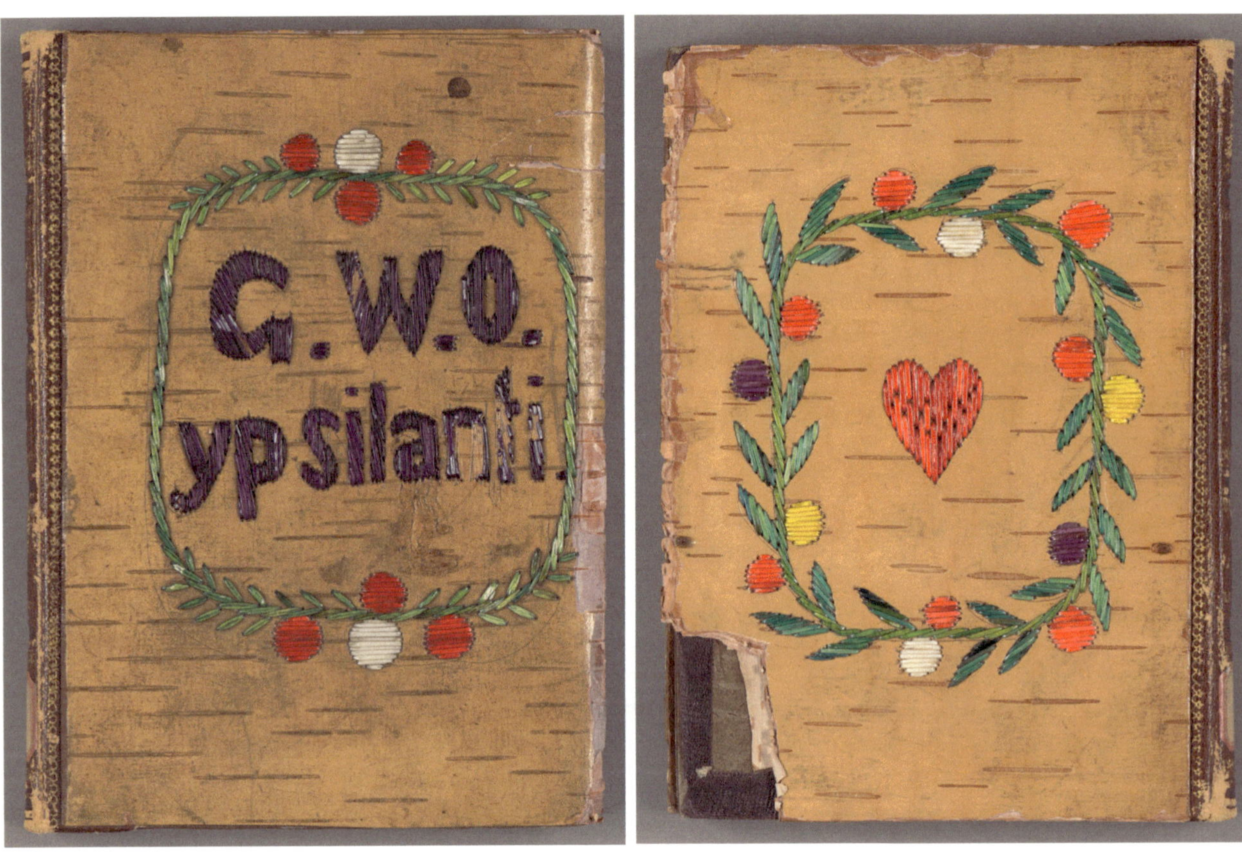

Figures 8a and 8b: Andrew Blackbird (Makadebinesi) (Odawa) and birch bark binding with porcupine quill decoration by Margaret Boyd (Odawa), *History of the Ottawa and Chippewa Indians of Michigan: A Grammar of their Language/Personal and Family History*, The Ypsilantian Job Printing House, Ypsilanti, Michigan, 1887. Amherst College Archives and Special Collections. Collection of Native American Literature. E99.O9 B6 1887 c.2.

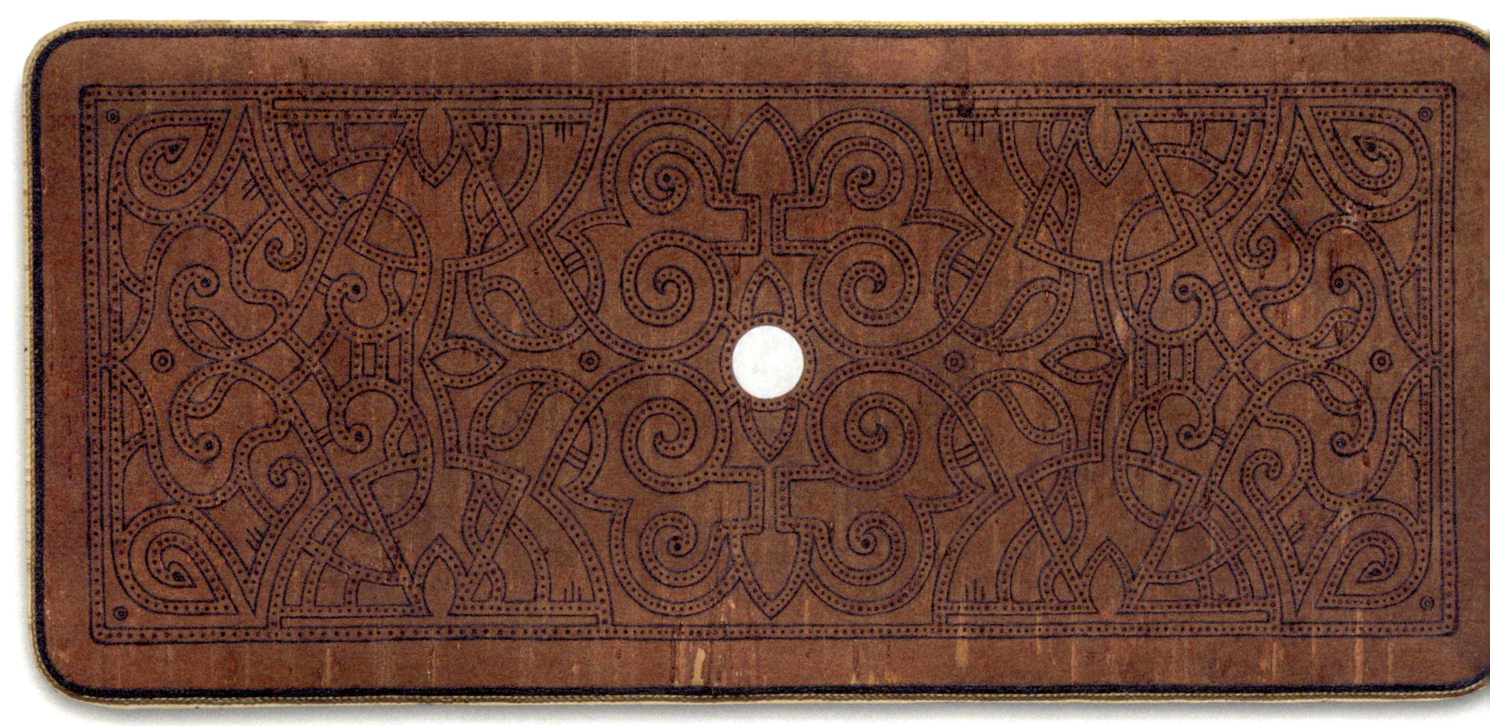

Figure 9: Sierra Henries (Chaubunagungamaug Nipmuc), *Pathways*, 2023. Freehand pyrography on winter birch bark, scallop shell, braided sinew. Courtesy of the artist. ©Sierra Henries.

ARTIST STATEMENT
Sierra Henries

Sierra Henries is Chaubunagungamaug Nipmuc and an artist from Maine who uses pyrography as a center of her practice. She is influenced by the Woodlands tradition of art using birch bark.

Pathways (Figure 9) is created on winter bark (birch bark) with another piece of summer bark as its backing. It has braided sinew as the trim detail, and a scallop shell disc at its center, which was made by forming the basic shape with a belt sander, but then doing all of the refining and finish work with files and sandpaper by hand. The design itself was created freehand, aside from the occasional use of pencil marks on scraps of paper to confirm that I had the lines balanced and even on both sides (no rulers, stencils, and so on). I sketched most of the design with a pencil, and then burned in the design using a pyrography tool. This project was particularly challenging because the winter bark doesn't burn quite as easily as summer bark does, which meant that I had to have the temperatures on my machine much higher and move much slower during the burning process. Consequently, I was consistently cooking my fingers throughout the process, and had to rely on wrapping them in cotton pads and bandages each day to try to shield them from the heat and prevent burning. Even parts of the tool itself ended up melting!

The white shell disc at the center represents the place where we all come from. As you follow the lines out from there, you'll notice that they go in many directions, take twists and turns, have seemingly dead ends....But in reality, they are all one continuous line that connects directly back to the source at the center no matter which way you follow it. Hence, *Pathways*. The dots along those pathways are people.

INTERVIEW WITH SIERRA HENRIES

Heid E. Erdrich in conversation with Sierra Henries

Heid E. Erdrich: How does place influence you as an artist?

Sierra Henries: I feel like in many ways, there's not much separation between art and place. The materials come from the land, the inspiration comes from the world around me, much of the energy I have for creating comes from being with places like the woods and the ocean. And when that energetic well starts to run dry, those are the places where I return to refill it. How could I not be influenced?

HEE: Describe the type of art you make, noting the materials you use and giving examples of a range of works you create, not just those included in *Boundless*.

SH: I create freehand pyrography line-work on birch bark. Many of these pieces are also cutting works made with an exacto knife. All are then framed to protect the bark. Other media I have worked on or with are wood, shell (lobster, crab, wampum, and so on), antique clay pipes, and other "found" objects. I have also expanded copies of my work onto prints, canvas prints, stickers, pocket mirrors, T-shirts, bags, mugs, postcards, notecards, and more, though I only carry a few of these presently!

HEE: Do you consider your work in the context of a particular tradition or arts practice? If so, how did you come into your practice?

SH: Though I'm deeply influenced by the traditional method of etching on birch bark, my style is different in that I burn into the bark instead of etching. I don't know of many folks who are creating works by burning into the bark, and those who are (that I've seen) are doing more mainstream styles of design such as portraiture and landscape works. I definitely pull on influence from traditional Eastern Woodlands designs, but my interpretations and line works are my own. When I first started, there was even less evidence of bark-burning artists.

HEE: Are there any materials you use that are threatened, scarce, or difficult to obtain? What are the issues surrounding those materials?

SH: Access to materials is a very real challenge. So much of the land where the birch bark, sweetgrass, and other important materials grow is privatized, and many of the owners (of the land) are not educated enough to allow access. Additionally, the bark I use in my art comes from mature trees, many of which are several hours travel away from me in western Maine. To find the time and resources and line it all up with proper weather is an undertaking that's not always accomplishable (mostly because of needing to prioritize work that pays the bills).

HEE: What is your vision for the future of your art for you and your community?

SH: I would love to start creating works that I can dedicate larger portions of time to, and that have a specific intention or purpose. In other words, not just pieces for sale at shows, but for museum exhibits and community projects. I would also love to do more collaborative pieces. I think I'd like to home in more on how art can help people, and how it can be a doorway into conversations, education, and community-building (especially for the local Indigenous communities).

Taubotne.

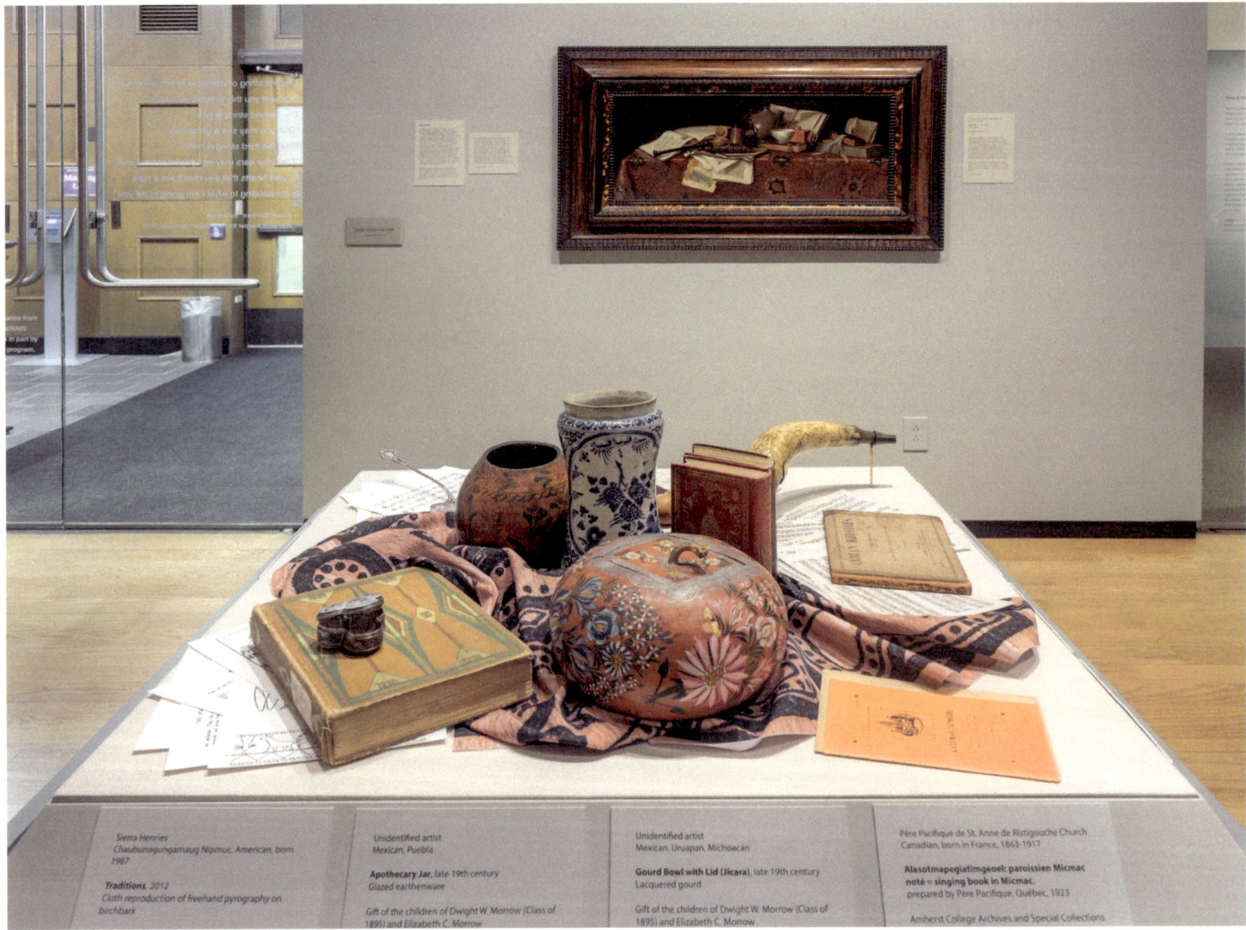

Figure 10: Installation photograph of a table group featuring works from the collections of the Mead Art Museum, the Amherst College Collection of Native American Literature, and Historic Deerfield. The fabric features a cloth reproduction of *Traditional*, a 2012 birch bark work with freehand pyrography by Sierra Henries (Chaubunagungamaug Nipmuc). The painting on the wall from the Mead's collection is *Still Life*, ca.17th century, attributed to Pieter Gerritsz van Roestraten (Dutch, 1630–1698). Museum purchase. 1976.12

Inspired by the Dutch painting placed nearby, this group of objects (Figure 10) imagines a still life celebrating Indigenous intellectual richness. It considers Indigenous people in the Northeast owning items made for trade—perhaps made by Indigenous people of Mexico and the Arctic. It presents an abundance of Native artistic accomplishment, especially in music, including hymns composed by Thomas Commuck (Narragansett), an ethnomusicologist who honored individual Native men and women, as well as Wabanaki, Mohican, Pawtucket, and other tribes with his hymns (Figure 39). Also highlighted are the diverse roles of Indigenous people—printer, baker, preacher, craftsperson, author, and soldier. The gunpowder horn honors the service of Nathaniel Sunsaman (spellings vary), a Niantic or Mohegan man who was in the 6th Connecticut Regiment in 1775.

Also nearby was a portrait of Hepsibeth Hemenway, a Nipmuc woman well-known for her wedding cakes (Figure 1). Listed in the will of her daughter Hannah were half a dozen silver teaspoons.[1] Imagine one of Hemenway's cakes being presented with a cake server similar to the one displayed. Among the books and musical scores are items made for global trade by the Dutch, Chinese, English, and French. Much like Indigenous artists, they used clay, gourds, horn, and ivory, which became scarce due to commercial and environmental practices. Soon Indigenous art became regarded as rare and collectible, not unlike these objects. While Native communities were forced into cultural loss, institutions were collecting what is our material and cultural legacy. Long cut off from parts of our histories and intellectual traditions, artists and writers reclaim and recover the important stories that objects tell.

—Heid E. Erdrich

NOTE

1 Hannah Hemenway lived with her mother as an adult, as did some of Hepsibeth's other children. While the teaspoons were not accounted for among Hepsibeth's belongings after her death in 1848, they were documented in the will of Hannah Hemenway. The family seemed to enjoy some economic advantages, particularly toward the end of Hepsibeth's life. See Hannah Hemenway probate records, docket #13525, filed 1892, Office of Probate, Worcester County Court House, Worcester, Mass. For more research on Hepsibeth and her portrait, see Holly V. Izard, "Hepsibeth Hemenway's Portrait: A Native American Story," *Old-Time New England* 77, no. 267 (Fall/Winter 1999): 49–85, https://www.historicnewengland.org/explore/collections-access/gusn/170023.

SHADOW RIVER
E. Pauline Johnson

Muskoka

A stream of tender gladness,
Of filmy sun, and opal tinted skies;
Of warm midsummer air that lightly lies
In mystic rings,
Where softly swings
The music of a thousand wings
That almost tones to sadness.

Midway 'twixt earth and heaven,
A bubble in the pearly air, I seem
To float upon the sapphire floor, a dream
Of clouds of snow,
Above, below,
Drift with my drifting, dim and slow,
As twilight drifts to even.

The little fern-leaf, bending
Upon the brink, its green reflection greets,
And kisses soft the shadow that it meets
With touch so fine,
The border line
The keenest vision can't define;
So perfect is the blending.

The far, fir trees that cover
The brownish hills with needles green and gold,
The arching elms o'erhead, vinegrown and old,
Repictured are
Beneath me far,
Where not a ripple moves to mar
Shades underneath, or over.

Mine is the undertone;
The beauty, strength, and power of the land
Will never stir or bend at my command;
But all the shade
Is marred or made,
If I but dip my paddle blade;
And it is mine alone.

O! pathless world of seeming!
O! pathless life of mine whose deep ideal
Is more my own than ever was the real.
For others Fame
And Love's red flame,
And yellow gold: I only claim
The shadows and the dreaming.

E. Pauline Johnson, *Flint and Feather: The Complete Poems of E. Pauline Johnson (Tekahionwake)*, (Toronto: Musson Book Co., 1917), 46–47.

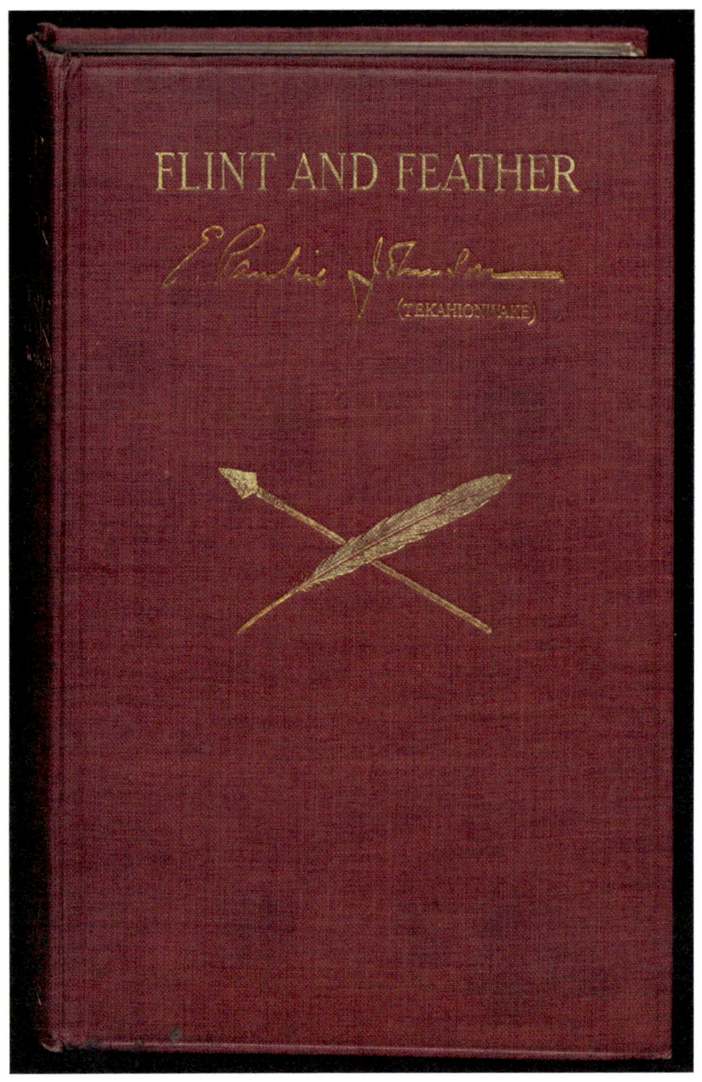

Figure 11: Cover of E. Pauline Johnson (Tekahionwake) (Mohawk), *Flint and Feather, Revised and Enlarged Edition*. Musson Book Company, Toronto, Canada, 1913. Amherst College Archives and Special Collections, Younghee Kim-Wait (Class of 1982)/Pablo Eisenberg Collection of Native American Literature. PR291199.2.J64 F5 1913.

THE HISTORY OF THE KIM-WAIT/EISENBERG COLLECTION OF NATIVE AMERICAN LITERATURE

Mike Kelly

Mike Kelly is the Head of the Archives and Special Collections at Amherst College.

The story of the Amherst College Collection of Native American Literature, generally known as the Kim-Wait/Eisenberg Collection or "the KWE," begins with the arrival of professors Lisa Brooks and Kiara Vigil at Amherst College in the fall of 2012. Lisa and Kiara both made a point of visiting the Archives and Special Collections Department on the A-Level of Frost Library to introduce themselves and inquire about incorporating archival materials into their teaching. At that time, however, support for Native American and Indigenous studies (NAIS) was extremely thin in the college's special collections. Apart from excellent copies of the *History of the Indian Tribes of North America* by Thomas McKenney and James Hall (Philadelphia, 1836–44), and Edward S. Curtis's *The North American Indian*, the collection had very little to support NAIS classes. Representation of Native authorship was limited to Sherman Alexie's and Leslie Marmon Silko's most popular works. Even Charles Eastman, who lived in Amherst while he wrote some of his most popular books in the early twentieth century, was completely absent from the shelves of the rare book collection. We made do with the limited materials available at that time, but we wanted to find a way to build our collections to meet the teaching and research needs of our newly arrived faculty.

Fortunately, the universe sent a solution our way in the form of a brochure advertising the sale of the private library of Pablo Eisenberg, professor of philanthropy at Georgetown University, and lifelong advocate for social justice. He had assembled a collection of nearly 1,500 books written by Native American writers and had decided to sell the entire collection as a single unit. Thus did Amherst's near-total lack of Native representation in special collections become a boon: other institutions that already held collections of NAIS materials passed on purchasing a collection that duplicated much of their holdings. As soon as I shared the collection description with Lisa and Kiara, they were enthusiastically on board, and we began talking up the opportunity to anyone who would listen. Younghee Kim-Wait (Class of 1982) heard our plea and made a generous donation that enabled us to purchase the collection. It was delivered to the Archives and Special Collections in August 2013.

Once the collection arrived, the real work began. We prioritized work on the Kim-Wait/Eisenberg collection and added 1,395 records to the library catalog by May 2014. The oldest item in the collection was a copy of the fourth edition of Mohegan minister and cultural leader Samson Occom's *A Sermon, Preached at the Execution of Moses Paul, An Indian* (New London, 1772), generally regarded as the first published book by a Native author. Eisenberg's collection included excellent coverage of other Native authors writing before the turn of the twentieth century, including William Apess, George Copway, Elias Boudinot, John Rollin Ridge, Peter Dooyentate Clark, Elias Johnson, Sarah Winnemucca, William Warren, Alice Callahan, Simon Pokagon, and E. Pauline Johnson. Books by more recent authors were present, but it was clear that Eisenberg's collecting was more focused on historical works than contemporary writing.

Through the process of unpacking and cataloging the books, we learned the strengths and gaps of the collection and drafted a formal policy for expanding the collection and addressing those gaps. The shortest version of this policy is that we seek to hold a copy of any book published by a Native author, regardless of format, subject, or audience.

The process of researching and cataloging the books revealed different ways that traditional library tools and systems erase Indigenous identities, but also offered opportunities to push the boundaries of those systems. Library of Congress call numbers for literature follow contemporary colonial boundaries; Canadian writers are classed in the PR 9000 range, while American writers receive call numbers in the PS range. E. Pauline Johnson, a Mohawk writer from Canada, is in the PR class; Maurice Kenney, another Mohawk writer who lived on the U.S. side of the border, is shelved in the PS range. One small intervention we made in our catalog records is to include a nonstandard note about the tribal identity of the author, wherever that information is clear. Both Johnson and Kenney have the searchable note "Mohawk Indian authors" in their catalog records to restore that common identity in spite of the colonial identities (Canadian author, American author) imposed by the Library of Congress classification system. Searching for books by writers from a particular tribe or community is one of the most frequent questions about the collection.

In spite of these limitations, there are ways we have used traditional rare book cataloging practices to be as transparent as possible about how and where we are acquiring books for this collection. Provenance notes that record former owners and other acquisition details are standard cataloging practice for rare book collections. The history of collecting Native American and Indigenous materials in museums, archives, and libraries has generally followed an extractive model of institutions removing unique materials from communities, often destroying or obscuring the cultural context of those materials in the process. Our goal is to avoid recreating those colonial practices; including detailed information about the sources of the items in our collection is one way to do that. All of the books that belonged to Pablo Eisenberg include a note that identifies them as such. As we have expanded the collection, we have made a point of including detailed provenance notes about our sources of acquisition.

Ten years after the arrival of the Eisenberg books in the Archives and Special Collections reading room in Frost, we have more than doubled the size of the collection. The collection now includes more than 3,350 books and we expect it to double in size again within the next decade. As news of the Kim-Wait/Eisenberg acquisition spread, we received many offers of donations to the collection; one of the earliest significant gifts came from Amherst alumnus Peter Webb (Class of 1972) who donated an earlier edition of Occom's *Sermon* along with an assortment of books by writers such as Apess, Copway, and Eastman. Visits from Native authors to campus have resulted in many additions to the collection, such as the 181 items we purchased directly from Gerald Vizenor after he saw our holdings of his works were less than complete. Most recently, we have partnered with Lee Francis, founder of Red Planet Books and Comics and A Tribe Called Geek, to ensure that Amherst holds as complete a collection of Native-authored comics and zines as possible. There is a tremendous amount of activity as a new generation of Native authors, artists, and creators engage with the world of print in the twenty-first century. The goal of the Native Literature Collection in the Amherst Archives and Special Collections is to continue to document this engagement in the past, present, and—most importantly—the future.

SELECTION OF TEXTS

Heid E. Erdrich

The feel and smell of old books is a pleasure I find distinct, sensual, intrinsic to knowing an author's work. Since childhood, some of my best memories are about handling books and pages in libraries, bookstores, and archives. My desire to be in an archive or library or museum had haunted me during the pandemic. The sensual aspects of book-handling, the texture and heft of old leather, the sound of a page turning, the smell of books! When I arrived at Special Collections at Amherst College's Frost Library, I'd hardly been anywhere outside of my home in Minneapolis. When I was shown into the collection, I nearly swooned.

The staff at Special Collections graciously guided me to works I had become interested in as I read entries for the entire online catalog. Staff and students also showed me works they found of interest. Head of the Archives and Special Collections at Amherst College, Mike Kelly, helped me kick off the process, and there could not have been a better instigator because Mike is an expert on Samson Occom, a Mohegan preacher and hymn maker who is considered the first Native American author in what became the United States. Later in the process, project coordinator (at that time) of Mapping Native Intellectual Networks of the Northeast, Brandon Castle guided me toward books on Indigenous foods, which became a section of *Boundless* that delighted visitors. Library staff, interns, and student researchers contributed enormously to my ability to select works from a distance. I also took student suggestions and included works they found interesting.

TEXT IN ART

Throughout the museum, visitors found visual art I selected for *Boundless* because it contained text. Some of these artworks were by white artists of the previous centuries—including an artwork I have been aware of since I was a child, one of the sixty-some iterations of *Peaceable Kingdom* by Edward Hicks (1780–1849). I came into my selection process for *Boundless* knowing that many works by today's Native artists use text in English or Indigenous languages within their images. The reasons for inclusion of texts are many and could be subject of an entirely other essay, but I was attracted to such works as a bridge between the texts that I was selecting and visual works.

In addition, I selected art that contained maps or other record-keeping systems that convey meaning through images. I made these selections so that visitors could read the art as well as the texts from the library. In both iterations of *Boundless* at Mead, I wrote labels that contained poems and quotes from Native writers that "spoke" from the walls. I included novels, play scripts, political statements, photo essays, and every manner of Native-authored literature. My intention in creating the labels and other didactics was to include as many Indigenous voices as possible, not just mine. I wanted to expand visitors' curiosity and understanding of Indigenous intellectual and artistic traditions by presenting visual art that could be read, next to texts from the Collection of Native American Literature.

Another aspect of my selection worked toward my desire for visitors to learn about the many Indigenous languages that were suppressed by colonization. My approach presented a further bridge between text and image in that it considered the visual aspects of language. Guests found texts in languages that do not use the same writing system as English: a poem in Cyrillic, ancient reliefs, a clay nail in cuneiform, a nineteenth-century lithograph in Cherokee syllabary—all works in symbol systems that might look like design or art to one who cannot read them. Similarly, the meaning of a string of wampum, which was part of *Boundless*, might be lost on someone whose idea of "document" meant paper copies. It is vitally important to show how diverse record-keeping and recognition of agreements look so that we can imagine what it would be like to negotiate vast land transfers without both parties recognizing and understanding one another's languages.

Museum collections often illustrate that Native people have been creating art for millennia. More often now than in the past, they might show contemporary Native art as part of the story, which allows for our representation as alive, even thriving, when it is not unusual to encounter people who think we no longer exist—especially on the East Coast. *Boundless* was a chance to show we are still here and that we have been writing and publishing for centuries, and doing so alongside our visual art or even within it.

TEXTS AND ASSIMILATION

Some of the works by Native authors that I chose for *Boundless* both charmed and horrified me, but I was determined to present a selection from the earliest to current Native authors. Some of the first Native-authored books were weapons of forced assimilation and were used hand in hand with the tactics of genocide: Christian Bibles, hymns, lessons, and dictionaries, in Indigenous languages helped Christianize and assimilate Indigenous populations. Often becoming Christian was the only way Indigenous people could remain in their homelands. Removal to distant lands was all too common a tactic of the colonial populations who forcibly displaced Indigenous peoples. These tactics fostered forced education, in English, and removal of children from their homes for such education. Today these methods are defined as genocide under global law.

Once Native Americans became Christian converts, Indigenous languages were banned in schools and churches. It's a bitter irony that those early books in Indigenous languages are now vital to many tribes as resources in the recovery and revitalization of their Indigenous languages. For many, but not all of us, the idea of documents printed in the original languages of America can be surprising. But the first Bible printed in colonial America was printed in the Algonquian language indigenous to what we now call New England.

READING AREAS

My visits to the actual collections at Amherst College were few. Most of my research was conducted using the online catalog and Amherst's excellent digital collection of early works. But the more I studied the remarkable books in the Collection of Native American Literature from a distance, the more I wanted *Boundless* guests to be able to engage with these texts in some physical way. I couldn't imagine creating an exhibition about books without offering visitors a chance to sit down and pick up an actual book. I wanted people engaged in reading to be part of *Boundless*. Mead staff understood this desire and together we made certain *Boundless* exhibitions at the Mead Art Museum would have reading areas where visitors of all ages could sit down with copies of books and excerpts reproduced from texts that are in Amherst's collections. Four reading areas offered Native-authored poems, stories, studies, musical scores, and even recipe cards they could take with them. If I couldn't bring everyone who visited *Boundless* into Special Collections, then I would give them the next best thing, room to read.

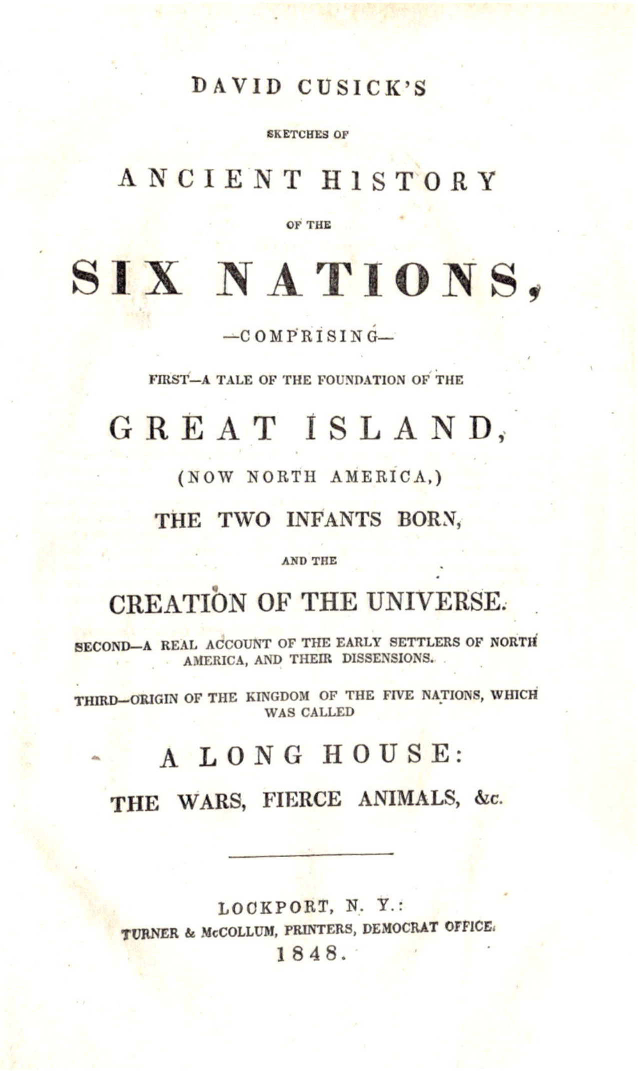

DAVID CUSICK'S

SKETCHES OF

ANCIENT HISTORY

OF THE

SIX NATIONS,

—COMPRISING—

FIRST—A TALE OF THE FOUNDATION OF THE

GREAT ISLAND,

(NOW NORTH AMERICA,)

THE TWO INFANTS BORN,

AND THE

CREATION OF THE UNIVERSE.

SECOND—A REAL ACCOUNT OF THE EARLY SETTLERS OF NORTH AMERICA, AND THEIR DISSENSIONS.

THIRD—ORIGIN OF THE KINGDOM OF THE FIVE NATIONS, WHICH WAS CALLED

A LONG HOUSE:

THE WARS, FIERCE ANIMALS, &c.

LOCKPORT, N. Y.:
TURNER & McCOLLUM, PRINTERS, DEMOCRAT OFFICE.
1848.

Figure 12a: David Cusick (Tuscarora), Title page from *David Cusick's Sketches of Ancient History of the Six Nations*, 1848. Third edition with illustrations, Lockport, N.Y.: Turner & McCollum, printers. Amherst College Archives and Special Collections, Younghee Kim-Wait (Class of 1982)/Pablo Eisenberg Collection of Native American Literature. E99.I7 C87 1848.

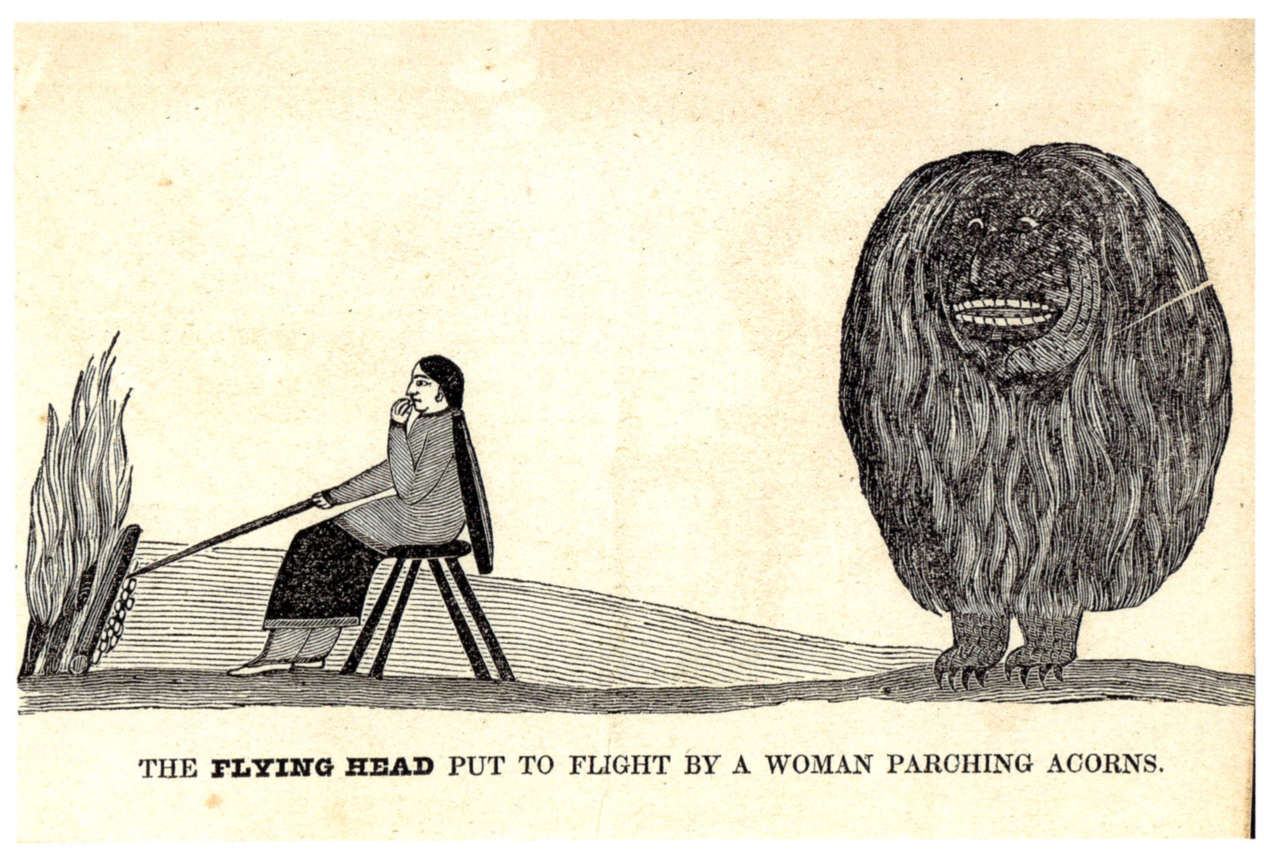

Figure 12b: David Cusick (Tuscarora), An illustration from *David Cusick's Sketches of Ancient History of the Six Nations*, 1848. Amherst College Archives and Special Collections, Younghee Kim-Wait (Class of 1982)/ Pablo Eisenberg Collection of Native American Literature. E99.I7 C87 1848.

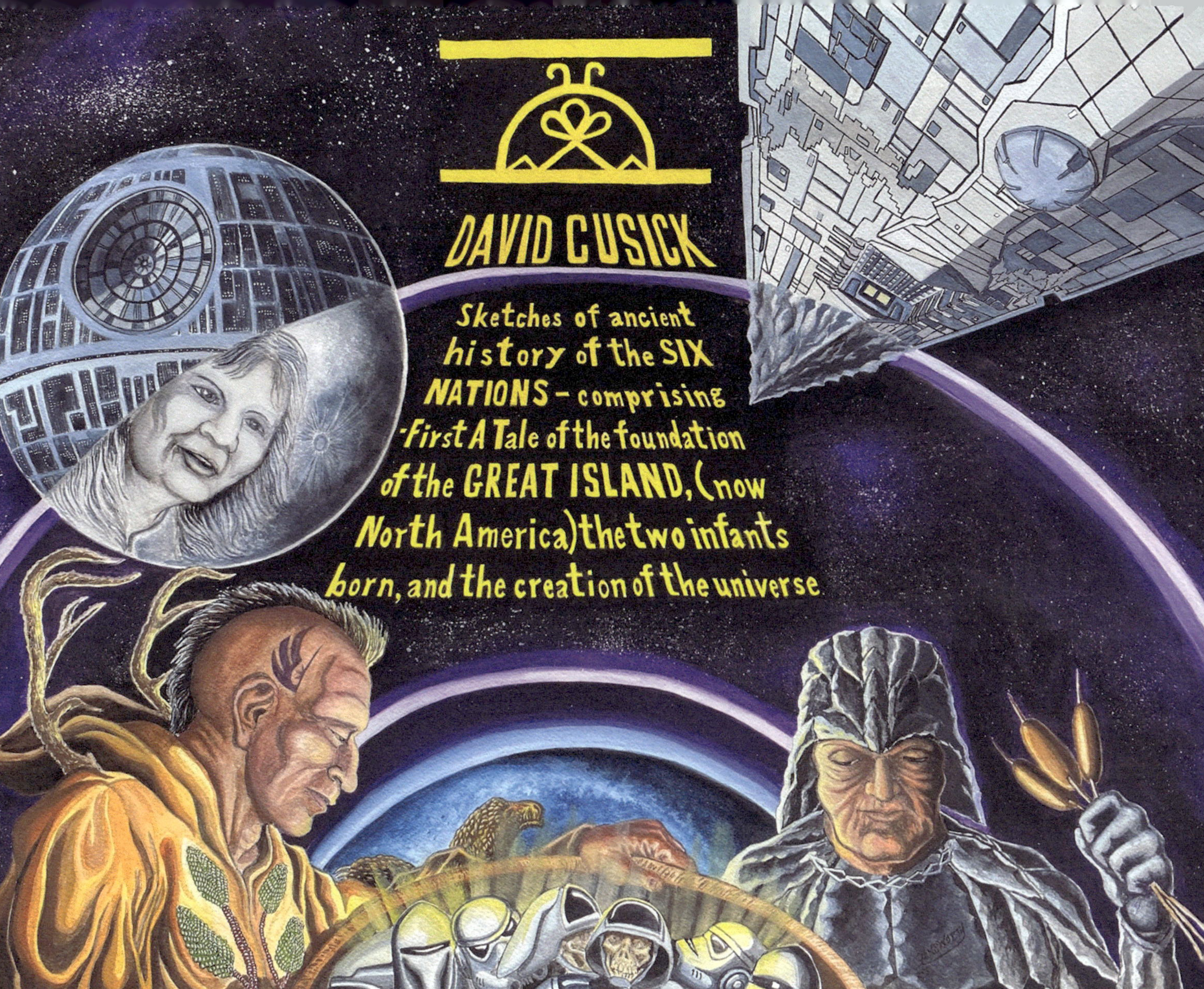

Figure 13: Eric Gansworth (Onondaga), *A long time ago on a turtle's back, not far away…*, 2023. Gouache and archival ink on Arches watercolor paper, 18″ × 24″ ©Eric Gansworth. Image credit: Petegorsky/Gipe.

A LONG TIME AGO

Eric Gansworth

Eric Gansworth is a visual artist and Lowry Writer-in-Residence at Canisius University in Buffalo, New York. He is Onondaga living on the Tuscarora Reservation.

Sometimes you encounter an idea and suddenly understand your life better. As a child, I fell in love with the hall of mirrors, the maze where variants of you mimicked your movements to infinity, as you might charge headfirst into a wall instead of finding the maze's next hallway.

Endless multiple possible views was a nice visual shorthand to one of my culture's most complicated foundations. In Haudenosaunee thought, there is no definitive version of any story. Even in reciting our cosmology, the teller's prerogative is to choose which elements to emphasize, which to play down, and which to eliminate entirely. These choices are determined by what the teller believes the audience needs most in the moment. I'd somehow picked up this complex nonwestern philosophy—the malleable relationship among teller, audience, and story—despite not being from a traditional family. It has resurfaced throughout my life, often when I least expect it.

Fresh from grad school, preparing to teach my first classes as a college faculty member, I encountered an American literature anthology. Rather than beginning with "exploration narratives," this book had editors committed to early Indigenous narratives first. Among them was a man named David Cusick, a family name I immediately recognized. He was a Cusick from the Tuscarora Nation, the community where I was raised. I had complex lifelong friendships with Cusicks. They had to be related, but I'd never heard of him. How was it that no one in his family thought his work important enough to pass that information down? The further I read, the further I headed down that hall of mirrors. I discovered he's among the very first Indigenous writers to document his culture from the inside. However, I also noticed immediately that his version of our cosmology has a heavy Christian overlay to its narrative threads, and I've often wondered if this is why his current living family didn't mention his work, or seem to know of his significant contribution to Indigenous culture, literature, and history.

Even in our small community, faith traditions were varied and often at odds. It's been long rumored that members of an aggressive Christian movement burned down the last longhouse early in the twentieth century. But as with so much else, this event isn't written, lingering only in the memories of those who were told the story and have passed it on. The major narratives of our cultures are largely transmitted through oral storytelling, aided with visual assistance in the form of wampum belts, rows of alternating purple and white beads, forming emblematic images to draw from.

I hadn't formally studied our cosmology when I encountered Cusick's work but, strictly through community interaction, I knew the basic highlights. Still, Cusick's Christian overlays were immediately visible, and I felt conflicted about presenting to undergraduates a version of our creation story obviously influenced by the Book of Genesis. If you went looking, you'd find many contradictory versions accepted as legitimate versions. That knowledge satisfied my immediate need of dealing with American literature survey students, but it was a complicated discovery for me.

My mother was raised in the Baptist Church, though only stepped inside for funerals and weddings. My five oldest siblings had been baptized in their full-immersion culture. By the time my closest brother and I came along, and her life had grown increasingly more complicated, she hadn't bothered to put us through that initiation. Whatever beliefs I was exposed to came in a haphazard and uncurated way, so I could pick and choose whichever funhouse mirror hallway I wanted, knowing I might smack my head against a rude surprise at any moment. Consequently, I also pull my own metaphors from any source that seems suitable to me, and this has shaped my artistic career.

We view the story as a living thing, understood by multiple generations in ways meaningful to them. Over the years, I've come back to Cusick's version over and over, as a window into his world. Grasping the reasons for his story's oddness allowed for a major shift in my understanding of our cosmology. As he was a product of his time and culture, I am a product of mine too. Popular culture, a major force in my world, gave me a closer understanding of reconciling the discrepancies he did not have available to him. I was well-versed in comics. The infinite possible versions of our cosmology felt akin to the "Infinite Earths" of DC Comics or the "Multiverse" of Marvel Comics.

Fusing those narratives of superheroes and supervillains onto the story of Skywoman/Mature Blossom and her Twin Sons/Grandsons felt like an oversimplification. However, multiple valid versions also fit neatly with my undeveloped understanding of our culture's rejection of the "definitive story" idea so prevalent in western culture. When I began teaching, my professional life as an artist started as well. I had work in a show with established Indigenous visual artists in the same six-month period I'd had fiction and some poems accepted for publication. Cusick had illustrated his book with key moments from the three major narratives he chose, and I realized that in some way, he'd helped shape my path, over a hundred and fifty years before.

My professional creative work draws on my experiences as an enrolled member of the Onondaga Nation, raised at the Tuscarora Nation in Western New York, including elements of this epic story I'd first seen fully documented by Cusick. My father's family was Tuscarora, like Cusick, but my mother, her female ancestors, and all her children are Onondaga. Though Tuscaroras had joined the other five nations of the Haudenosaunee in 1722, they still have their own close but different history and cultural shape. That cultural influence remains and shapes my aesthetic in ways I can't possibly be aware of. I suspect I'm more open to the idea of multiple legitimate narratives, because my family's consciousness was always divided, always a little hall of mirrors, even in my small community of a thousand people.

Because my work relies heavily on cultural experience, fragmented stories and repeated patterns always speak to me. The layers of my multiple cultural lives dance and reabsorb one another, like concentric radiating circles in a lake when a stone gets dropped in. Thought threads, observations, encounters with another artist's work, all enter my imagination and lie dormant for years until the right triggers release them. Even years beyond the impact, the radiations emerge unexpectedly, overlapping a new vibration. I've come to trust that feeling.

Given the strong Christian influence, I rarely returned to Cusick's version of our foundational narratives. I'd later discovered versions with less of that particular double exposure. Just the same, something kept drawing me back to reconsider it. Sometimes all it takes is a sliver of an idea to wedge open a new door.

The full title of his book (Figures 12a and 12b) is *David Cusick's Sketches of Ancient History of the Six Nations, —Comprising—First—A Tale of the Foundation of the Great Island (Now North America), The Two Infants Born, and the Creation of the Universe. Second—A Real Account of the Early Settlers of North America, and Their Dissentions. Third—Origin of the Kingdom of the Five Nations, Which Was Called a Long House: The Wars, Fierce Animals, &c.* Absurdly long titles with built in subheadings were not uncommon in his era, but the breadth of his choices also suggests his epic desire to capture our cultures. It suggests his urgency in sending it out. In an author's note, he asserts that he'd waited much of his life for someone to document these stories. Aging, he recognized mortality's limitations, so he did what so few people do. He committed, and wrote the book he'd been waiting for, even as he had reservations about his ability to do so.

Numerous threads keep drawing me back to this volume. With the story's blatant Cain and Abel double exposure on Flint and Sapling, the twins of our cosmology, I suspected more Christian imagery awaited inside. I didn't understand that other things awaited me, too. Revisiting *Star Wars*, some time later, in one of its many iterations, I realized another stone had dropped into my Lake of Unconscious. Its concentric rings began to surface, triggered by George Lucas, that story's teller, and his choice to begin changing his narrative, to suit a new audience's needs.

Adherents to American culture are nothing if not unyielding in their love of their unexamined story. Lucas tinkered in small ways with these three stories, clearly labeling his activities, calling the new versions the "Special Edition." Rabid fans, mostly middle-aged men, groused constantly, ludicrously claiming he "raped my childhood." This "epic violation" amounted to a few scenes enhanced by new technology. Perhaps more critically, he made small narrative changes that his obsessive believers claimed were the ruination of some sacred text.

I suspect Lucas knew early on this would happen one day. At the beginning of *Return of the Jedi*, Luke must face a gluttonous, self-absorbed slug, his gang of parasitic thugs, and monsters he'd cultivated that included a voracious giant called a rancor and a sarlacc—another unseen monster, a sentient digestive tract living in a pit, which would devour you and slowly continue to digest you over a thousand years. Among the changes, he added further clarifying titles. He changed the succinct title from *Star Wars* to *The Star Wars Trilogy Special Edition: Episode IV—A New Hope*. In interviews, Lucas also told numerous conflicting stories about the development of the *Star Wars* universe, each anecdote inserted or deleted, depending on the audience of the moment.

Looking at these new absurdly long titles, I felt Cusick's impossibly long title resurface, so detailed a reader was offered major highlights before ever accessing the text. Many years later, witnessing Indigenous communities feverishly embrace the new character, Baby Yoda, I revisited Lucas's increasingly long story, and understood why immediately. Baby Yoda's story resonated with stories familiar from many Indigenous families, a lost child, removed from family, forced to rely on the kindness of strangers, and, well, we know how that turned out for most of our ancestors. His real name is not even revealed for an extended amount of time.

Also in that moment, I began to see how deeply *Star Wars* had always resonated with Indigenous communities, and how most Indians I met didn't seem to care that the stories had minor changes, or that some parts of the story were concerned with events happening generations before the initial stories. They didn't care that our initial understanding didn't even include the identity of the true main character, and that some parts of those stories didn't all line up quite as exactly as they might have anticipated.

There were stories of brothers, at odds with one another, one seeking balance and the other seeking domination, each defined partly by the other's actions and desires; stories of twins on different paths; stories of major characters falling from one world to another, beginning a journey all over again; stories of a moon that turns out to be a malevolent force, and of a moon that saves lives. Lucas claimed he was interested in the universals of myth, but maybe he was really engaging the universals of truth in variation, the universals of our foundations in stories. *Star Wars* begins not with action, but with an absurdly long opening, an orienting scroll that stretches out before the audience like David Cusick's title, setting the stage for all that's to come. These two concentric circles colliding in my life reopened the door to another old image, made new again by variation, shaped by my needs in the moment. This is the way my life path has been shaped.

And I am now well into middle age. Consequently, like so many others, this story can also begin: A long time ago....

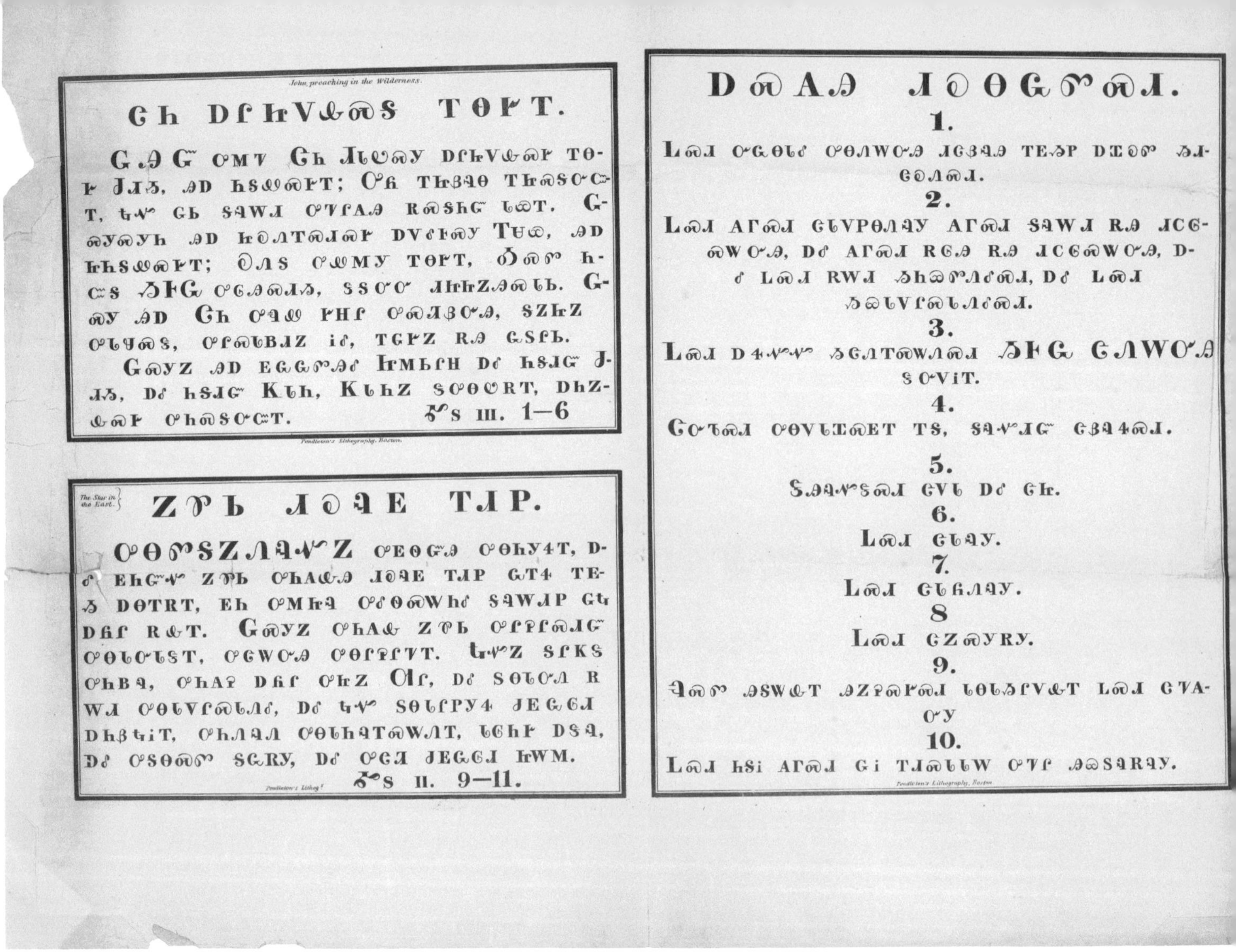

John preaching in the Wilderness.

Pendleton's Lithography, Boston.

The Star in the East.

Pendleton's Lithog.

Pendleton's Lithography, Boston

Figure 14: Installation photograph featuring Asa Hitchcock, translator (American, 1800–1849): *John Preaching in the Wilderness; The Star in the East;* and *The Ten Commandments* (Pendleton's Lithography, Boston, 1836). Amherst College Archives and Special Collections. Collection of Native American Literature. File PM784.H58 S37 1836. Image credit: Petegorsky/Gipe.

Asa Hitchcock served at Dwight Mission within Cherokee territory where he was a mechanic in 1826. In 1828 Dwight Mission relocated to Oklahoma when the Cherokee were forced to move; it is now owned by the Cherokee Nation. Dwight Mission and other missions were involved in printing Cherokee language material. Cherokee syllabary uses a symbol for each syllable in a word. Sequoyah, the inventor of the syllabary, lived near Dwight Mission briefly and was a Cherokee blacksmith who did not read or write. He first used symbols for numbers, eventually developing them into the syllabary between 1809 and 1812.

ODE TO SEQUOYAH
Alexander L. Posey

The names of Waitie and Boudinot—
    The valiant warrior and gifted sage—
And other Cherokees, may be forgot,
    But thy name shall descend to every age;
The mysteries enshrouding Cadmus' name
Cannot obscure thy claim to fame.

The people's language cannot perish—nay,
    When from the face of this great continent
Inevitable doom hath swept away
    The last memorial—the last fragment
Of tribes,—some scholar learned shall pore
Upon thy letters, seeking ancient lore.

Some bard shall lift a voice in praise of thee,
    In moving numbers tell the world how men
Scoffed thee, hissed thee, charged with lunacy!
    And who could not give 'nough honor when
At length, in spite of jeers, of want and need,
Thy genius shaped a dream into a deed.

By cloud-capped summits in the boundless west,
    Or mighty river rolling to the sea,
Where'er thy footsteps led thee on that quest,
    Unknown, rest thee, illustrious Cherokee!

Alexander Lawrence Posey, *Poems of Alexander Lawrence Posey* (Topeka, Kans.: Crane & Company Printers, 1910), 184–185.

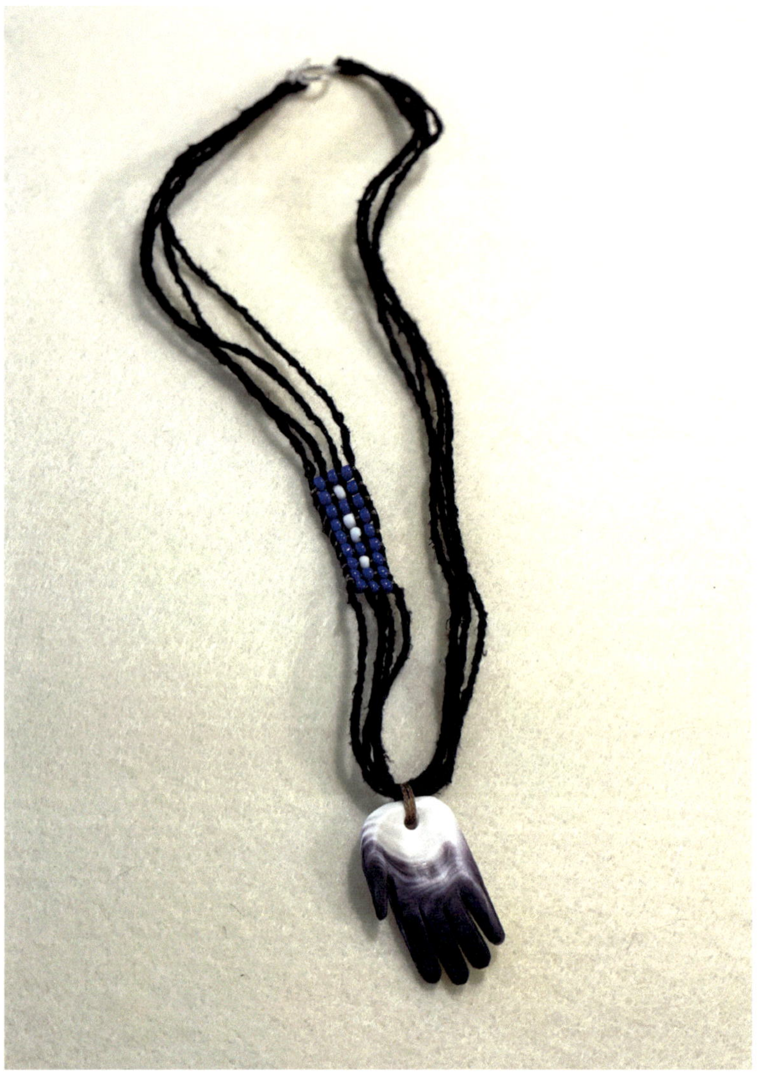

Figure 15: Elizabeth James-Perry (Aquinnah Wampanoag), *At Waters Edge*, 2022. Necklace in wampum, milkweed plant, logwood dye, glass trade beads, sterling silver. Courtesy of the artist.

Hand motifs have always fascinated me, and I've been incorporating them into my wampum art for decades. In Wampanoag jewelry, the purple and white inside of the shell is often featured.

In this case both sides are interesting: with layers of tans and grays exposed on the back, the hand appears to be dipping into water; hence the title. It has been strung on handspun, rather silken, dyed milkweed cordage.

—Elizabeth James-Perry

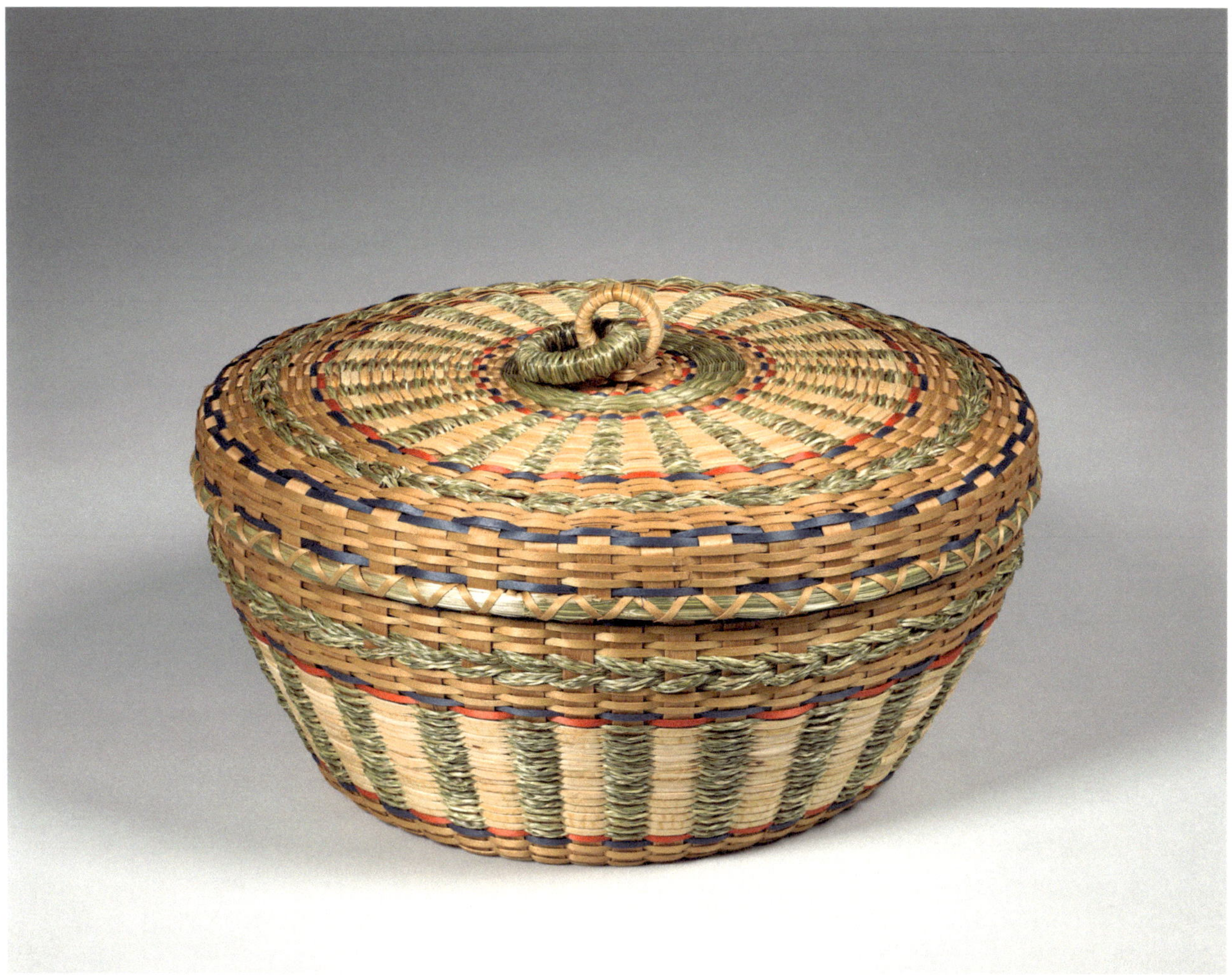

Figure 16a: Theresa Secord (Penobscot), *Penobscot Sewing Basket* (closed), 2023. Ash and braided sweetgrass, cedar bark, velvet photograph. 6″ × 11″ × 11″ (15.2 cm × 27.9 cm × 27.9 cm). Mead Art Museum at Amherst College. Museum purchase with William K. Allison (Class of 1920) Memorial Fund. AC 2023.03.

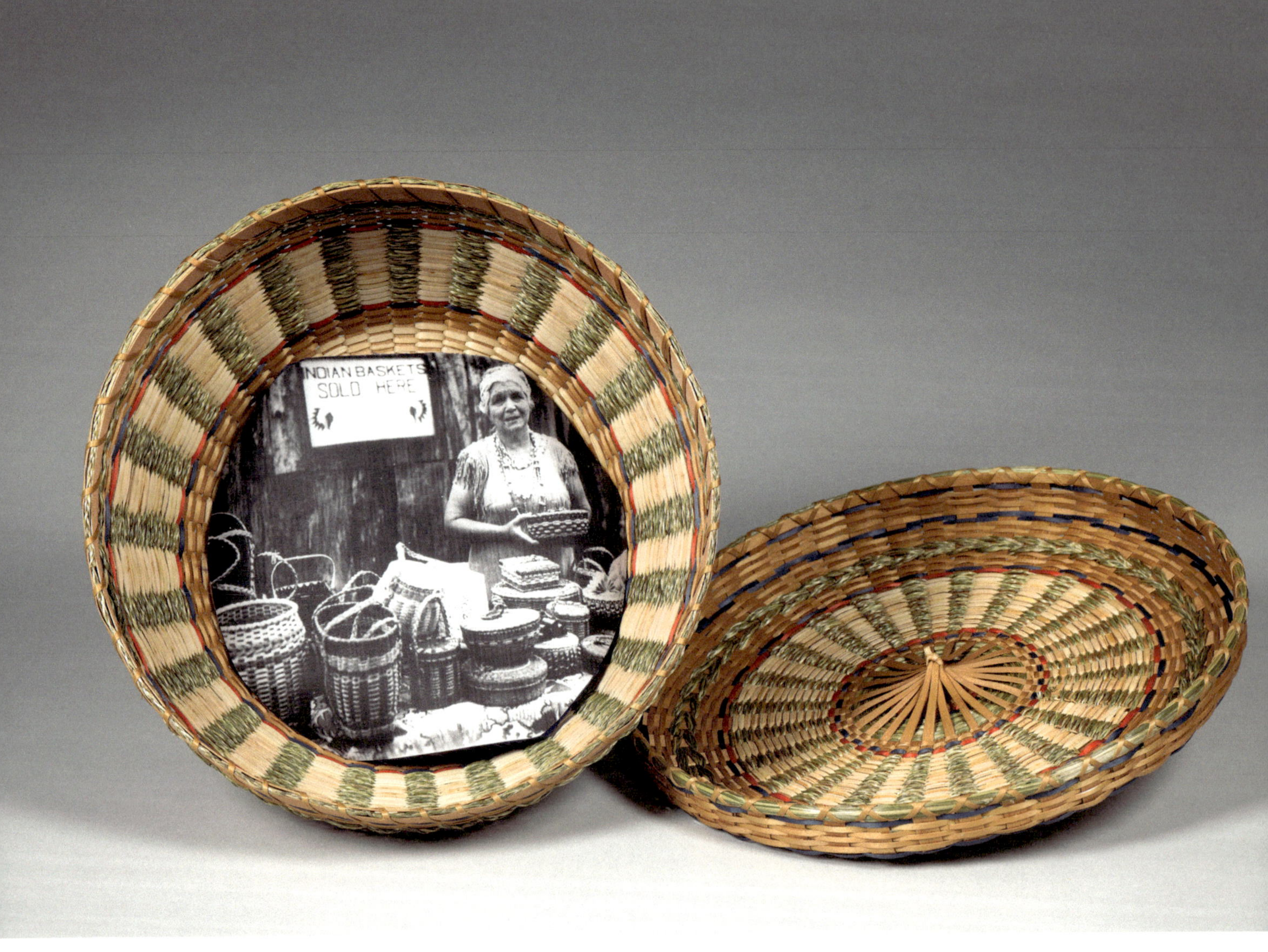

Figure 16b: Theresa Secord (Penobscot), *Penobscot Sewing Basket* (open), 2023. Ash and braided sweetgrass, cedar bark, velvet photograph. 6″ × 11″ × 11″ (15.2 cm × 27.9 cm × 27.9 cm). Mead Art Museum at Amherst College. Museum purchase with William K. Allison (Class of 1920) Memorial Fund. AC 2023.03.

The basket was woven on my great-grandmother's wooden form and handed down to me from the 1800s. Inside, a photograph shows her holding a similar basket in 1953. I backed the photograph with velvet, which would have been used for associated sewing basket notions such as a pin cushion.

—Theresa Secord

CURRENTS OF KINSHIP

3

CURRENTS OF KINSHIP

Heid E. Erdrich

As *Boundless* developed, the image of being carried on water through all that I was learning continued to guide me. Jacquelyn Cabarrubia '25, a student researcher assisting me in Special Collections, pointed out the traditional "Potawatomi Song" with its emphasis on movement, which seemed a perfect emblem for what I was experiencing with my persistent feeling that my research is a journey by water: "Now we all move, we're moving with this earth,/ The earth is moving along, the water is moving along,/the grass is moving, the trees are moving,/The whole earth is moving/So we all move along with the earth, keeping time with the earth."[1]

The song is also a beautiful illustration of Gerald Vizenor's notion of transmotion in art and literature by Native Americans as he defines it: "Natural motion is a heartbeat, ravens on the wing, the rise of thunderclouds and the mysterious weight of whales. Transmotion is the visionary or creative perceptions of the seasons and the visual scenes of motion in art and literature."[2]

These two passages from writing found in Amherst's Collection of Native American Literature helped in shaping *Boundless* by reminding me to keep moving and follow currents as they presented themselves to me. One current I became particularly interested in was how authors were related to one another by kinship and ancestry as well as place. As I got to know Brothertown, Mohegan, Nipmuc, Shinnecock, and Wampanoag artists creating weaving, ceramics, paintings, birch bark art, and music today, I learned that many consider specific early Native American authors tribal ancestors or actual relatives. I learned that from the very first published Mohegan authors, an entire family of writers spanning generations had sprung. Visual artists from the region also shared that they are related to early authors. Movement across generations moved me and I followed, carried by a current of kinship.

There are further hallmarks of kinship within *Boundless*. Some of the living artists included in the show created works with their families in mind. Penobscot weaver Theresa Secord's basket (Figures 16a and 16b) includes a photograph printed on velvet of her great-grandmother selling baskets. Kimberly Toney's notes on Wawaus, the Nipmuc printer, accompany three pages of the first Bible ever printed in what became the United States; the wampum work of Elizabeth James-Perry (Figure 15) shares the room with two canoe paddles carved by her brother, Jonathan James-Perry (Figures 5 and 6) and both share an ancestor with Paul Cuffe, Jr., whose book was in the first iteration of *Boundless*.

The kinship that exists between Native American culture groups of the Northeast can be explained by the shared Algonquian language and political alliances in the past as well as the shared land, shared place. We also see bonds of intermarriage persisting into the present. Wampanoag, Mohegan, Mahican, Montauk, Narragansett, Nipmuc, and other marriages took place in the early Americas as they take place today. Groups no longer established as tribal entities also married into these tribes. There are no "extinct" Natives of New England; they live on in current tribes. As Natives often have to assert: *We are still here*.

I wasn't surprised to find focus on relationality within early Native American writing. The two earliest published Native American writers were Samson Occom and Joseph Johnson, Occom's son-in-law, a Mohegan man also identified as Montauk/Mahican.[3] Johnson is ancestor to Gladys Tantaquidgeon, Melissa Fawcett, Madeline Sayet, Rachel Beth Sayet, and likely others included in the exhibition.[4] In 1772 both Occom and Johnson published sermons for a Mohegan man who was sentenced to death in New Haven, Connecticut. Occom highlighted the notion of relatedness in his *Sermon on the Execution of Moses Paul*, calling Paul "My poor unhappy brother Mose" and later asserting: "You are the bone of my bone, and flesh of my flesh. You are an Indian, a despised creature."[5] Perhaps being despised brought those Natives struggling to enact survivance into traditional kinships that have since been obscured but that still persist.

A good example is the assertion of the Brothertown Indians, a tribe once in Massachusetts, now located in Wisconsin, who published a calendar in 2022 that you can find in the Collection of Native American Literature. The handsome wampum-colored purple background of the cover contains the design of a colorful star quilt. We think of the star quilt as traditional to the tribes and culture groups of the west; however, these quilts have become symbolic of family and honor for many Native Americans. Tribal names feature within the star on the Brothertown Indians calendar showing the relationships that built the Brothertown and that are still honored. A subtitle states: "Seven Tribes; Seven Generations." At the top of the star is the name Mohegan; to the right moving downward are the names Montaukett, Narragansett, and Niantic. Moving up on the left, the names Pequot-Groton, Pequot-Stonington, and Tunxis nearest the top. At the center of the star is the word "Eeyawquittowauconnuck," which is the name Brothertown gave itself.

Similar values of tribal kinship were expressed by Hendrick Aupaumut, an early author who was likely Mohawk as well as Mohegan, who explained the breadth of Indigenous kinship:

> And according to the ancient covenant of our ancestors, the Delaware nation are our Grandfathers [...] The Shawanoe nation then called the Muh-hu-con-nuk nation to be their Elder Brothers, and promise obedience to them, which they still acknowledged to this day; and they are our Younger Brother, or Nkeeth-mon-nauk [...] Therefore the Miami nation are our Grandchildren to this day; and also their allies. [...] All these nations ever acknowledge this friendship; and whenever they met any of our people they call them Muh-so-mis, or Grandfathers. [...] Kut-tooh-waw, or Cherokees, are our younger brothers. [...] And the Seven Nations of Canada are our brothers also, who has renewed that covenant with us last Summer. And part of the Six Nations are our Uncles, to wit, Mohawks, Onondagas, Cayogas, and Senecas. But the Oneida and Tuscarora are our brothers. (The Oneidas were our younger brethren.)[6]

It didn't surprise me to learn that Aupaumut is ancestor to composer Brent Michael Davids, whose score *The Last of James Fenimore Cooper* was part of the first iteration of the *Boundless* exhibition (Figures 34a and 34b).

Beyond the Northeast, *Boundless* contains works by Dakota, Lakota, Ho-Chunk, and other culture groups, which are displayed together to highlight relationship and kinship. Some of the artists and authors relate to one another culturally while others, the Sully and Deloria families, who according to Phillip J. Deloria are related biologically. But blood doesn't always result in kinship. Drawings, paintings, and literature by one of the most well-known families of Native American authors, were written by the Dakota descendants of Alfred Sully, a white U.S. military officer who abandoned the family. In 1863, this officer ordered the massacre of Native women, children, and elders. He was a military artist and the son of an illustrious American portrait painter, Thomas Sully, whose work is in the Mead's collection, and who created the image of the infamous President Andrew Jackson (known as "Indian Killer") that we see on the twenty-dollar bill today.[7]

Art by Dyani White Hawk, Andrea Carlson, Fritz Scholder, and Jaune Quick-to-See Smith in the Mead's collection offered the opportunity to show how Native American artists related aesthetically and highlight how artists and authors credit influences from earlier generations, both Native and white. Each of the artists mentioned above also loaned images to authors, including for my own work. Covers of books by lauded authors Joy Harjo, Louise Erdrich, Gerald Vizenor, and other writers, included in *Boundless,* evidence the strong associations and collegial kinship that continues in an intertribal artistic and intellectual community at work today. These are just a few of the currents of kinship I followed as *Boundless* came together.

I see kinship between authors and artists over and between generations as a relational tradition that was important to highlight in the project. Much like the way many cultures express their kinship to water in their very names, the flow of *Boundless* tends toward revealing kinship, including direct ancestral connections between authors and artists, as well as cultural and collegial relationships. By the time I had mapped out these relationships, it occurred to me that the state of relationship is a transmotion that requires active engagement of place and, further, creating art from place engages transmotion vital to survivance.[8]

NOTES

1 "Potawatomi Song," in *Drink the Winds, Let the Waters Flow Free*, ed. Sharon Day and Pat Panagoulias, illustrated by Jaune Quick-to-See Smith (Minneapolis: Johnson Institute, 1983).

2 Gerald Vizenor, "The Unmissable: Transmotion in Native Stories and Literature," *Transmotion* 1, no. 1 (2015): 63, https://doi.org/10.22024/UniKent/03/tm.143.

3 Bernd Peyer, ed., *American Indian Nonfiction: An Anthology of Writings, 1760s–1930s* (Norman: University of Oklahoma Press, 2007), 63.

4 Rachel Beth Sayet, conversations with Heid E. Erdrich, 2022.

5 Samson Occom, "Preface," in *A Sermon Preached at the Execution of Moses Paul, an Indian* (Newhaven, Conn.: Printed and Sold by Timothy Green, 1772), 22.

6 Hendrick Aupaumut, "History of the Muh-He-Con-Uk Indians, 1790," in *American Indian Nonfiction*, ed. Peyer, 63.

7 Bruce Bartlet, "Thomas Sully's Influence on U.S. Coins and Currency," *The E-Sylum: An Electronic Publication of the Numismatic Bibliomania Society* 17, no. 1 (January 5, 2014), Article 16, https://www.coinbooks.org/esylum_v17n01a16.html.

8 Gerald Vizenor's term for the active and on-going persistence of Native American cultures beyond survival.

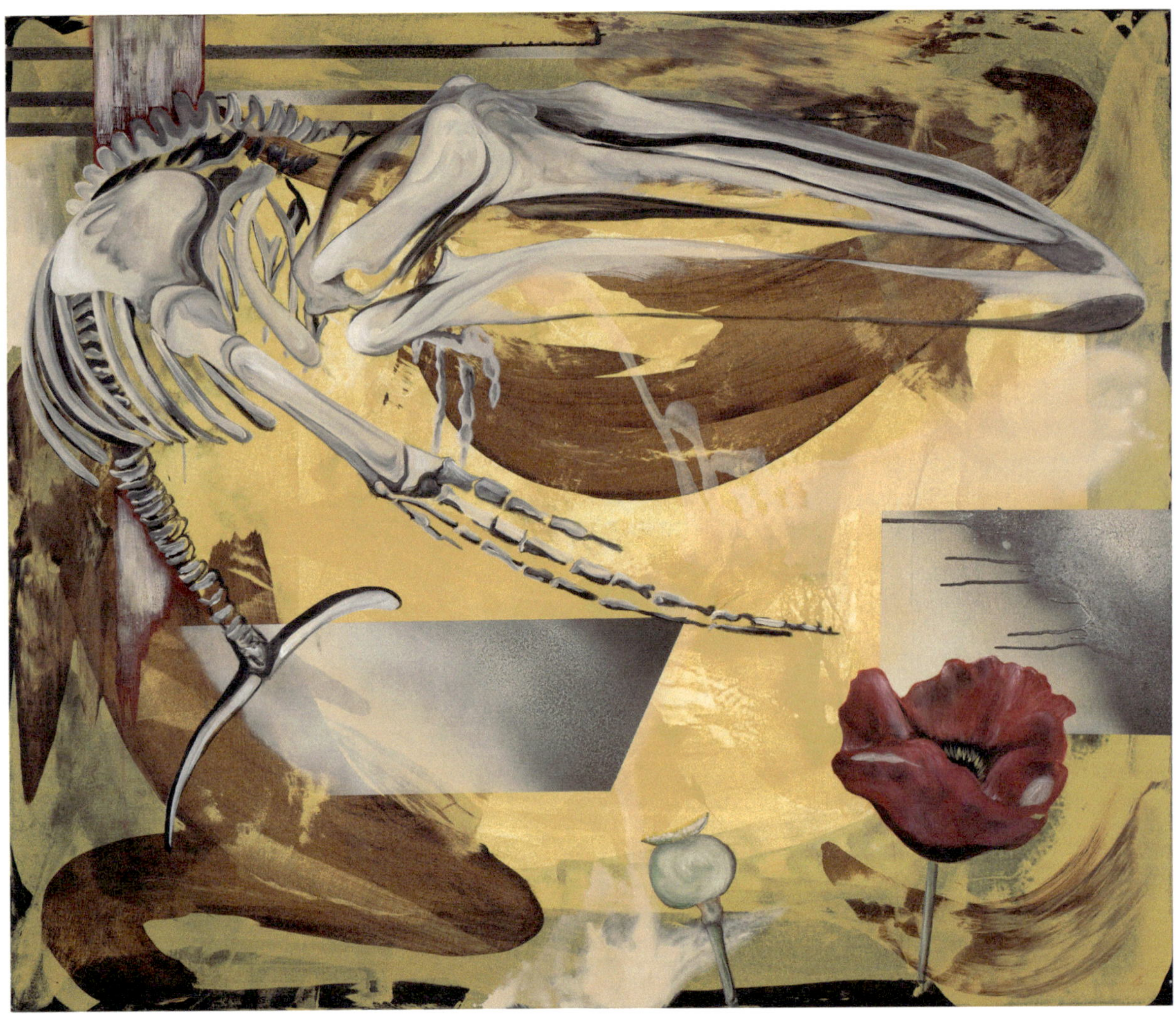

Figure 17: Courtney M. Leonard, *Collider Study #1*, from *BREACH: Logbook 21*, 2021. Mixed-media clay, acrylic on canvas, 60″ × 72″ × 2″. Mead Art Museum at Amherst College. Purchase with the Wise Fund for Fine Arts. AC 2022.22. © Courtney M. Leonard. Image credit: Petegorsky/Gipe.

Collider Study #1 depicts the articulated skeletal remains of Tofu, a juvenile humpback whale that was struck by a shipping boat off the coast of New England in 2007. Its flipper extends in reach toward a red poppy in bloom. Both the remains of the whale and the symbolism of the poppy are reflective of how pain and loss can also lend to healing and continuity. When a whale passes away, its remains fall to the bottom depths of the ocean and its carcass feeds an entire ecosystem. This knowledge of reciprocity and symbiosis is akin to how the whale would also traditionally feed the entire Shinnecock Nation during harsh times. Indigenous communities are often at the forefront of climate issues as the first to be impacted from rising waters, lack of access to healthy waters, and the need to protect our interspecies ecological relationships as stewards of our respective cultural landscapes.

—Courtney M. Leonard

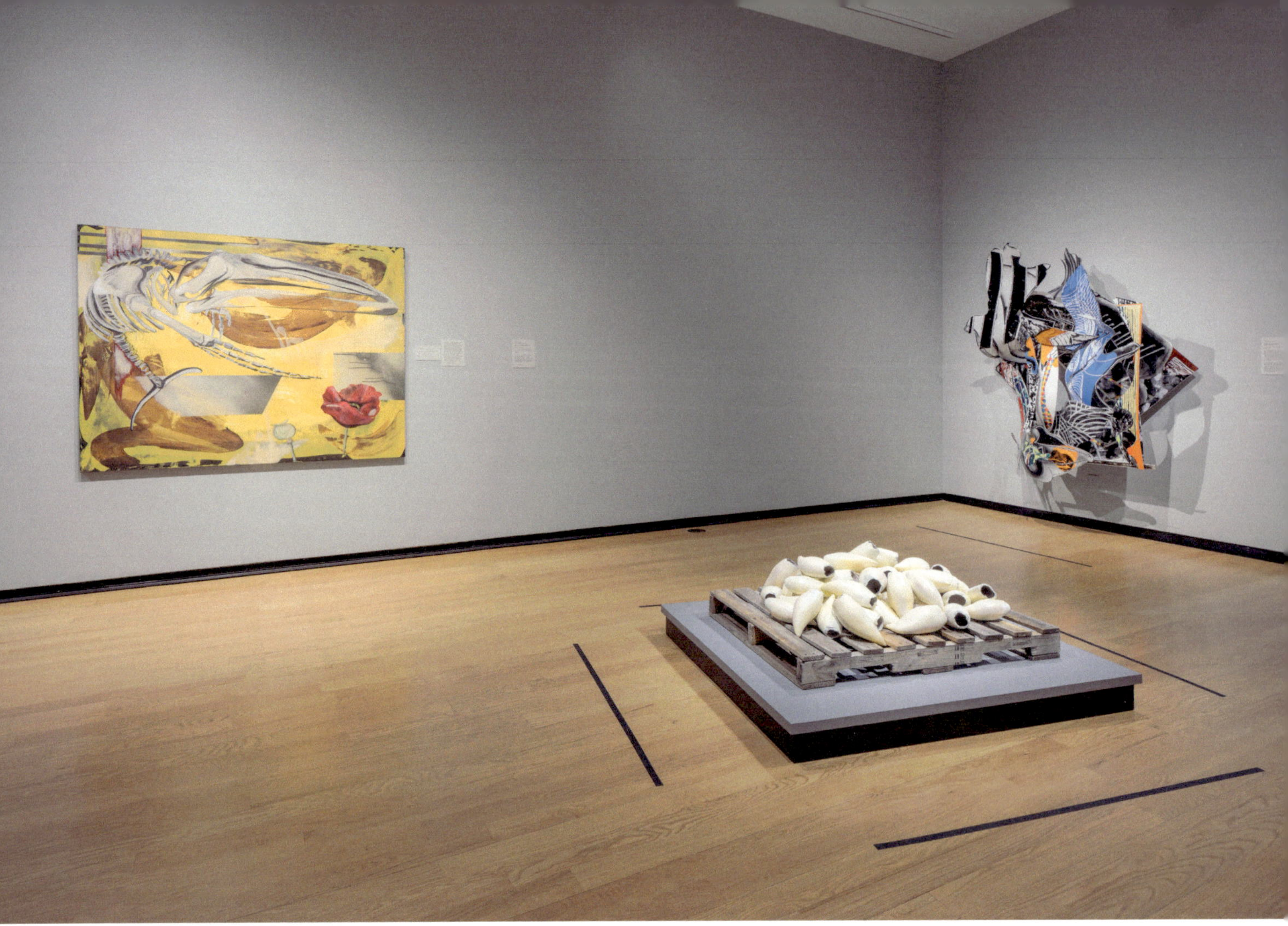

Figure 18: Installation photograph of *Boundless*, fall 2023. Left to right: Courtney M. Leonard (Shinnecock), *Collider Study #1*, from *BREACH: Logbook 21*, 2021. Mixed-media clay, acrylic on canvas, 60″ × 72″ × 2″. Mead Art Museum at Amherst College. Purchase with the Wise Fund for Fine Arts, AC 2022.22; Courtney M. Leonard (Shinnecock, born 1980), *BREACH #2, (BREACH: Logbook 21)*, 2016–21. Ceramic on wood pallet. Mount Holyoke College Art Museum, South Hadley, Massachusetts. Purchase with the Jean C. Harris Art Acquisition Fund, MH 2021.12; Frank Stella, *Of Whales in Paint, in Teeth, &c.*, 1990. Acrylic on aluminum. 83¼″ × 68″ × 32¾″ (211.5 cm × 172.7 cm × 83.2 cm). Mead Art Museum at Amherst College. Gift of Steven M. Jacobson (Class of 1953), AC 1994.8. © 2024 Frank Stella / Artists Rights Society (ARS), New York TBD. Image credit: Stephen Petegorsky.

Stella's work displayed near Leonard's artworks in the first iteration of *Boundless* creates a conversation on the whaling industry as well as on art practices and Indigenous and colonial viewpoints. Stella made his sculpture *Of Whales in Paint, in Teeth, &c.*, in relation to chapter 57 of Herman Melville's *Moby-Dick*. In this chapter, while describing Native, white, and ancient people as savage, the main character, a white man named Ishmael, makes comment on a kind of universal artistic and sculptural urge:

> As with the Hawaiian savage, so with the white sailor-savage. With the same marvelous patience, and with the same single shark's tooth, of his one poor jack-knife, he will carve you a bit of bone sculpture, not quite as workmanlike, but as close packed in its maziness of design, as the Greek savage, Achilles's shield; and full of barbaric spirit and suggestiveness, as the prints of that fine old Dutch savage, Albert Durer.

A PICTURE
Olivia Ward Bush-Banks

I drew a picture long ago—
  A picture of a sullen sea;
A picture that I value now
  Because it clears Life's mystery.

My sea was dark and full of gloom;
  I painted rocks of sombre hue.
My sky alone bespoke of light,
  And that I painted palest blue.

But e'en across my sky of blue
  Stretched troubled clouds of sodden gray,
Through which the sun shone weak and dim,
  With only here and there a ray.

Around my rocks the yellow foam
  Seemed surging, moaning in despair
As if the waves, their fury spent,
  Left naught but desolation there.

Three crafts with fluttering sails I drew,
  And one sailed near the rocks of gray,
The other on its westward course,
  Went speeding out of danger's way.

The other still outdistanced them
  Where sky and water seemed to meet.
I painted that with sails full set,
  And then my picture was complete.

My life was like the sullen sea,
    Misfortune's woes, my rocks of gray,
The crafts portrayed Life's changing scenes,
    The clouded sky Life's troubled Day.

I longed to paint that picture o'er
    Without the rocks of sombre hue;
Without the troubled clouds of gray,
    I'll paint the sky of brightest blue.

My sea shall lay in calm repose,
    No hint of surging, moaning sigh.
My crafts, unhindered by the rocks,
    Shall speed in joyous swiftness by.

But this shall be when brightest hours
    Of hope and cheer are given me.
I'll paint this picture when Life's sun
    Shines clear upon Prosperity.

Olivia Ward Bush-Banks, "A Picture," Academy of American Poets, November 21, 2020, https://poets.org/poem/picture. Originally appeared in *The Colored American Magazin*e 1, no. 2 (June 1900): 77–78.

TOWARD AN INDIGENOUS LIBRARY, ARCHIVE, AND MUSEUM: PRACTICES AND CONSIDERATIONS

Brandon Castle

Brandon Castle was the project coordinator for Mapping Native Intellectual Networks of the Northeast at Frost Library and is now Native American and Indigenous Studies Librarian at the University of Massachusetts Amherst. He is from Ketchikan Indian Community, Ts'msyen.

Indigenous communities have varying needs when it comes to accessing, sharing, and connecting to their cultural knowledge. A unifying similarity across Indigenous communities is that the need to protect cultural traditions and customs are real and deep, especially for communities aiming to preserve and promote their cultural knowledge for future generations.

Indigenous peoples have become increasingly involved in managing, organizing, documenting, and locating cultural knowledge that has been displaced from their original contexts and placed in repositories such as libraries, museums, and archives across the country and world. One such way Indigenous people have been managing cultural knowledge is taking on the role of librarians, curators, and archivists to meet the preservation needs of their communities and by applying an Indigenous lens on western museum, library, and archival practices. Indigenous interventions into western practices are focused on reparative justice and cultivating professional practices which center Indigenous sovereignty and epistemologies. On a library level, this includes integrating accurate descriptions of Indigenous materials in library catalogs, and contextualizing materials within Indigenous ways of knowing.

For example, accurately classifying and applying metadata schemas which reflect and contextualize Indigenous materials in their original knowledge systems allows for Indigenous community members, researchers, and the public to access and engage with Indigenous materials in respectful ways. On a broader level, changes in practice should be of benefit to Indigenous peoples and uplift their self-determination and liberation while advancing Indigenous knowledge in a relational way. Indigenous scholars in the field of library and information science define these changes as "Indigenous librarianship," or practices of librarianship which privilege Indigenous communities and the relationships they have to cultural knowledge.

By applying an Indigenous lens to western practices, the cultural values of reciprocity, responsibility, and respect of Indigenous knowledge can be adopted by institutions when done in a collaborative, intentional way such as building relationships with Indigenous communities who are represented in institutional collections. One such practice that has been instrumental at Amherst College's Frost Library is the push for culturally sensitive cataloging of Indigenous authored materials, many of which have been featured in *Boundless*.

To catalog a book in a culturally sensitive way is a process of determining the original context of the book. What is the author's Indigenous background? Is the author Indigenous? If not, does the book feature the writings of Indigenous people? How widely accepted is this piece of literature as being an accurate portrayal of a certain peoples and/or communities? These probing questions, while seemingly investigative, are a critical part in determining the relational quality and the impact a book has within Indigenous communities and wider intellectual networks. It is important to note that only Indigenous communities can make these determinations and it is the responsibility of institutions, as stewards of Indigenous collections, to consult and collaborate with Indigenous communities whose cultural knowledge is represented in collections, stacks, archives, and exhibitions. To be culturally sensitive in practice means to take time to reflect on the reciprocal nature of stewarding Indigenous materials and relationship building with Indigenous communities.

In a library, building relationships with Indigenous communities can look like purchasing and acquiring books directly from Indigenous bookstores and vendors. In 2016, an Amherst College student attended the first Indigenous Comic Con held in Albuquerque, New Mexico and purchased several comics published by Red Planet Books and Comics, an Indigenous-owned comic book store based in Albuquerque. Since then, Archives and Special Collections has made additional purchases from Red Planet including in the fall of 2022 and spring 2023. Dr. Lee Francis IV (Laguna Pueblo), the founder of Red Planet and the Indigenous Comic Con (now known as IndigiPop Expo), visited the Archives in November 2022 and felt right at home among a nearly complete collection of books, zines, and comics published and or distributed by Red Planet. We continue to develop our relationship with Dr. Lee Francis IV and his publishing and outreach efforts aimed at engaging Native youth. In the spring of 2023, Dr. Francis IV visited us again and brought posters that once lined the walls of the Red Planet shop in Albuquerque, which are now on display in the Archives. Additionally, Amherst College supported the IndigiPop Expo 2023 as an official sponsor. We are committed to maintaining a comprehensive collection of that work and building the foundation for future Indigenous students, authors, creators, and communities to connect and envision Indigenous futures through literature.

The Amherst College Library Archives and Special Collections are open to thinking collaboratively with regional partners, Indigenous organizations, and community members on initiatives and interventions into the library and information science field to uplift tribal sovereignty and respect Indigenous ways of knowing. We invite everyone to review resources and protocols developed by Indigenous communities, librarians, scholars, and organizations who are leading the way toward restorative justice and an Indigenous museum, library, and archive.

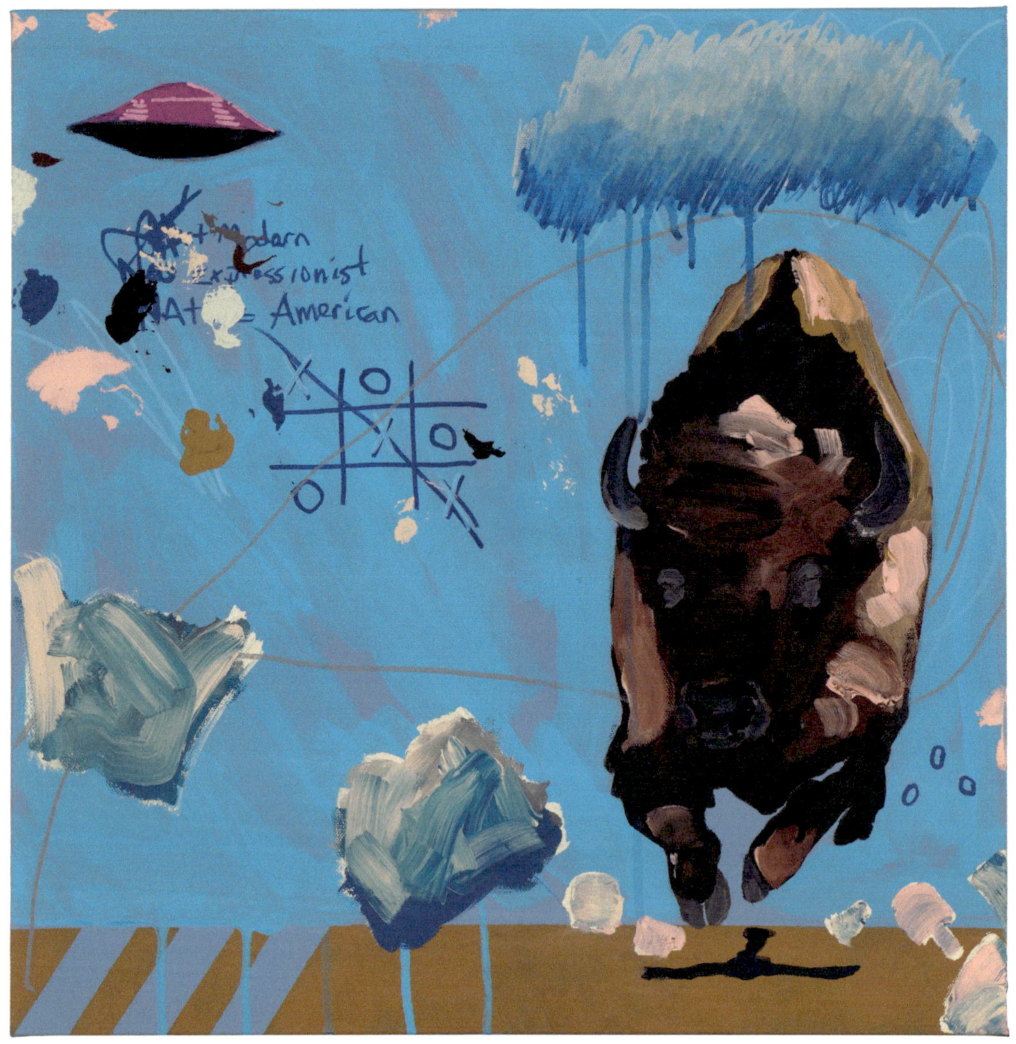

Figure 19: Frank Buffalo Hyde, *I Got Rambling on My Mind*, 2021–2022. Acrylic on canvas. Stretcher: 20″ × 20″ × 2″ (50.8 cm × 50.8 cm × 5.1 cm). Mead Art Museum at Amherst College. Purchase with Wise funds. AC 2022.08. © Frank Buffalo Hyde. Image credit: Petegorsky/Gipe.

ON FRITZ SCHOLDER

Frank Buffalo Hyde

Frank Buffalo Hyde is a painter who grew up on the Onondaga Reservation and in Santa Fe, New Mexico. He is Onondaga and Nez Perce.

In the lexicon of contemporary Indigenous painters there are but a few that have been elevated from the level of kitsch or craft. For most people those artists are distant romanticized titans that changed the course of contemporary Native art, but for me those people are real and exist in three dimensions. I grew up around them, heard stories about them and what it was really like during the "Golden" age at the Institute of American Indian Arts in the early to mid-1960s. Among them was Fritz Scholder, an abstract expressionist painter from California. One part Bill Soza and two parts Nathan Olivera, his work skyrocketed in both renown and market value. Fritz was rubbing elbows with the show business elite, even having Andy Warhol paint his portrait. Depicting garish superhuman figures with headdresses, seemingly effortless mastery of paint drips and dry brush techniques, his art embodied the era of changing attitudes around what contemporary Indigenous art was, the era and the civil rights movement and counterculture music.

Fritz Scholder's legacy, however, has been tainted a bit for me. At first he claimed no Native ancestry, then he did, then he didn't, then he did again. That ambiguity is a luxury not afforded to the rest of us. Yet I respect the painterly qualities and mysterious composition paired with a Bay Area figurative color palette that creates an undeniable alchemy recognized as Fritz Scholder's style. His influence on my work is in his immediacy. When I saw the PBS profile of him painting in his studio, something just registered in my psyche as if I were seeing a blueprint or signpost.

FRITZ SCHOLDER: *UNTITLED*

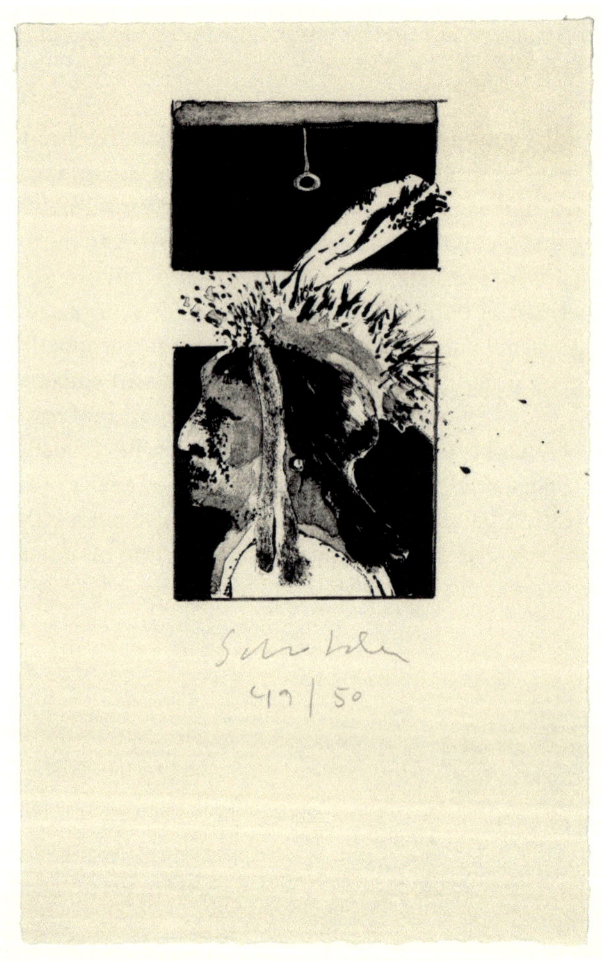

Figure 20: Fritz Scholder (Luiseño). *Untitled*, 1972. Lithograph Sheet: 11 1/8 in × 7 1/16 in; 28.3 cm × 17.9 cm; Image: 6 1/16 in × 3 1/4 in; 15.4 cm × 8.3 cm; Frame: 18 3/4 in × 14 3/4 in. Mead Art Museum at Amherst College. Gift of Richard H. Templeton (Class of 1931); AC 1981.126. Image Credit: Petegorsky/Gipe Photography.

FRITZ SCHOLDER: *RANDOM THOUGHTS AND MEMORIES*

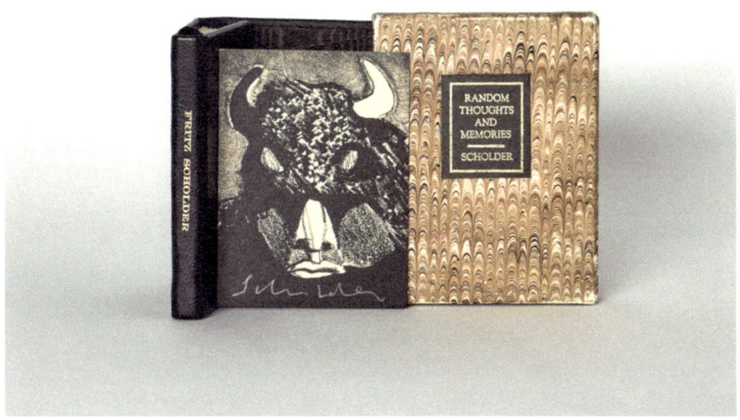

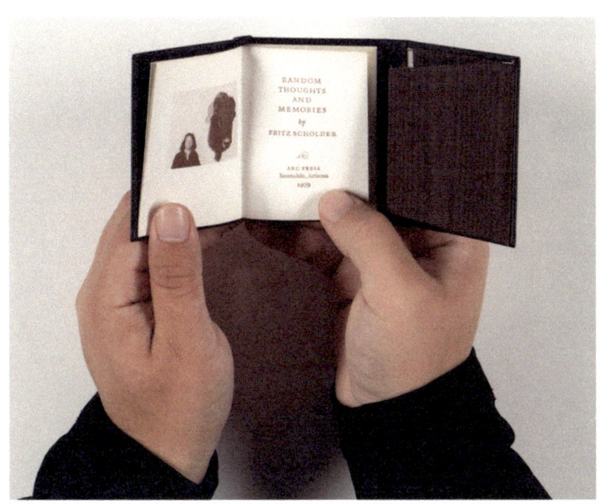

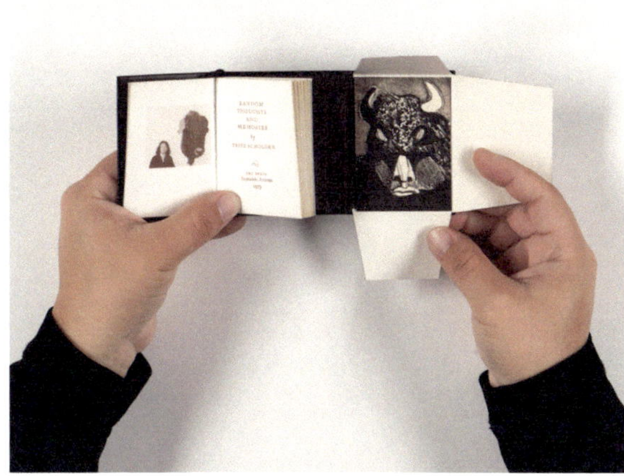

Figure 21a-c: Fritz Scholder (Luiseño). Lithograph in *Random Thoughts and Memories*, 1979. Lithograph in poetry book, 8 x 6 cm. Scottsdale, AZ: ARC Press; amc.014757165 21 unnumbered pages : 1 portrait, 1 lithograph 8 x 6 cm. Amherst College Archives & Special Collections. Collection of Native American Literature. PS3569.C52533 R3 1979.

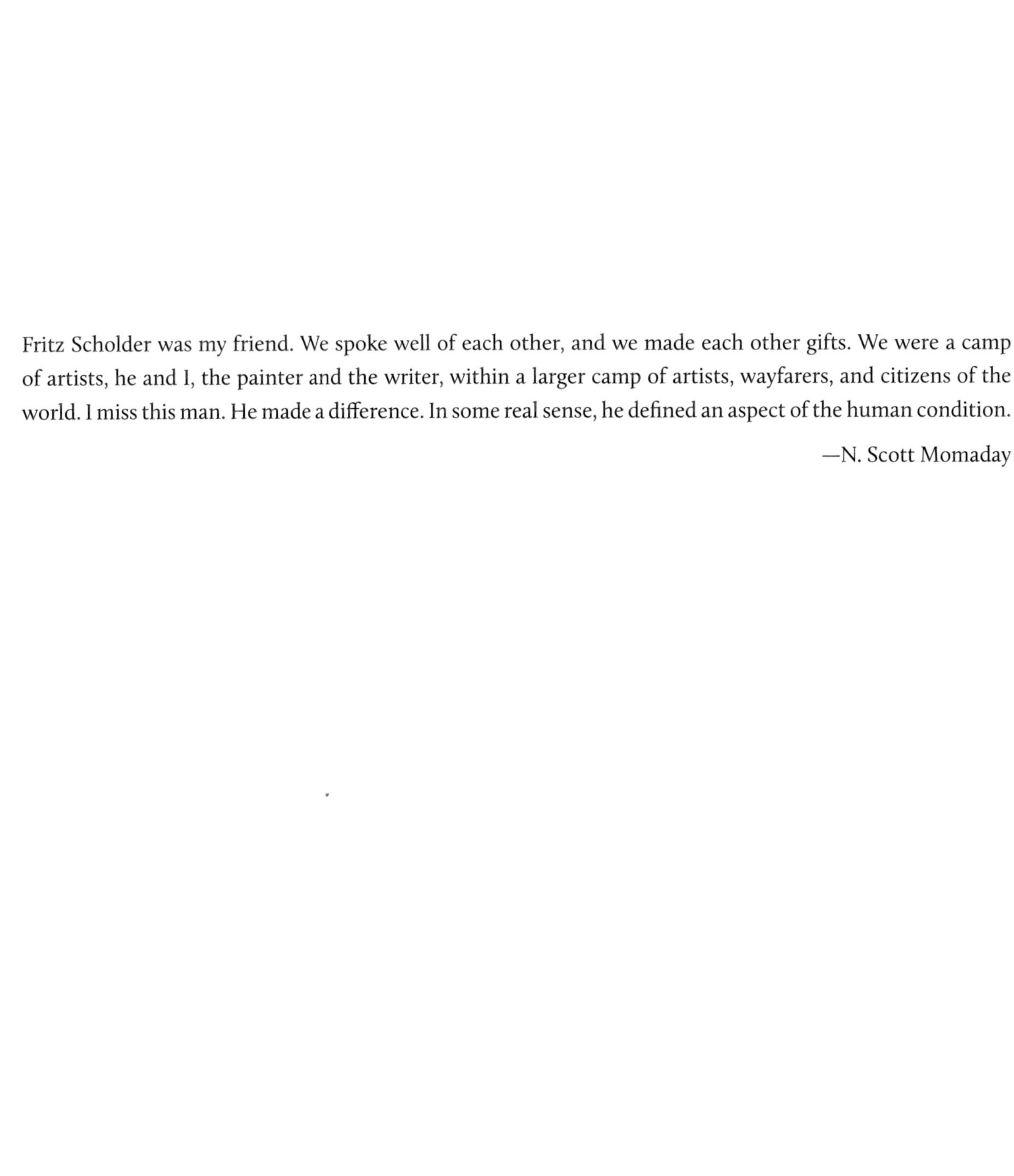

Fritz Scholder was my friend. We spoke well of each other, and we made each other gifts. We were a camp of artists, he and I, the painter and the writer, within a larger camp of artists, wayfarers, and citizens of the world. I miss this man. He made a difference. In some real sense, he defined an aspect of the human condition.

—N. Scott Momaday

The shaman-artist has now drawn the line
And has begun the fight against the cyber-technocrat.
It's not that I'm against computers.
But I think that the human being
Has to be very careful in the coming millennium.

—Fritz Scholder

Both quotes from Joseph M. Sánchez, ed., *Fritz Scholder: An Intimate Look* (Santa Fe, N.M.: Institute of American Indian Arts Museum, 2008).

JAUNE QUICK-TO-SEE SMITH: *CHARLO #7*

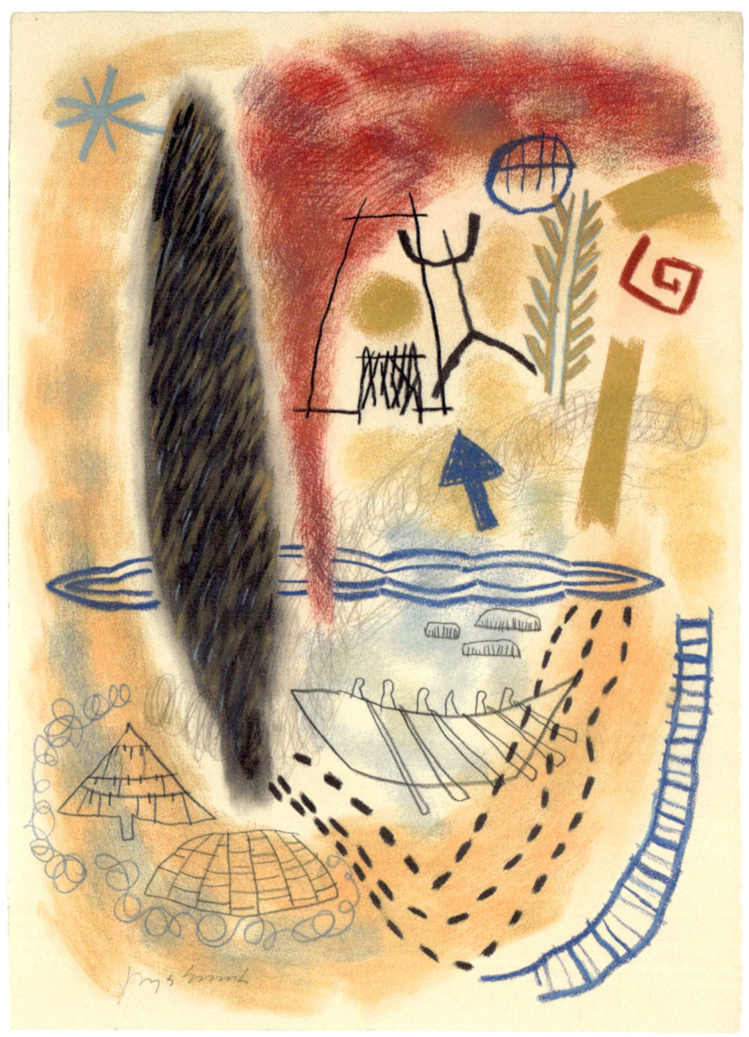

Figure 22: Jaune Quick-to-See Smith (Salish/Kootenai), *Charlo #7*, 1985. Pastel on paper. Sheet: 30⅛″ × 22¼″ (76.5 × 56.5 cm). Museum purchase with Charles H. Morgan Fine Arts Fund. AC 2022.26.

JAUNE QUICK-TO-SEE SMITH: *WAITING FOR RAIN*

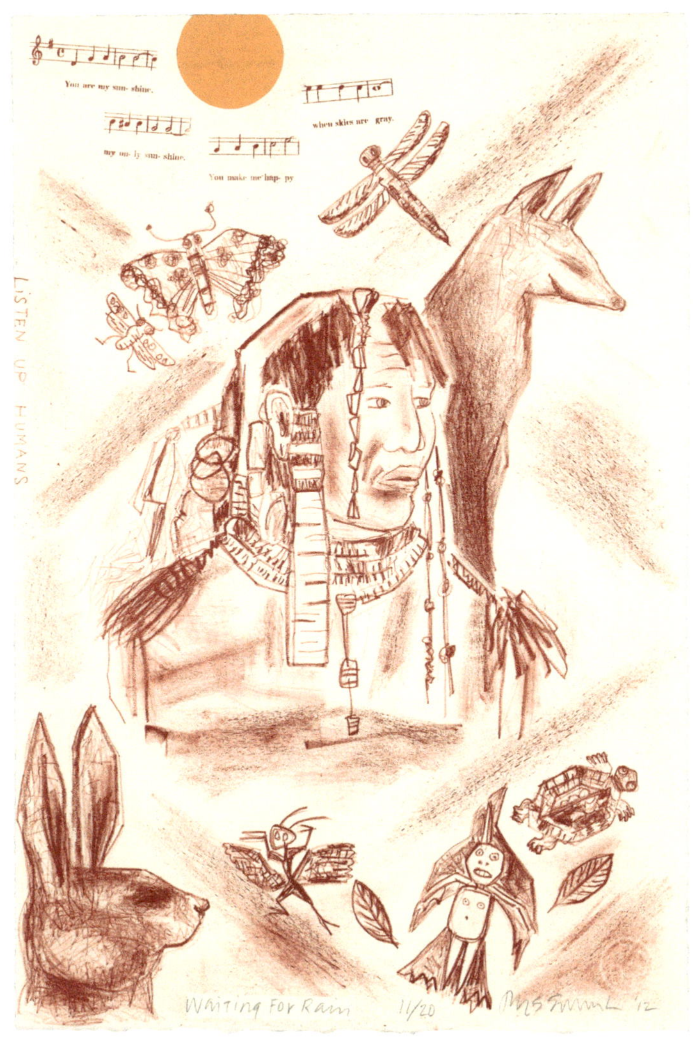

Figure 23: Jaune Quick-to-See Smith (Salish/Kootenai), *Waiting for Rain*, 2012. Lithograph. Sheet: 22⅛″ × 15″ (56.2 cm × 38.1 cm). Museum purchase with William K. Allison (Class of 1920) Memorial Fund. AC 2022.04.

IMASUUGTUA

Abigail Chabitnoy

Abigail Chabitnoy is Assistant Professor of English at the University of Massachusetts Amherst. She is a Koniag descendant and member of the Tangirnaq Native Village in Kodiak.

Have I told you one about the apocalypse?

A/lone woman
an island, having been
one to survive

(on/the backslide)

Soon discovered
Soon (in) a cave hid
and ~~k~~-----

The woman not found
The woman came out

painfully

surprised

To know she was
(only) human
(only) [on] the island. Seven years

She lived this way
neither smiled
neither laughed. In the eighth year

"Bright raft"   an arrival
Others like her
came to be/the island and she

No longer
alone
was wind

No longer
was ------

Still
                    in these channels
wind
in all directions

I am learning to say

                                        I am searching for my contents

Still

                                        I am searching for my contents

Disclaimer: To preserve the meaning of the poet's lineation, this chapter is also available in its original, non-reflowable format as a PDF here: https://doi.org/10.3998/mpub.14513702.cmp.1.

INUIT ARTIST: UNTITLED SOAPSTONE SCULPTURE

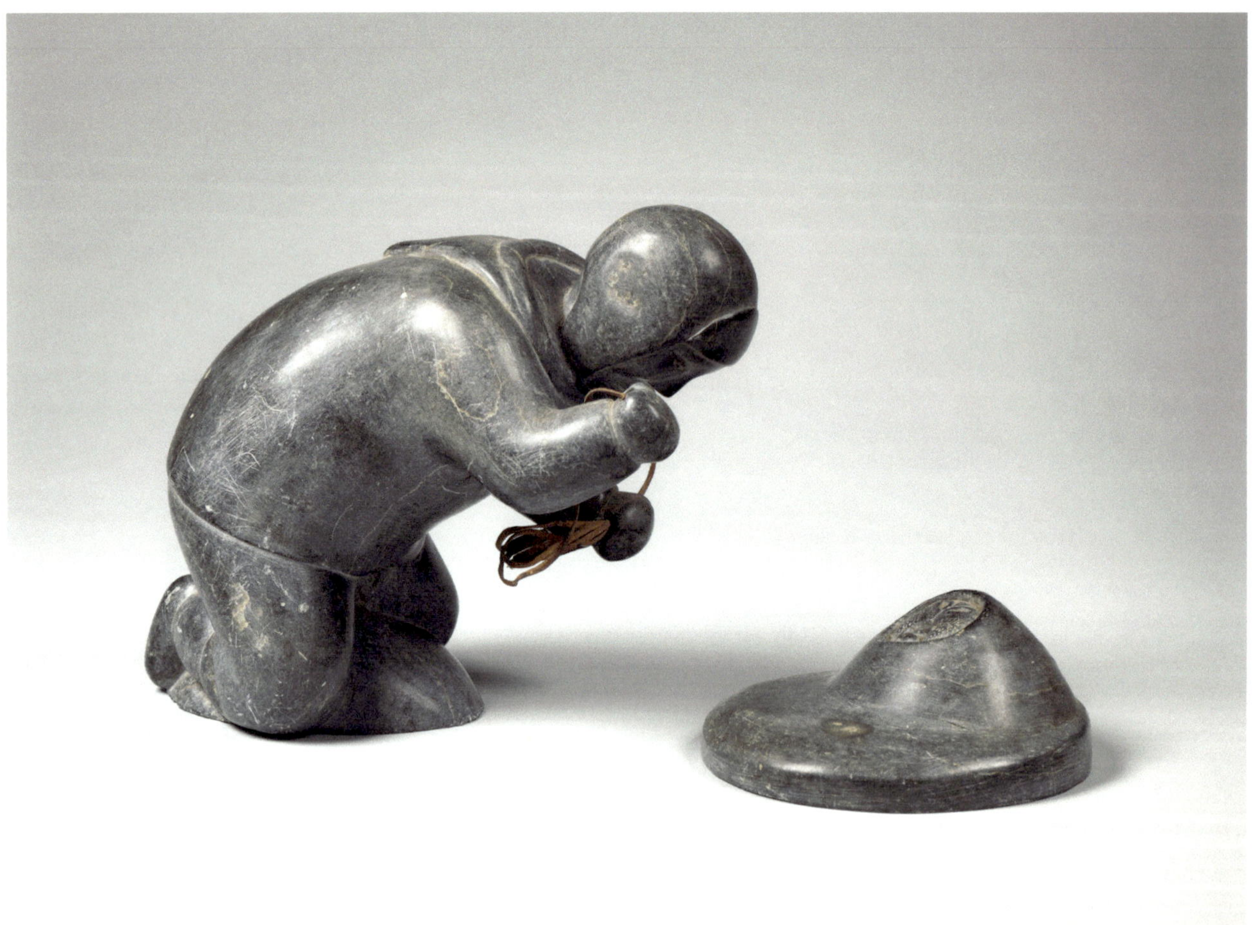

Figure 24: Inuit artist (likely Povungituk or Inukjuak community, Canadian), Untitled, n.d., soapstone. Found in Collection. Mead Art Museum.

While working on *Boundless*, Mead staff found this sculpture at the museum. No information accompanied the artwork. This carving shows an Inuit hunter hovering over a smaller figure, a walrus head peering up at the hunter in the moment before the hunter strikes. The hunter holds a leather rope or tether. A missing weapon, most likely carved of ivory, would fit in the figure's hand.

Inuit art has been signed and labeled, often in syllabics—an Inuit writing system—since the 1960s. There's no signature on this sculpture which suggests the artwork was made in the early to mid-1950s. The type of stone used in this sculpture also suggests the timeframe (it appears to be made of a stone mined for one decade only) and the location where it was made, most likely in the Inuit communities of Povungnituk or Inukjuak.[1]

NOTE

1 Heid E. Erdrich, social media exchanges with various Inuit community members and arts professionals, 2023.

BOUNDLESS STUDENT INTERN REFLECTION

Catherine Charnoky

Catherine Charnoky is an enrolled member of the Citizen Potawatomi Nation and class of 2024 at Amherst College. Catherine was a 2022 curatorial intern for *Boundless*.

Small signs saying "No Colonizing" and "No Colonizing, Anytime" by the Massachusetts-based artist Justin Beatty (Ojibwe, Garden River First Nations) greet me as I approach the Mead Art Museum. I am pleasantly surprised and filled with excitement. It's the *Boundless* exhibition opening reception and the museum is bustling with over three hundred people, the most I've ever seen in the Mead during my three years as a student at Amherst College. I am blown away by how different the artworks look all in one place, in their full size, and in relation to each other. They are so different from how I'd become accustomed to seeing them: an image on the computer screen or disjointed in the museum's study room. It feels as if I'm being reunited in person for the first time with Zoom class friends. In the far corner I see a heap of ceramic pieces shaped as large whale teeth placed on a pallet made by Courtney M. Leonard (Shinnecock)—a cry against the settler-colonial destruction of whales similar to the settler-colonial destruction of humans (Figure 18).

In the entry gallery, there are multiple display cases containing books, items I rarely see displayed at an art museum. One book is *A Sermon: Preached at the Execution of Moses Paul* written and preached by Samson Occom (Mohegan) in 1772. The sermon advocates for abolition and is the first published book written by a Native American. As I continue, I stop to read an excerpt of the "Potawatomi Song" on the wall. The lyric: "So we all move along with the earth, keeping time with the earth" strikes me, filling me with peace as I contemplate the normality and inevitability of cyclical change. In the next gallery, I see myself reflected in the photograph *Eufaula Girls* (Figure 25) by Cara Romero (Chemehuevi). The female figures in the photograph are suspended in deep water, their arms open up to the light, and their shawls twist about them. The stillness of the photograph makes them look elegant and peaceful—yet the scene is foreboding. As I look around me, I observe how each artwork comes alive when engaged with: speaking to each visitor, educating, acting as a mirror, and creating a conversation. I am awed by curator Heid E. Erdrich's mind, the connections she makes between all of the artworks and literature, and how the exhibition does in fact flow like water.

While researching artworks and artists for *Boundless*, I was struck by the complex way with which each artist engages with the concept of Indigeneity and expresses their own Indigeneity in their artwork. For example, Fritz Scholder (Luiseño), a famous and influential twentieth-century painter, distanced himself from his Luiseño affiliation at the beginning of his career and vowed to never paint a Native American. However, later in life Scholder retracted his vow and painted a series of Native Americans in abstract expressionist, surrealist, pop art styles with the intention of disrupting Indigenous stereotypes. In contrast, Sky Hopinka (Ho-Chunk, descendent of Pechanga Luiseño) centers Indigenous perspectives in his films from the beginning of his career and explores themes including decolonization and land rights. Other artists in this exhibition express Indigeneity through their use of traditional

Indigenous materials, designs, and techniques. For example, the activist Margaret Blackbird Boyd (Odawa) used dyed porcupine quills to embroider the birch bark–bound book *History of the Ottawa and Chippawa Indians of Michigan* (1887) written by her brother (Figures 8a and 8b). I am inspired by how Margaret used the money from selling this book to travel to Washington, D..C., to meet with President Ulysses S. Grant and advocate for her people. I love how the exhibition brings stories of Native American presence to life, emphasizes the profound influences of these works, explores unique fusions of artwork styles, and highlights the ever-changing ways we use art and literature to amplify our voices. We are boundless.

As an artist and enrolled member of the Citizen Potawatomi Nation I often contemplate what my Indigenous identity means to me personally, to my community, to society at large, and how my identity influences my work. Researching for *Boundless* deepened my understanding of how one expresses identity and how one can use positionality to strengthen their work. I am incredibly grateful to be part of the process of curating an exhibition that uplifts Indigenous voices and is a step in decolonizing the Mead Art Museum. I thank all who were a part of this process.

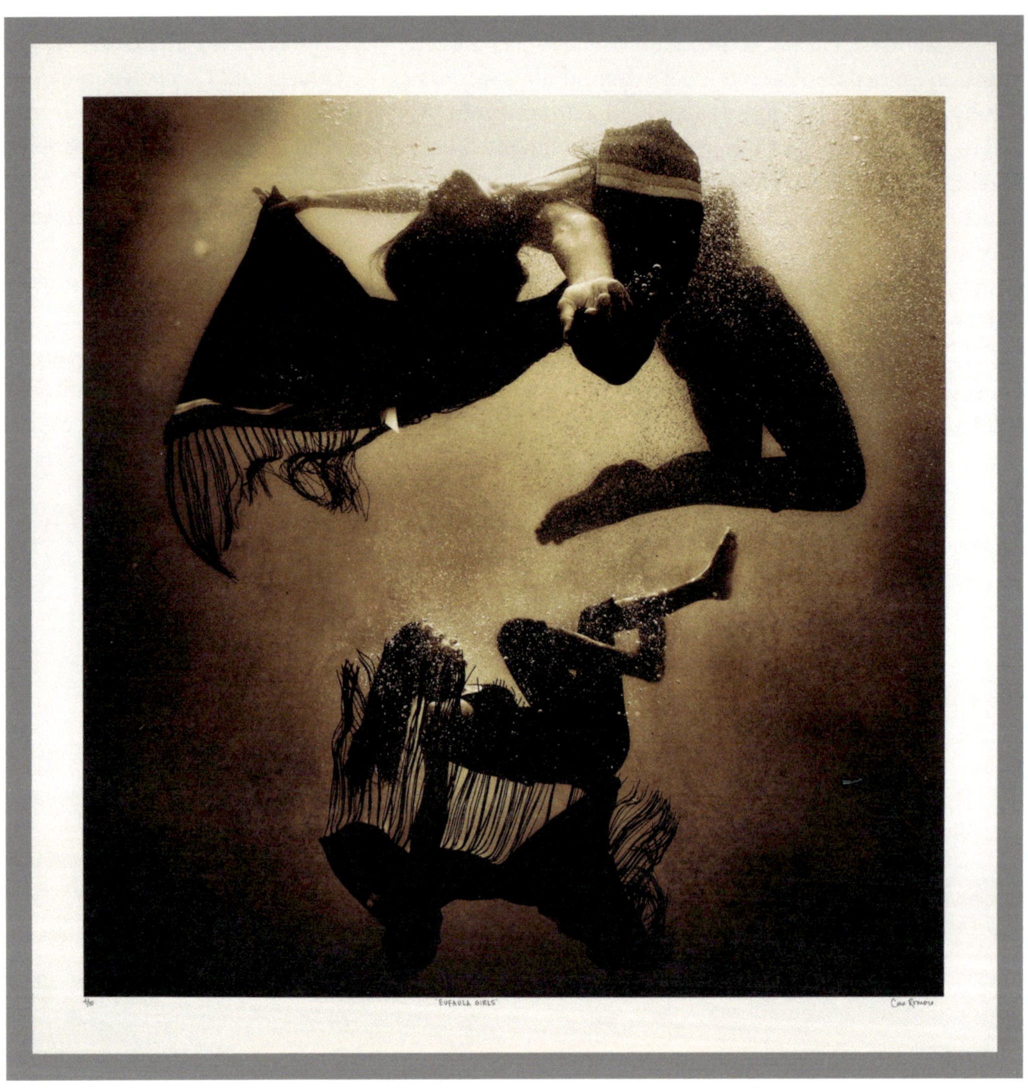

Figure 25: Cara Romero (Chemehuevi), *Eufaula Girls*, 2015. Pigment print mounted on plexiglass. Sheet: 33 3/4″ × 33 1/4″ (85.7 cm × 84.5 cm); Image: 30″ × 29 5/8″ (76.2 cm × 75.2 cm). Mead Art Museum at Amherst College, Museum purchase. AC 2022.07.

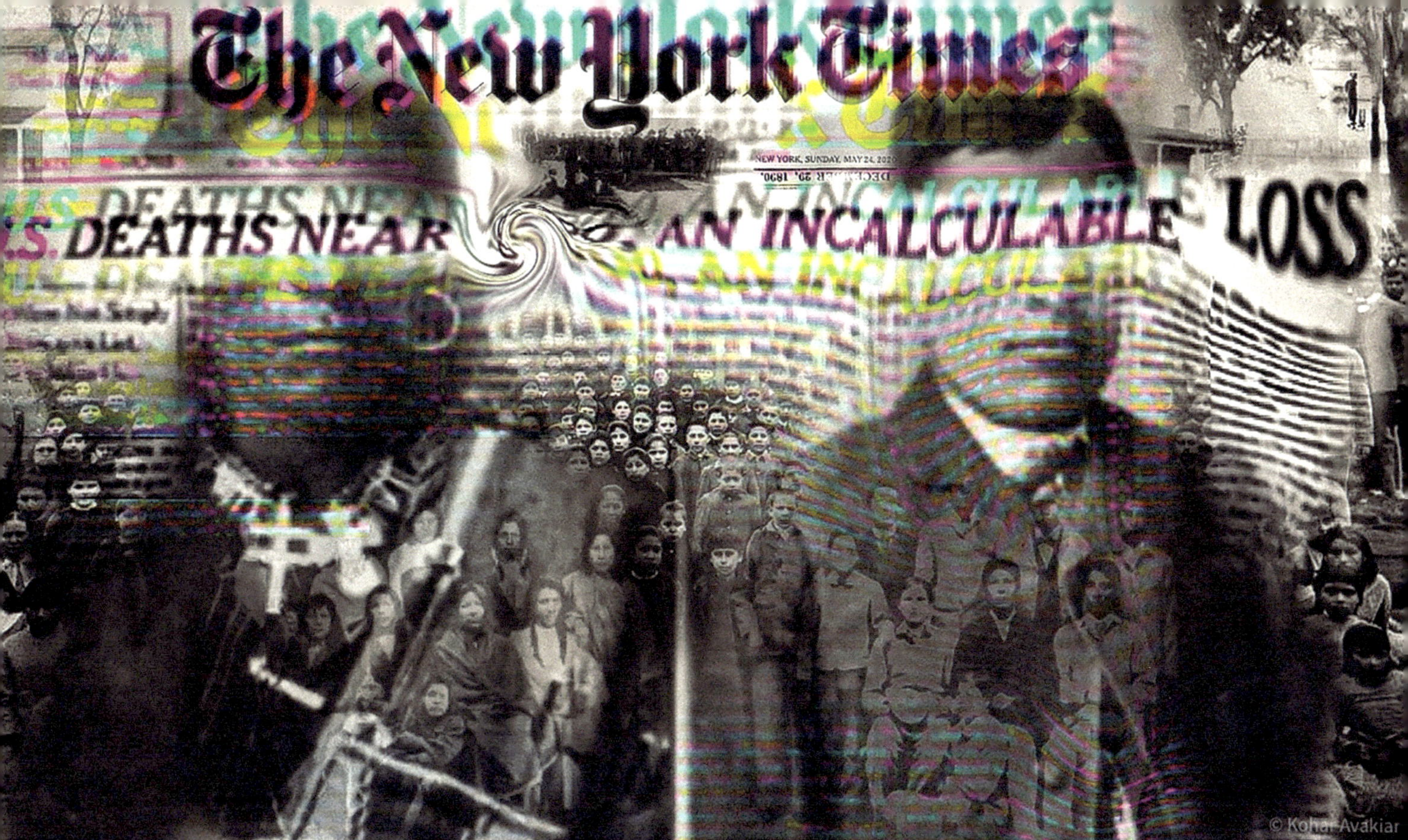

Figure 26: Kohar Avakian, *U.S. Deaths Near An Incalculable Loss*, 2021. Digital media. ©Kohar Avakian.

U.S. DEATHS NEAR AN INCALCULABLE LOSS

Kohar Avakian

Kohar Avakian is a doctoral student at Yale University. She is Nipmuc, Black, Armenian. This piece first appeared in *3Views on Theater*, issue 7 in June 2022, edited by Sarah Rose Leonard and Brittani Samuel. Reprint by permission of the author.[1]

U.S. Deaths Near An Incalculable Loss (Figure 26) is a time-collapsing collage and a political commentary on genocide, photography, representation, and time created in response to *Between Two Knees* by the 1491s. The Native comedy troupe's new play is about the generation-altering legacy wrought by the Wounded Knee Massacre of 1890 and committed at Indian boarding schools across what is now North America. On May 11, 2022, the United States government finally answered to the genocidal crimes it sponsored against Indigenous youth at the 400+ federally funded Indian ~~boarding schools~~ concentration camps founded between 1819 and 1969. The U.S. Department of the Interior released an investigative report formally detailing the incalculable losses that generations of Indigenous people already knew and felt. There were over five hundred "confirmed student deaths" across nineteen institutions, and still many more unaccounted for and unnamed. In 2021, the stolen remains of over 1,300 Indigenous children were unearthed at former "Indian residential schools" in Canada. A federally funded genocide was committed in plain sight.

This piece was inspired by the play's poignant, yet beautiful analogy that compared the survivors of boarding schools to shadows. I combine the solemn and sobering *New York Times* headline "U.S. DEATHS NEAR 100,000, AN INCALCULABLE LOSS," published on May 24, 2020, with twelve archival images forcibly captured at these sites of genocide, perhaps most notable being the "Before and After" portraits taken at the Carlisle Indian Industrial School in Pennsylvania. What happened in the space between that before and after? This palimpsestic visual represents the accumulation of death committed at the hands of the U.S. government, the piercing palpability of intergenerational trauma, and the amnesiac simultaneity of time experienced by survivors and their descendants in the aftermath of such unspeakable loss. Like the one million souls taken too soon by COVID-19, the pronounced yet invisible presence of their collective absence will remain imprinted upon generations. Like shadows of light, the survival of their memory radiates and reverberates eternally, transcending space and time. I commemorate the losses—the countless children, parents, siblings, cousins, friends, and relatives—whose lives extend beyond a number.

It was no coincidence that I ended up in a room full of other Natives to see *Between Two Knees* on the day that the United States released that monumental report on boarding schools. When dealing with histories as genocidal as ours, laughter has been a constant salve for our pain. We had the opportunity to watch the play as a dress rehearsal right before its final release. I wouldn't have wanted it any other way. The experience of being with a Native audience was joyous, hysteria-inducing, and at times somberly silent. The vaudeville-inspired set was ornately orchestrated and the room was thick with ripe laughter, thanks to Truman, a member of the Indigenous community at Yale whose laugh echoed throughout the room seconds into the play. After the show, I told Truman that he's got a laugh so good that people should pay *him* to be an audience member. Throughout the course of the play, I lost complete track of time. Hysteria took over the room, and I felt the magic of live performance for the first time in a long time.

Between Two Knees was a reminder that like the circularity of pain, intergenerational trauma, and life itself, joy always returns (often in the form of lewd jokes, silly dance sequences, and spontaneous song breakouts). Following multiple generations of a family between their experiences at Wounded Knee during the massacre of 1890 and the American Indian Movement occupation in 1973, the play brings to life this universal truth: everything circles back. The Wounded Knee massacre—an event of many names—did not end in 1890. Rather, an ending is simply a beginning. Life always comes after death. We are all caught in an intricately entangled web of time. We all represent the seventh generation to another, just as we are all ancestors in the making. In the aftermath of such unspeakable tragedy, our ancestors had no choice but to collect their things and keep walking. Their survival allowed us to experience the joy of being together in that room. As we walked out of the theater, I looked up at the moon. There was a radiant rainbow ring of light encircling it, hugging all of its deep shadow-filled crevices. I thought back to the image of our ancestors as loyal shadows and felt their presence walking with us. May their light continue to reach the darkest shadows and may their shadows find the light.

NOTE

1 https://www.3viewstheater.com/views/u-s-deaths-near-an-incalculable-loss.

CHANDLER: *THE MOON AS SEEN FEBRUARY 2, 1882 AT BALDWINVILLE, MASSACHUSETTS*

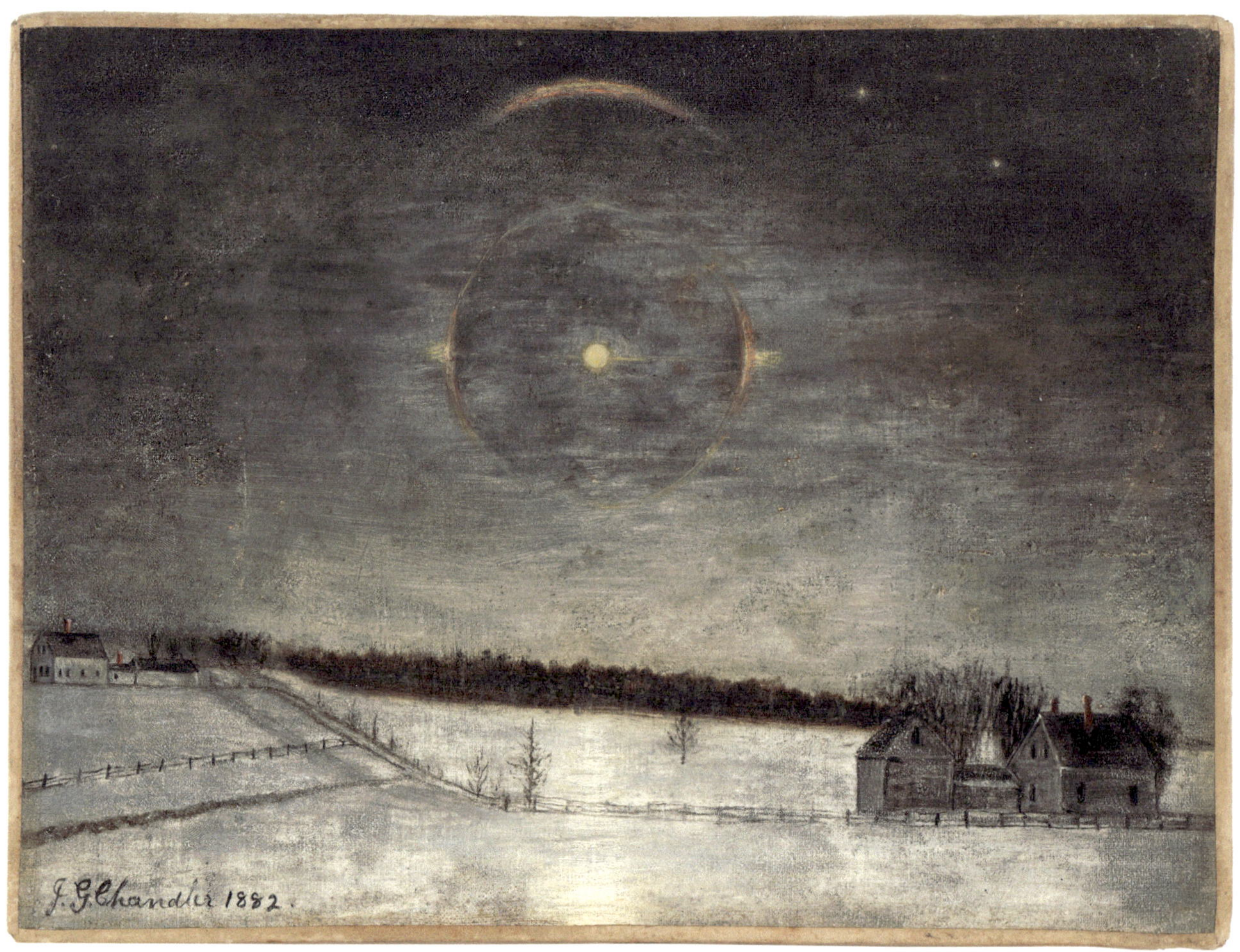

Figure 27: Joseph Goodhue Chandler, *The Moon as Seen February 2, 1882 at Baldwinville, Massachusetts*, 1882. Oil on canvas. Frame: 13¼″ × 17⅜″ × 1½″ (33.7 cm × 44.1 cm × 3.8 cm); stretcher: 11⅛″ × 15¼″ (28.3 cm × 38.7 cm). Mead Art Museum at Amherst College, Gift of Mary A.C. Ware. AC P.C.1890.4. Image credit: Petegorsky/Gipe Photography.

The circle around the moon in this painting (Figure 27) depicts what are commonly called moon dogs. The scientific term is paraselene. The optical phenomenon requires very cold weather, which the painting suggests with its snow-covered landscape. The location, Baldwinville, is part of current day Templeton, Massachusetts. The village was created from Narragansett Plantation, land set aside for men who fought against the Narragansett in King Philip's War in the 1670s.

THE CAMPER
E. Pauline Johnson

Night 'neath the northern skies, lone, black, and grim:
Naught but the starlight lies 'twixt heaven, and him.

Of man no need has he, of God, no prayer;
He and his Deity are brothers there.

Above his bivouac the firs fling down
Through branches gaunt and black, their needles brown.

Afar some mountain streams, rockbound and fleet
Sing themselves through his dreams in cadence sweet,

The pine trees whispering, the heron's cry,
The plover's passing wing, his lullaby.

And blinking overhead the white stars keep
Watch o'er his hemlock bed—his sinless sleep.

E. Pauline Johnson, *Flint and Feather: The Complete Poems of E. Pauline Johnson (Tekahionwake)* (Toronto: Musson Book Co., 1917), 33.

GEORGE WESLEY BELLOWS: *FERN WOODS*

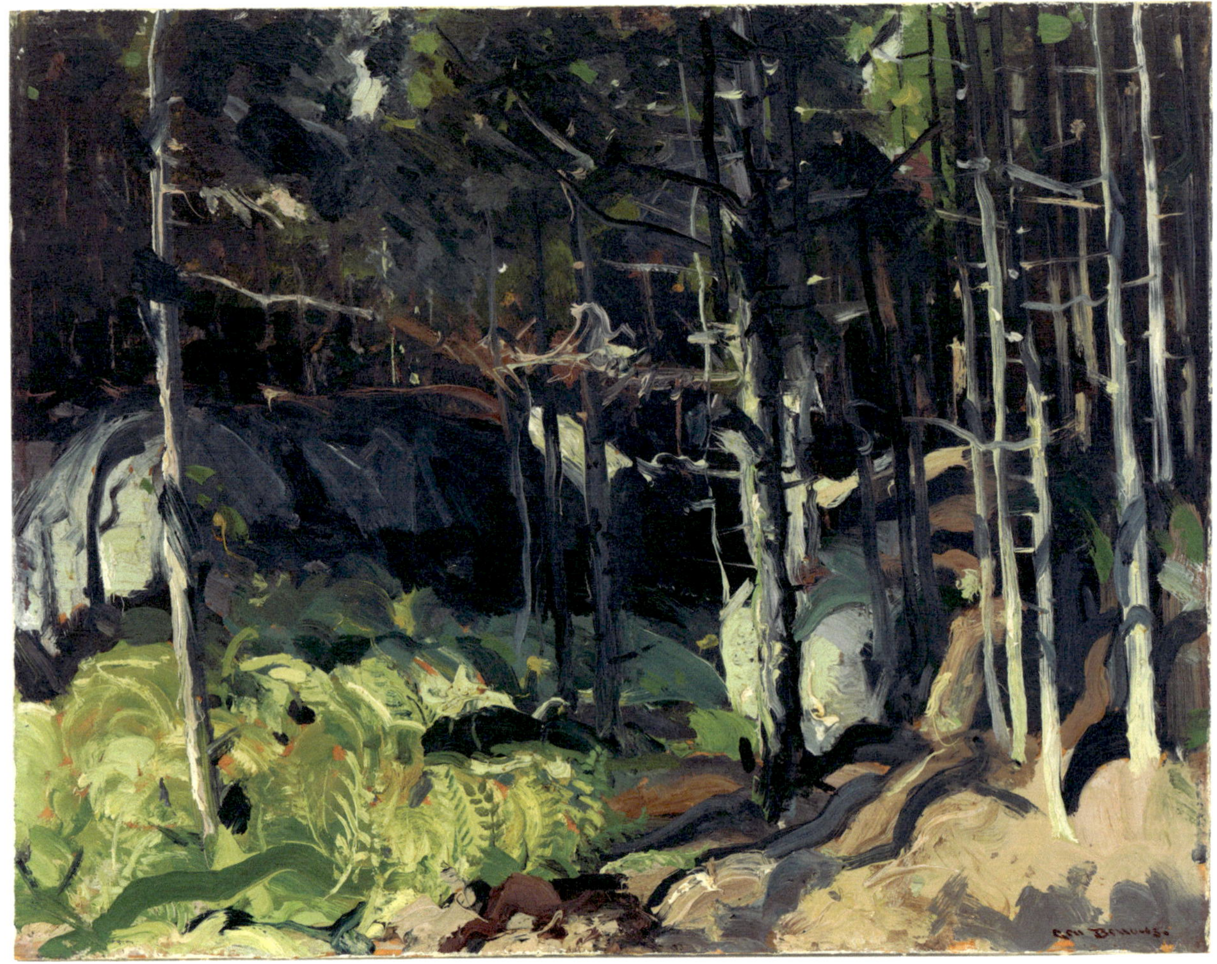

Figure 28: George Wesley Bellows, *Fern Woods*, 1913. Oil on board. Frame: 22″ × 26⅜″ × 2″ (55.9 cm × 67 cm × 5.1 cm); board: 15″ × 19½″ (38.1 cm × 49.5 cm). Mead Art Museum at Amherst College. Gift of Albert Sylvester (Class of 1956), Susan Hopwood, Amy Katoh, and Duncan Sylvester in memory of their parents, Elizabeth E. and Albert L. Sylvester (Class of 1924). AC 1986.124. Image credit: Petegorsky/Gipe Photography

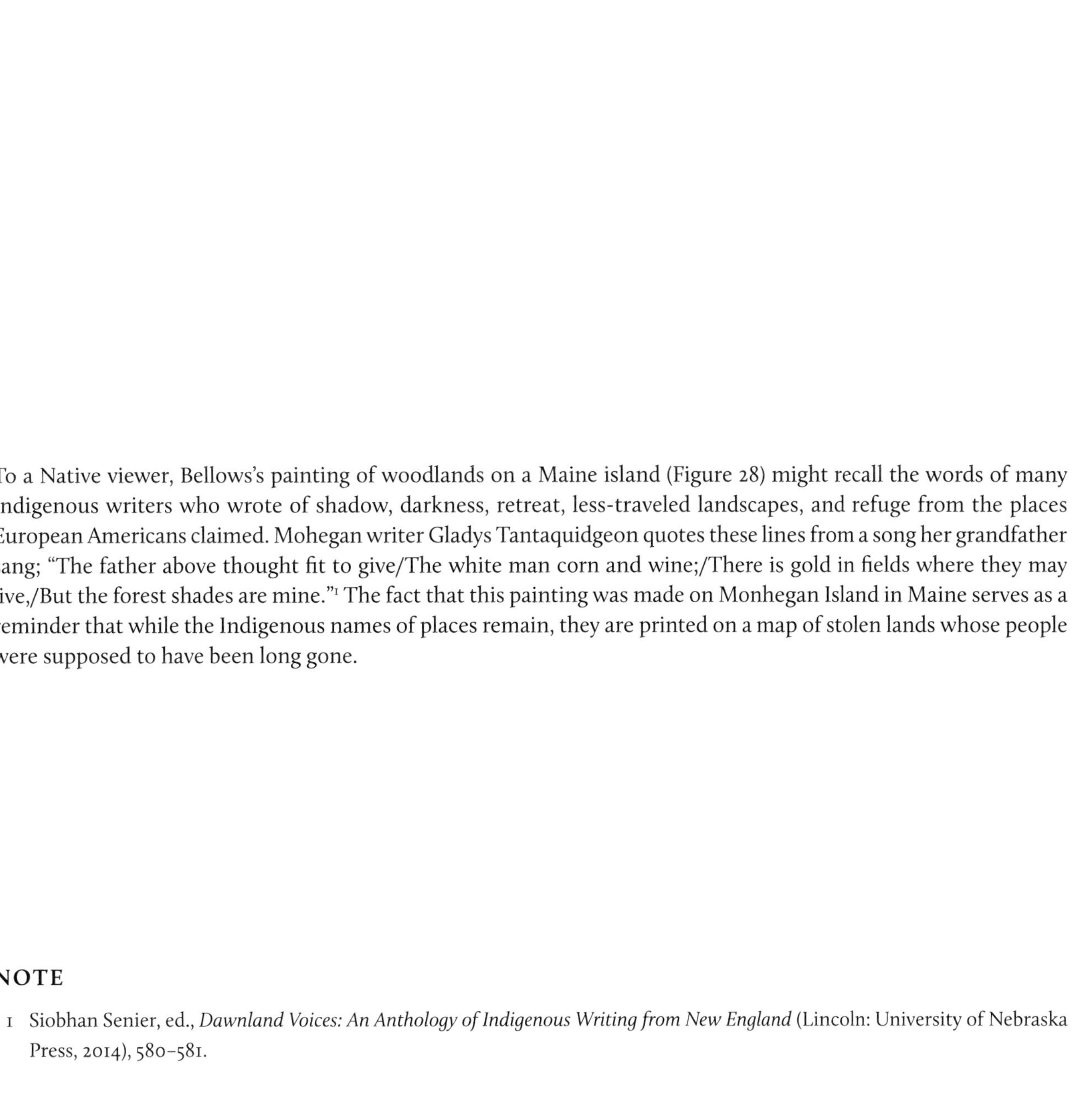

To a Native viewer, Bellows's painting of woodlands on a Maine island (Figure 28) might recall the words of many Indigenous writers who wrote of shadow, darkness, retreat, less-traveled landscapes, and refuge from the places European Americans claimed. Mohegan writer Gladys Tantaquidgeon quotes these lines from a song her grandfather sang; "The father above thought fit to give/The white man corn and wine;/There is gold in fields where they may live,/But the forest shades are mine."[1] The fact that this painting was made on Monhegan Island in Maine serves as a reminder that while the Indigenous names of places remain, they are printed on a map of stolen lands whose people were supposed to have been long gone.

NOTE

1 Siobhan Senier, ed., *Dawnland Voices: An Anthology of Indigenous Writing from New England* (Lincoln: University of Nebraska Press, 2014), 580–581.

JOHN SLOAN: *DOLLY READING*

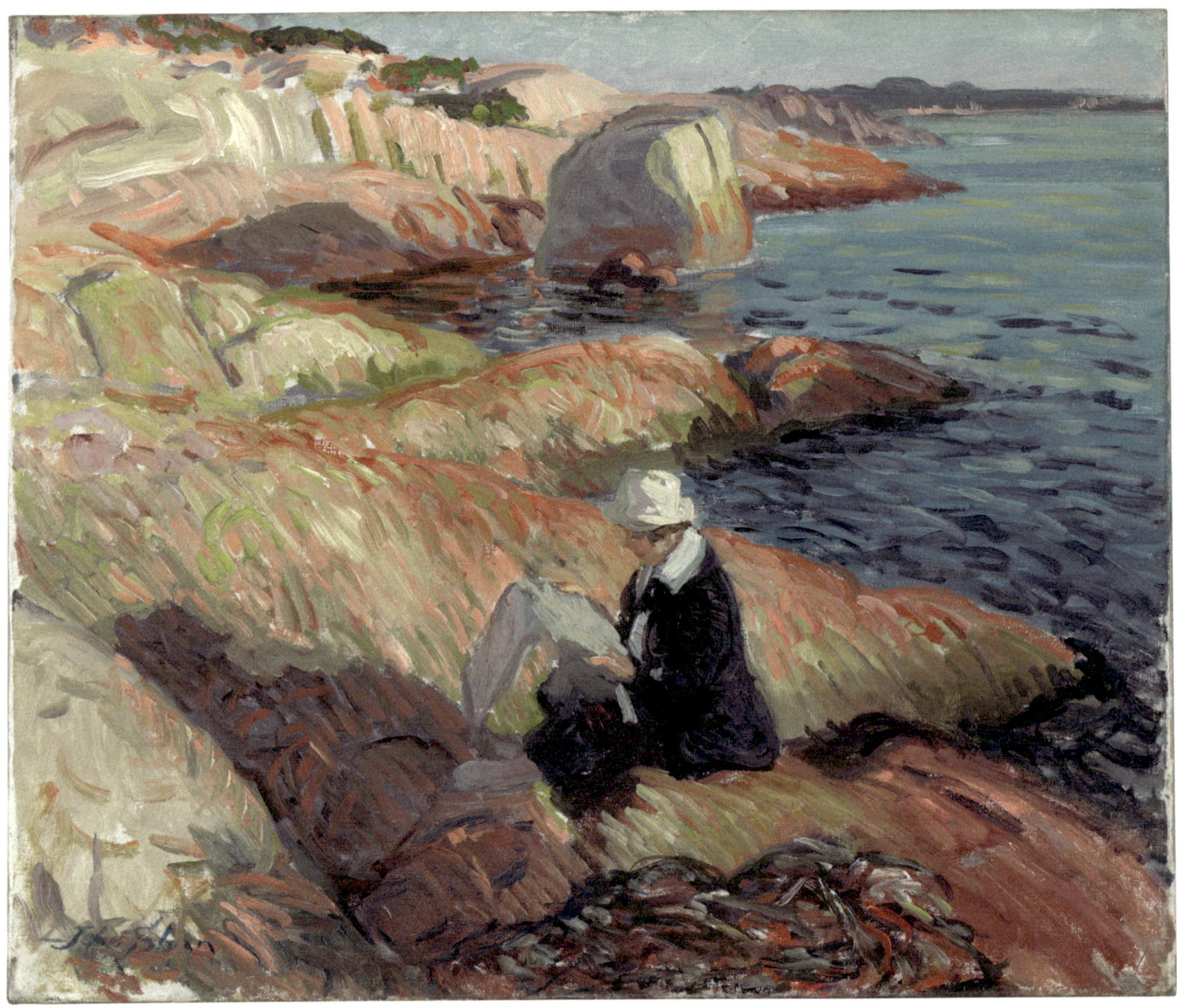

Figure 29: John Sloan, *Dolly Reading*, 1914. Oil on canvas. Frame: 26⅝″ × 31″ × 3″; stretcher: 19⅞″ × 24½″. Mead Art Museum at Amherst College. Bequeath of Dr. Sanford B. Sternlieb (Class of 1946). AC 2019.22. © 2024 Delaware Art museum / Artists Rights Society (ARS), New York. Image credit: Petegorsky/Gipe Photography.

Dakota artist Mary Sully, whose work was included in the first iteration of *Boundless*, admired artists from the Ashcan School—a group of painters whose subjects were ordinary sights, figures, and settings, and also had political commentary. Sloan's work such as *She's Got the Point,* also shown in *Boundless*, asserted the painter's respect for women's rights. This painting (Figure 29) does the same in that it shows a woman, whose name is given (Dolly) engaged in an intellectual pursuit. Many other artists of the era might have shown a woman lounging or in modest swimwear or strolling, but here she is reading—a moment perfect for *Boundless*.

ARTIST STATEMENT
Brittney Peauwe Wunnepog Walley

Brittney Peauwe Wunnepog Walley is a Massachusetts-based artist and a citizen of the Nipmuc tribe.

Weaving enables me to honor my ancestors while uplifting present and future generations. My hope is to share the beauty of Northeastern Woodland art through contemporary pieces crafted from traditional methods that have been used from time immemorial. A dear friend taught me this craft. Kuttabotamish to my teacher, weaving mentors, and the Nipmuc community that supports me in this craft and inspires me to continue in traditional arts.

The blue basket featured in *Boundless* (Figure 30) is part of a series I am working on entitled *Different Footprints*. It showcases a rich combination of patterns and designs, symbolizing the beauty and power of different peoples when they walk together. Nipmuc basket traditions, water motifs, and samples of still-existent seventeenth-century Eastern Woodland bags are seen throughout the series. The blue basket is the second of the series, featuring parallel lines and an eight-pointed star, which are characteristic of traditional Nipmuc pieces. Its moon phases contemplate the passage of time, pay homage to the various moons and ceremonies observed by Eastern Woodland peoples, and tie into the water theme of the series. The top pattern is a partial reproduction of a Mohegan bag from the seventeenth century. The first basket in *Different Footprints* features a similar sample from a seventeenth-century Narragansett bag. Learning from these baskets and including their patterns is both to honor the past seven generations of weavers and to inspire the next seven to come.

Future contributions to the series will continue to blend historical and contemporary patterns while meditating on themes of trust, relationship building, kinship, and unity.

Additionally, I use the methods of basket weaving to create earrings. Each round segment is woven exactly how round baskets are created. I make these smaller crafts with hopes to spread the art of Northeastern Woodland weaving as far as possible.

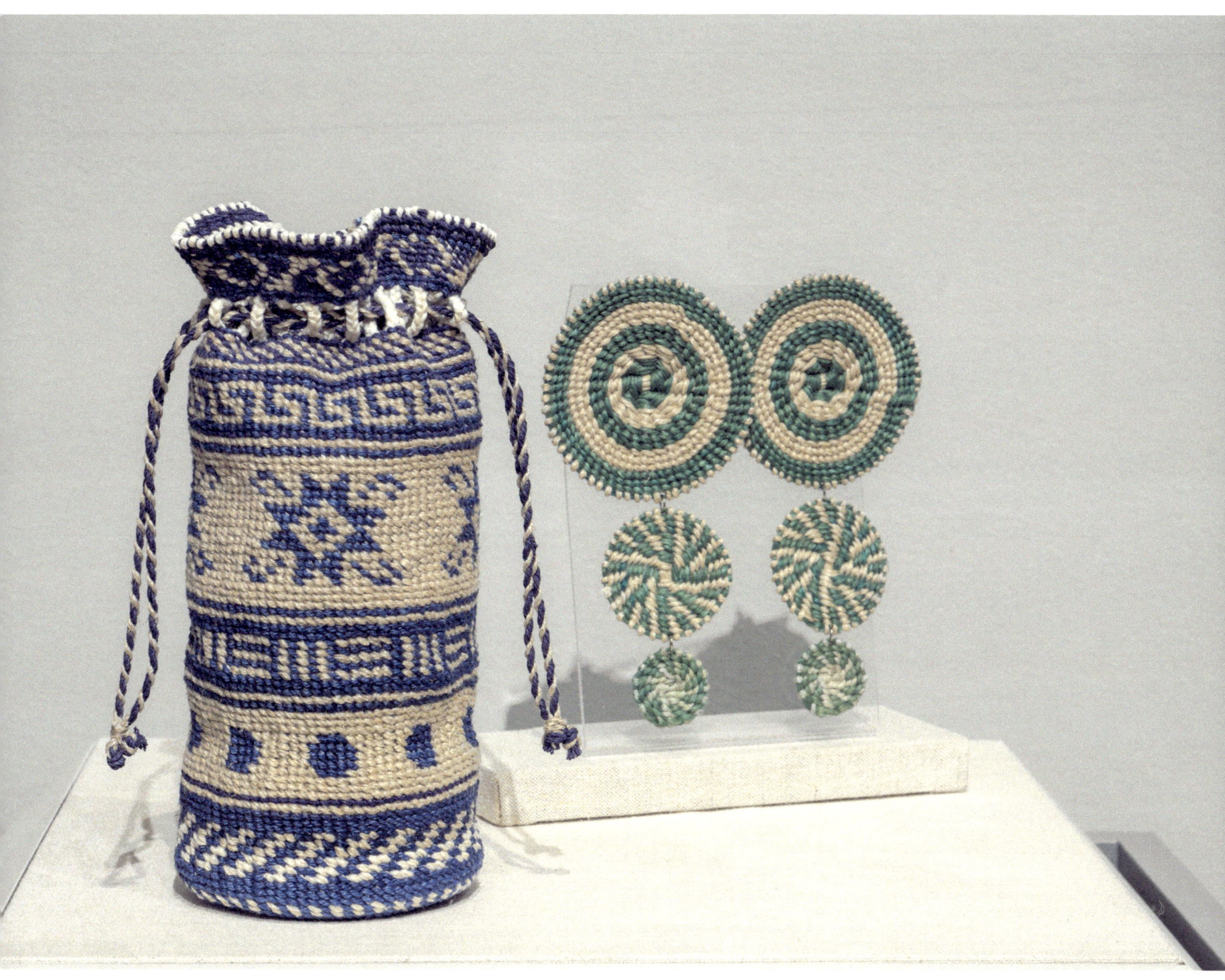

Figure 30: Brittney Peauwe Wunnepog Walley (Nipmuc), Installation view of *Different Footprints (continued)* and *3-Tier Statement Earrings,* 2023. Hemp fiber cordage. Courtesy of the artist. Image credit: Stephen Petegorsky.

A POEM FOR EASTHAMPTON, APRIL 2023

Jason R. Montgomery

Jason R. Montgomery is a Chicano/Indigenous Californian activist, writer, painter, and playwright from El Centro, California. In 2016 he cofounded Attack Bear Press and founded 50 Arrow Gallery in North Hampton. He is one of two 2021–23 Easthampton Poets Laureate.

I've wounds inflicted by you.
Black and blue newsprint bruises,
green cactus needle tattoos,
And Poetry paper cuts.

I have self-inflicted wounds.
Brillo pad scratched skin patches
Rubbed raw with hope of hiding
The scars of my brown birth caul.

I was told be more like King.
Keep us, we pray, in perfect peace.
Last I checked they shot him too.
Then put his face on a t-shirt

You're damn right I'm angry

It's a red-skinned Lordean rage.
It's Sun kissed, and sleep deprived,
A rage that's hollow bone deep
Twisted with cell memory

I don't have much more than this.

i have cried red trails of tears
down a face of banished dust.
With no more than a half glance
From you hurried passersby.

Redemption songs have called in
All those standing in earshot
Only to be an off tune
earworm as they walked away

Please hear this fair case for rage.
It's my black burning belief
That voices raised in anger
Will finally be heard true.

Rage is a hope.

Anger is my last screamed prayer.
I bellow it in the dream
You will join in communion
Because you see me as you.

Disclaimer: To preserve the meaning of the poet's lineation, this chapter is also available in its original, non-reflowable format as a PDF here: https://doi.org/10.3998/mpub.14513702.cmp.2.

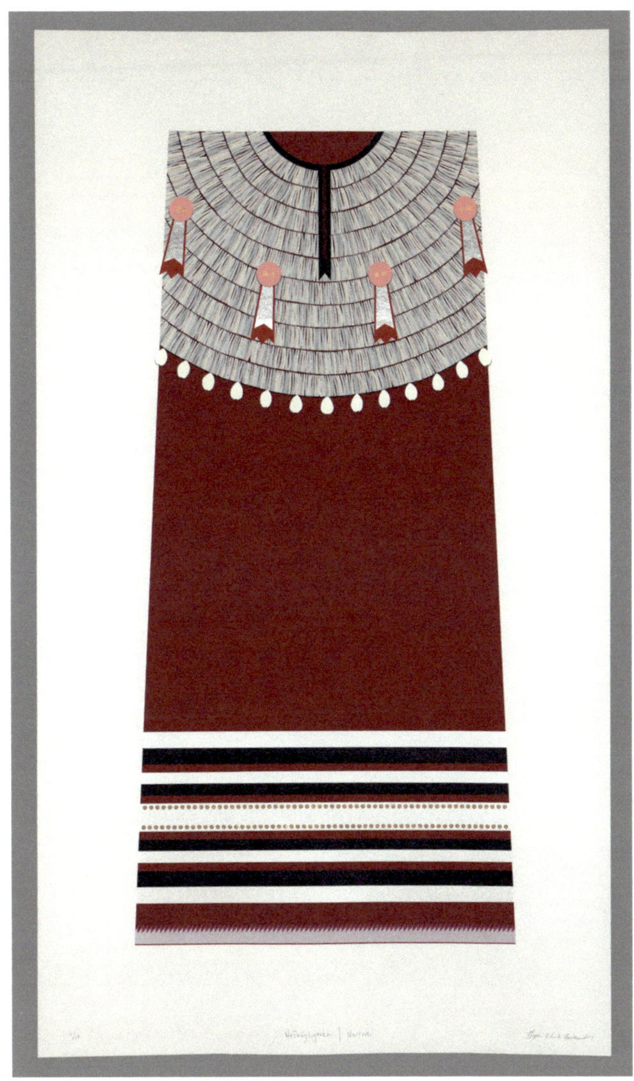

Figure 31: Dyani White Hawk (Sicangu Lakota, German and Welsh ancestry), *Wačháŋtognaka (Nurture)* from the suite *Takes Care of Them*, 2019. Screenprint with metal foil. Sheet: 55½″ × 32″ (141 cm × 81.3 cm); frame (approx.): 62″ × 38″. Mead Art Museum at Amherst College, Museum purchase with Trinkett Clark Memorial Student Acquisition Fund. AC 2020.05. © Dyani White Hawk.

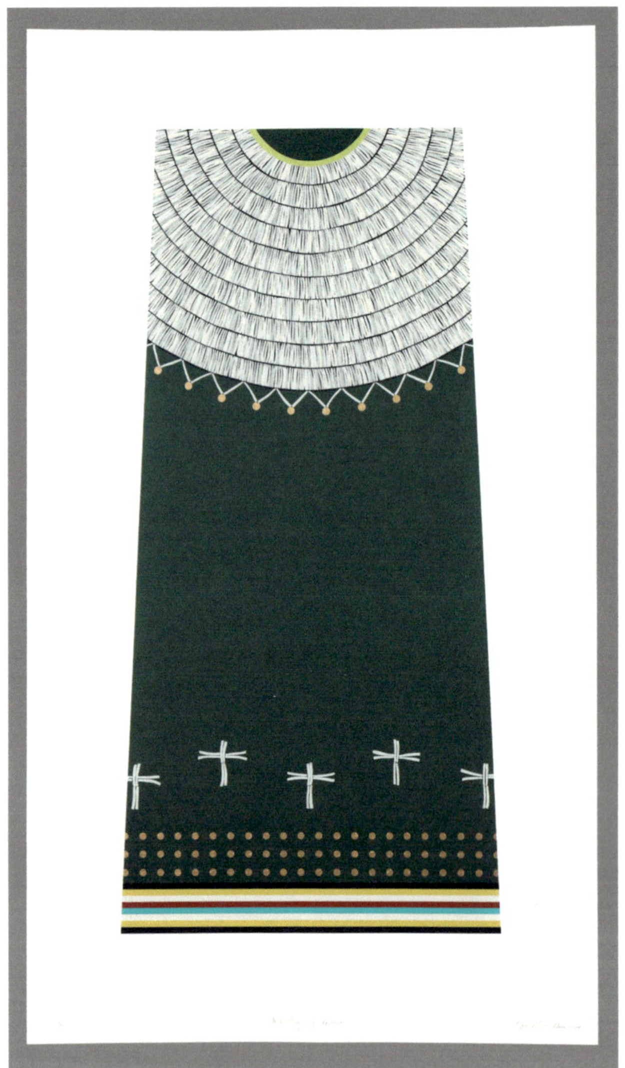

Figure 32: Dyani White Hawk (Sicangu Lakota, German and Welsh ancestry), *Nakíčižiŋ (Protect)* from the suite *Takes Care of Them*, 2019. Screenprint with metal foil. Sheet: 55½″ × 32″ (141 cm × 81.3 cm); frame (approx.): 62″ × 38″. Mead Art Museum at Amherst College, Museum purchase with Trinkett Clark Memorial Student Acquisition Fund. AC 2020.06. © Dyani White Hawk.

The image of Dyani White Hawk's *Wačháŋtognaka (Nurture)* is featured on her mother Sandy White Hawk's 2023 book *A Child of the Indian Race: A Story of Return* from Minnesota Historical Society Press. Sandy White Hawk is a Sicangu Lakota adoptee from the Rosebud Reservation, South Dakota. She is the founder and director of First Nations Repatriation Institute, which offers resources for First Nations people impacted by foster care or adoption to return home, reconnect, and reclaim their identity. Sandy White Hawk is also the director of healing programs for the National Native American Boarding School Healing Coalition and a former elder-in-residence at the Indian Child Welfare Law Office in Minneapolis. She is the subject of several documentaries, including *Blood Memory: A Story of Removal and Return*.

MARY SULLY: NATIVE VIEWS OF PERSONALITY AND CULTURE
Philip J. Deloria

Philip J. Deloria (Dakota descent) is the Leverett Saltonstall Professor of History at Harvard University, and the author of *Playing Indian*, *Indians in Unexpected Places*, and *Becoming Mary Sully: Toward an American Indian Abstract*.

Mary Sully's life and art cannot be detached from the work of her sister, the Dakota linguistic anthropologist Ella Deloria, for the two were companions for decades. Together, they set out to learn and practice the art of ethnography, and did so in the company of Franz Boas, Ruth Benedict, and the extraordinary circle of anthropologists at Columbia University in New York City. For Ella, ethnography meant an "insider" study of her own Dakota life and culture. For Mary Sully, ethnography came secondhand through her sister, and it expressed itself through a unique artistic vision. The object of Sully's ethnographic gaze was quite different from that of her sister, however. Sully embarked on an American Indian study of America—its celebrities, its media, and its popular culture.

Each of Sully's 134 "personality prints" reflect essential characteristics of an individual, while also offering the figure as a representative distillation of some aspect of American culture. In trying to capture the composer and conductor John Philip Sousa, for instance, Sully creates an evocative series of icons, shapes, and colors. We see musical notes. We sense the grass and the linear order of a band on a football field at halftime. We note the distinctive bell shape of the Sousaphone, a marching tuba invented by the bandleader. Sousa was tightly connected to the band program at the University of Illinois, and so Sully features the orange and blue colors of the school. There's a swirling sense of music, movement, and Americanness, with red, white, and blue emerging in the bottom of the three panels as an eye-catching design—the musical notes taking shape as a marching band formation and reminding viewers that Sousa was, among other things, the composer of *The Stars and Stripes Forever.*

But if Mary Sully was an acute observer of American culture, she was pulled by her sister into the ethnographic illustration of Dakota worlds. She drew shawls, pipes, parfleche boxes, dolls, dresses, hair ties, clothing, cradleboards, and more. Among Sully's personality prints are to be found a few curious images of animals adorned with Native material culture, as if modeling such valuables for the viewer. A fluffy dog dons a headdress and matching moccasins (Figure 34). A second dog wears a floral saddle blanket and sports, tied to its tail, a feather staff or sort of coup stick, standing at attention (Figure 33).

Dakota artists had deep traditions of ornamentation for and about animals, most notably in the elaborate decorative gear crafted for their horses. Horses replaced dogs as beasts of burden, and Lakota people recognized the historical and analogic relations between them. One prominent word for horse, *sunka wakan*—holy dog—suggests exactly that kind of relation. Indeed, a perusal of old Lakota dictionaries reveals a rich complex of concepts rooted in the phoneme *sunk or sung* that blur together horses, dogs, wolves, and foxes. Sully's horse-like, scruffy bearded dog with saddle blanket and tail decoration thus seems rich with Dakota cultural resonance, as does her fluffy pup, bedecked with rich adornment. Given the ways that Lakota people recognized the personhood of animals, might it be the case that Sully was expanding her canon to represent the distinct personalities, not just of humans, but of dogs as well?

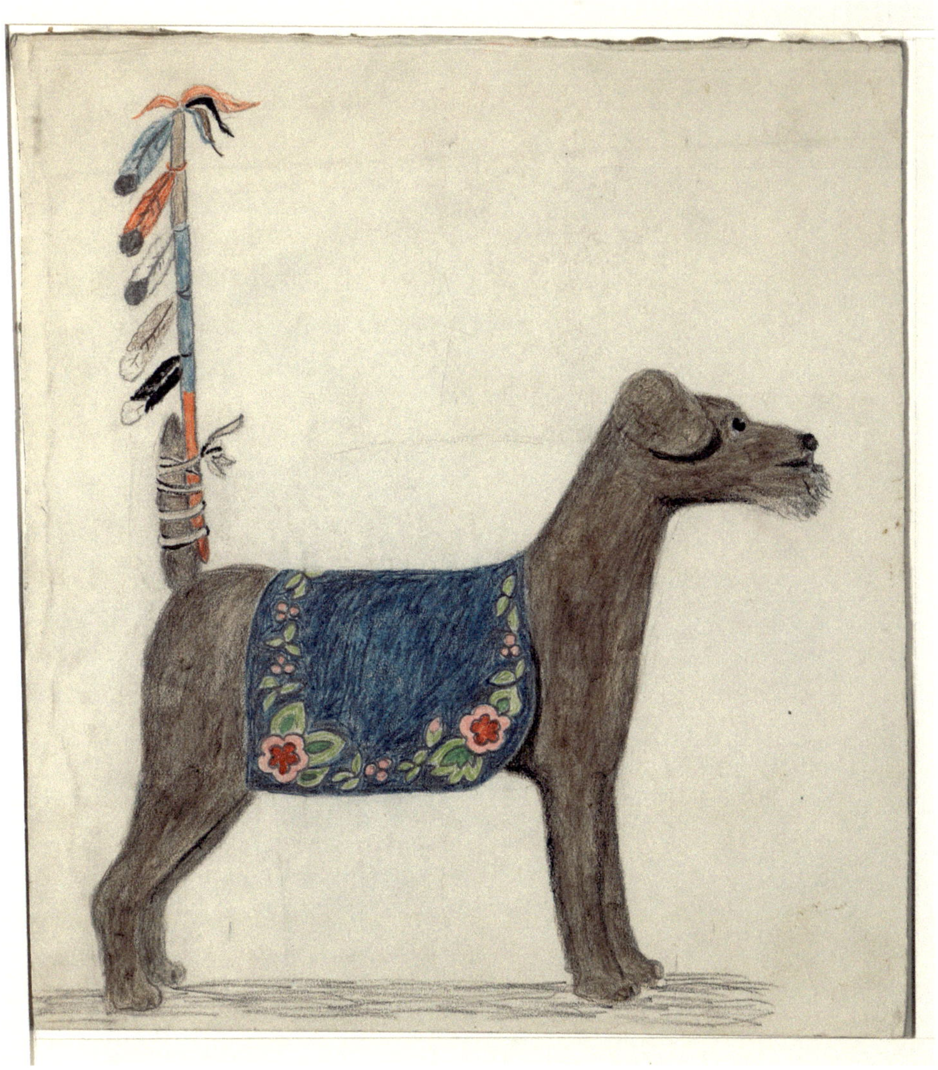

Figure 33: Mary Sully (Yankton Dakota), *Dog with Blue Blanket*, ca.1940s–1950s. Drawing, approx. 12″ × 8″; frame 18¾″ × 14¾″. Courtesy of the Mary Sully Foundation.

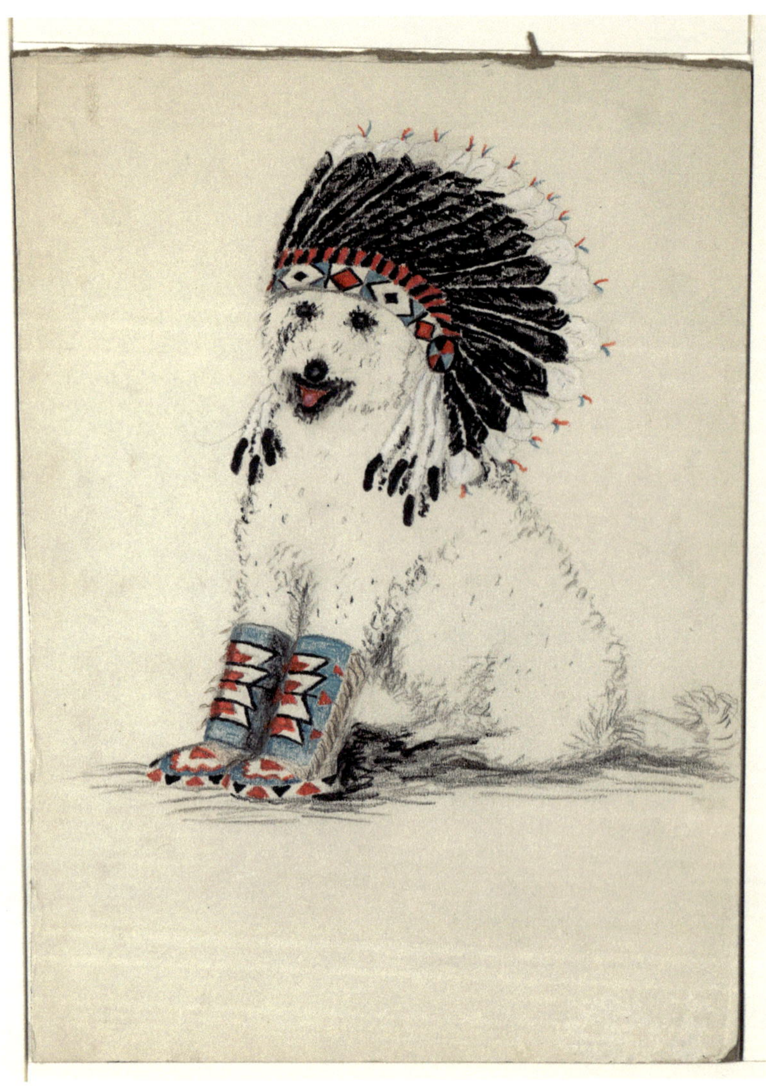

Figure 34: Mary Sully (Yankton Dakota), *Dog with Headdress*, ca.1940s–1950s. Drawing, approx. 12″ × 8″; frame 18¾″ × 14¾″. Courtesy of the Mary Sully Foundation.

WIOŚTE OLOWAN
Julia Yellow-Hair

WIOŚTE OLOWAN

Ehake wa*n*mayakuwe,
Ehake wa*n*mayakuwe.
Śice tecihilaqon!
Wa*n*na waya wamanikte.
Ehake wa*n*mayakuwe
Ehake nape-mayuza!

LOVE SONG

For the last time, come greet me again.
For the last time, come greet me again.
Dear friend, I loved thee alone!
Now to school I'm going away;
For the last time, come greet me again.
For the last time, come take my hand!

Publications in the early twentieth century, such as *The Indians' Book*, edited by Natalie Curtis, with illustrations by Ho-Chunk artist Angel De Cora, were read in Indian boarding schools. Perhaps they were intended for Native students on some level as evidenced by this bilingual song that is introduced with this note: "Holy Star (Julia Yellow-Hair) is in boarding school and that is why she has chosen this song for her contribution to *The Indians' Book*. She is granddaughter of the aged chief, Yellow-Hair, renowned among the Dakotas."[1]

NOTE

1 "Song by Julia Yellow-Hair," *The Indians' Book: An Offering by the American Indians of Indian Lore, Musical and Narrative, to Form a Record of the Songs and Legends of Their Race*, ed. Natalie Curtis (New York: Harper and Brothers, 1907), 58.

STORYING, SIGNS, AND SYMBOLS WITHIN THE OČETI ŠAKOWIŊ

Kiara M. Vigil

Kiara Vigil is Associate Professor of American Studies and Dean of New Students at Amherst College. She is Dakhota from the Sisseton Wahpeton Oyate.

Where to begin? Perhaps with Dyani White Hawk and Mary Sully. Or Mary's sister Ella Cara Deloria, "beautiful day woman", as she was known in Dakhodia (the Dakhota language). Her work as an anthropologist and writer made her more well-known than Mary during their lifetime, and Ella overlapped with important literary figures—authors like Charles Ohiyesa Eastman and Zitkala-Ša, who were also part of the Očeti Šakowiŋ and today are celebrated within the field of Native and Indigenous literary studies. All these Indigenous creators used texts and images to represent themselves and their views of a world where Christianity and western education overlapped with traditions and teachings stemming from the Očeti Šakowiŋ—the Seven Council Fires. This confederacy became widely known as the Great Sioux Nation but is better understood in Dakhodia as representing a larger thiošpaye or "extended kin network" of Dakhota, Lakota, and Nakota people.

This entry points to the long and complicated tradition of storying, which has always been a part of the Očeti Šakowiŋ. It has endured across generations even with the Christianization of Plains peoples and their adaptation of various colonial tools, like the horse, the English language, the printing press, the ledger book, and more. By emphasizing creative storytelling practices at the intersection of text and image with examples from the Seven Council Fires, my aim is to highlight the boundlessness of writing and art as well as the power of Native books as works of material culture.[1]

For Dakhota people, the ethic of kinship is central to one's life. This ethical relationship has often been reflected in the art and writings of Dakhota people to provide a map of knowledge that is collectively created and shared. Thus, storytelling required signs and symbols to represent the world imagined and the world experienced to guide members of the Oyate in how they should engage with one another. The exhibition *Boundless* offers contemporary viewers multiple entry points into this rich linguistic and cultural history of Dakhota people as artists and writers. Although most published in English, I contend that the epistemologies and cosmologies carried by Indigenous languages were also at play in their thinking and provided guiding frameworks for their representational work, which could run counter to dominant narratives provided by American society. Ella Deloria, as a practicing Christian from an Episcopalian family, also worked on translating between Dakhodia/Lakota and English and was perhaps best equipped with understanding the power of language.

In a letter from 1928 to her spiritual advisor, Bishop Hugh L. Burleson, Deloria wrote extensively about her linguistic work under the guidance of Dr. Franz Boas. She writes, "I am very thoroughly convinced that you cannot really get at the heart of a people without knowing their language." The contents of her letter have been published posthumously in 2022 in *The Dakota Way of Life,* so that readers today can learn more about Deloria's legacy in relation to Dakhodia, story, and culture.[2]

Deloria's translation work remains useful for current language revitalization and teaching efforts. At the same time, because of the different structures of Dakhodia and English, most translations between the two languages are partial and imperfect at best, which makes any discussion of "translation" tenuous and complicated. I will focus on a particular example of a partial translation between Dakhodia and English to illustrate this complicated relationship and the key differences between these two linguistic systems that could have influenced artists and writers coming out of an Očeti Šakowiŋ tradition.

Some of the earliest examples of Plains artistry and writing come from waníyetu wówapi, or as scholars have translated these words: "winter count."[3] The notion of the "count" as a reference to marking the passage of time from one winter to another aligns with Dakhota traditional practice. At the same time, wówapi is best understood as more than a mere accounting of the passage of chronological or clock time. Wówapi itself is less a "count" than instead referring to writing and the creation of a text. In Dakhodia, wówapi means any writing: a note, a letter, a message, or a book. The library is wówapi thipi or "the book house." Wówapi káǧa is to make writing, to write a book or letter, and relatedly "owá éhnaka" is to put something into writing and to record something. This is the work of the Oyáte (the People) in relation to waníyetu wówapi. Together, with a keeper who does the creating of the image, they collectively write, remember, and record history. Today, when Dakhota people ask one another about their age, the question is: How many winters are you? For the number of winters reveals one's survival during a time of scarcity and struggle. Similarly, to ask about one's enrollment in a tribal nation and belonging within a particular reservation is to ask: Where are you written? So, waníyetu wówapi is more fully understood as a winter book. These books are art objects, archives, and collective memories of the passage of time and events. They are in fact *boundless* when it comes to writing and art, to story and time, and to the boundary that might separate the individual from the collective.[4]

Waníyetu wówapi fused images and oral traditions together within a material culture object that became an archive of pivotal events in the life of a band, community, or family. The keeper of the book safeguarded this object and was responsible for creating the images that were arranged upon it. The choice of image depended on conversations with elders to help choose which event was the most important to represent. But the winter book was not an object unto itself. The images presented depended upon everyone in the community acting as listeners and storytellers to fully populate the narratives surrounding each image. Individuals would mark momentous events in their lives by indexing them to images on "the count." Both the action of indexing and those of listening and retelling that accompanied this symbolic system helped everyone remember their survival from one winter to the next. Since Dakhodia is a verb- and not a subject-object-based language, one's actions matter. One's relationships matter. Everything about "the count" was relational, as was the knowledge it carried. Ella Deloria writes this in *Speaking of Indians* about the importance of relationality in Dakhota society: "Before going further, I can safely say that the ultimate aim of Dakhota life, stripped of accessories, was quite simple: One must obey kinship rules and be a good relative."[5] Looking at the creation of winter books points to the enduring power of the "ethics kinship" that binds Dakhotas to one another.[6]

The Dakhota and Lakota writers and artists presented within *Boundless*, and those who are absent, well-known artists like Oscar Howe, were deeply enmeshed in both an Indigenous worldview, that of the Očeti Šakowiŋ, and an

American social and political system that often sought to limit the reach and impact of their perspectives. A collaborative and complicated text that combined visual vocabularies from U.S. settler society and Dakhota narratives, which began in 1871 and remained in print until 1939, is the now-rare Dakhota-language newspaper *Iápi Oaye*. Translated by its missionary founders as "The Word Carrier," it offers another example of a boundless approach to knowledge, thought, and image where Native and non-Native writers documented life in Dakhota society alongside world events.

Published by a Christian missionary press, *Iápi Oaye* circulated to a largely Dakhodia-reading and -speaking audience to share local and global stories as well as important notices concerning the negotiation of treaties, the emergence of boarding schools, and other assimilatory processes like allotment that followed the end of violent conflict over Native-held lands. Alongside these news reports, Christian missionary writers inserted their own English-language lessons and Bible stories printed in Dakhodia hoping to convert Indigenous readers. Despite such aims, the paper's run—the longest of any Indigenous-language newspaper in United States history—remained in Dakhodia, with only small subsections in English. This preservation of the language, and the epistemological and cosmological systems encoded within it, offers an opportunity to engage with the paper not as the "Word Carrier" (a reference to the Gospels and the English language) but as the "Language Carrier."

In linguistic terms *Iápi* refers to language, so Dakhota readers may have subscribed to this periodical to read news in their own language. Indeed, the *imagined communities* that this newspaper helped nurture were also communities where the creation of waniyetu wówapi continued to flourish.[7] In fact, references to these winter books appear in at least two issues of the paper, from December 1, 1895 and February 1, 1921, revealing a complicated intertextual system of meaning-making that brought older and contemporary sign systems into dialogue with one another. The more ephemeral and mass-produced newspaper enabled writers and readers of Dakhodia to continue the process of storying, recording events, and making memories and meaning out of their shared experiences of colonization. Thus, the newspaper's emergence did not threaten but perhaps enabled and archived the practice of waníyetu wówapi creation that remained a part of Očeti Šakowiŋ experience.

In fact, as the more permanent archiving of knowledge was made possible by waníyetu wówapi, the printers from the Santee Normal Training School in Nebraska, who published both *Iapi Oaye* and its English-language companion paper *The Word Carrier*, embraced the fundraising potential of these periodicals to support the school by selling bound volumes of previously published issues. An advertisement from the last page of the November–December issue of *The Word Carrier* in 1908 reads: "Iapi Oaye and Word Carrier—Bound Volumes—Two copies. Volume I. From 1871–1887. Bound in cloth with leather back and corners. Scarce. Price...$6.00 each Twenty copies Volume II. From 1888–1900. Same binding, price...$4.00." This ad highlights a potentially rare and special opportunity for subscribers, who had excess income, to purchase one of these bound volumes. There are several bound volumes of both *Iapi Oaye* and *The Word Carrier* in the Archives and Special Collections at Amherst College, as part of the Kim-Wait/Pablo Eisenberg Collection of Native American Literature, which include the two date ranges described in this ad from 1908, suggesting the school's effort at selling the volumes was a success.[8]

In addition to winter books and Indigenous-language newspapers, ledger book art circulated widely among Native and non-Native audiences throughout the late nineteenth and early twentieth centuries. Although not featured in

Boundless, these are another important aspect of Plains artistic traditions that intersected directly with bookmaking technologies and in many cases were drawing on representational strategies developed much earlier that are kin to winter books.

The Plains Ledger Art Digital Publishing Project promotes further preservation and research concerning ledger drawings produced between 1860 and 1900, with well over two hundred books of Plains Indian ledger art that exist across various collections today. These ledger books offer individual and collective histories of cultural, social, ceremonial, and aesthetic information of life as experienced by Plains peoples during times of increasing violence, both in terms of military conquest and Christianization as well as the push to remove Indigenous peoples from their historic homelands and the forced residential schooling of Indigenous children, which further disconnected them from their Native languages, cultures, and people. This departure into ledger art points to another critical example of adaptation by Indigenous creators that brought visual and book history together into one object. As a transitional form of Plains Indian artistry that corresponds with a period of dispossession and dislocation with the expansion of an allotment system, destruction of buffalo herds and other game animals, and the aftermath of the Civil War, the use of ledger paper in lieu of painting on buffalo hide, as well as the introduction of new coloring materials points to a time when Native artists told new stories with new tools while drawing on older pictorial traditions.[9]

The waníyetu wówapi saw a similar sort of transition as the earliest images created by keepers were done on rock walls before shifting their work to hides and later to muslin cloth, paper, and canvas. Just as Plains peoples had transitioned from using dogs (to help transport their belongings from one seasonal encampment to another) to horses after the expansion of the Spanish empire, so too do we see a trend toward adaptation and incorporation. Dakhota writers, who were both practicing Christians and members of the Oyate, whose articles appear in the pages of *Iápi Oaye*, provide additional examples of this power of adaptation. Many of their writings point to the changing landscape of the Oyate, which was not vanishing but was in flux as further evidence of survival in the context of colonization. Like the many artists and writers featured in *Boundless*, these brief examples speak to a long tradition of overlap where people of the Očeti Šakowiŋ fine-tuned their aesthetic representations of life and knowledge by engaging in an array of image-making and storytelling technologies pointing to the boundless world of Native books and art.

NOTES

1 For more about the figures mentioned in this opening paragraph, see Philip Joseph Deloria, *Becoming Mary Sully: Toward an American Indian Abstract* (Seattle: University of Washington Press, 2019); Kiara M. Vigil, *Indigenous Intellectuals: Sovereignty, Citizenship, and the American Imagination, 1880–1930* (New York: Cambridge University Press, 2015); and María Eugenia Cotera, *Native Speakers: Ella Deloria, Zora Neale Hurston, Jovita González, and the Poetics of Culture* (Austin: University of Texas Press, 2010).

2 Ella Cara Deloria, *The Dakota Way of Life*, ed. Raymond J. DeMallie and Thierry Veyrié (Lincoln: University of Nebraska Press, 2022), xi.

3 Throughout this essay, "waníyetu wówapi" will be used interchangeably with "winter books."

4 Candace S. Greene and Russell Thornton, eds., *The Year the Stars Fell: Lakota Winter Counts at the Smithsonian* (Lincoln: University of Nebraska Press, 2007).

5 Ella Cara Deloria, *Speaking of Indians* (Lincoln: Bison Books, 1998), 25.

6 Christopher J. Pexa, "Transgressive Adoptions: Dakota Prisoners' Resistances to State Domination Following the 1862 U.S.–Dakota War," *Wicazo Sa Review* 30, no. 1 (2015): 29–56, https://doi.org/10.5749/wicazosareview.30.1.0029.

7 Benedict Anderson, *Imagined Communities: Reflections on the Origin and Spread of Nationalism* (London: Verso, 2016).

8 Advertisement, *The Word Carrier*, Santee Normal Training School, Nov.–Dec. 1908, 24 (Archives and Special Collections, Amherst College Library).

9 Colin G. Calloway, ed., *Ledger Narratives: The Plains Indian Drawings in the Mark Lansburgh Collection at Dartmouth College* (Norman: University of Oklahoma Press, 2017).

EARTH EATERS

4

BRENT MICHAEL DAVIDS: *THE LAST OF JAMES FENIMORE COOPER*

Brent Michael Davids is a celebrated composer and co-director of the Lenape Center in Manhattan. He is Mohican/ Munsee-Lenape.

—

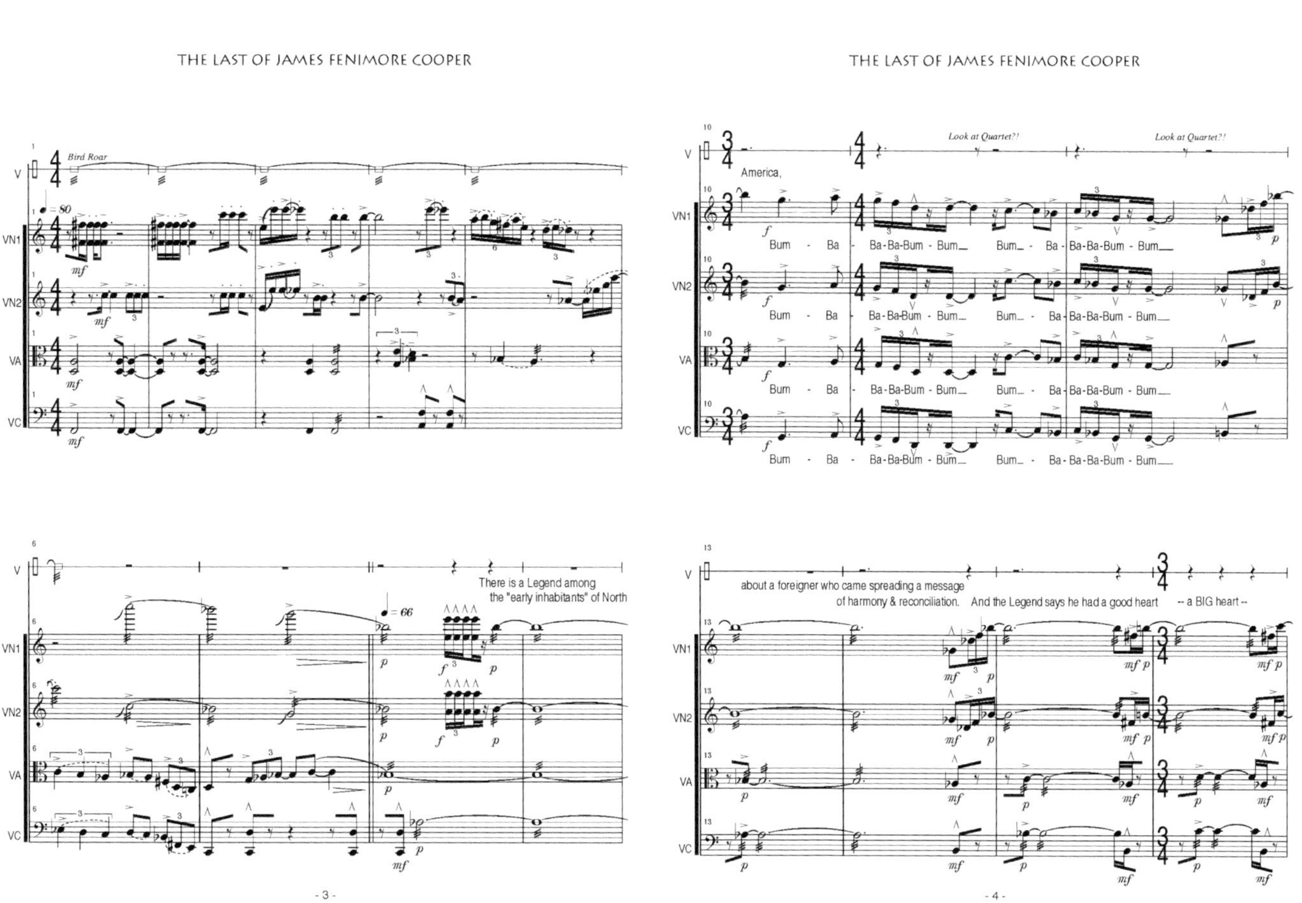

Figure 35a and 35b: Brent Michael Davids, *The Last of James Fenimore Cooper*, Measures 1 to 9 (left) and Measures 10 to 16 (right), 2001. ©Brent Michael Davids. Reprinted by permission of the artist.

EARTH EATERS
Lisa A. Crossman

Lisa Crossman is Director of Curatorial Affairs at the Mead Art Museum.

> "I never knew how many variations of a vision we can spin to make one image that might not even have been true but now is now and now I know we do."
>
> —Heid E. Erdrich, excerpt from "Variations True," *Little Big Bully*[1]

The sight of the hairy spider or the yellowjacket in Andrea Carlson's *Gore Hounds* (2010) might make one person jump and another person laugh. Somebody may see beauty in Thomas Cole's *Daniel Boone at His Cabin at Great Osage Lake* (1826) and someone else violence. Yet another individual might experience an uncomfortable blend of contradictory emotions. But what can you make of the silver *Cake Server* (1768–69) (Figure 10)? It could be appreciated for its artistry or the imagined delight of such an object's use. Do these interpretations preclude an examination of the underlying conditions in which silver was produced at that time? How have portraits like the eighteenth-century painting by Joshua Reynolds of Sir Jeffery Amherst, the town of Amherst's infamous namesake, been interpreted?

As I ponder the many stories that can be told about an object, centering on a few works that were displayed or considered for *Boundless*, I ask: Can we create new narratives without replicating the structures of preexisting ones? Does speaking of the violence of colonialism give it more power or diminish its might? Can its power be consumed and transformed?

I don't know the answers.

I consider these words in the Toronto Biennial catalog, *Water, Kinship, Belief*: "...the desire for fixed meanings is a colonial anxiety...."[2]

I look at the art.

Gore Hounds by artist Andrea Carlson (Figure 37) is a kaleidoscope of colors and shapes that form a jagged foreground, beyond which I read the sea and sky. A giant spider hovers on one side of the work, a yellowjacket on the other. The red text, evocative of writing on a horror film poster, reads "GUT MUNCHING GORE HOUNDS." The gap between the work's four sections gives the impression of a creased paper, folded or torn, and then placed back together—an intentional decision by the artist, among others, to disrupt reading the image in a singular way, as complete or whole. *Gore Hounds* is part of the series *VORE* that Carlson began in 2008. It can be exhibited alone or with other works from the series, the order of each work interchangeable.[3]

Carlson has described her artistic role as "filter or translator, fully digesting [her] sources as a complication to the craft of appropriation."[4] Her language references cannibalism; *Gore Hounds* alludes to the 1980s film *Terreur cannibale*

(Cannibal Terror) and, by extension, to the genre of gore or exploitation film—a genre that traffics in graphic violence and sexual content. But Carlson wields the symbol of cannibalism with the purpose of recovery.

Carlson, who is Anishinaabe with lineal descent from the Grand Portage Band, has explained: "The idea of cannibalism, or cultural cannibalism, referenced through the film's text is a metaphor for the assimilation and consumption of cultural identity."[5] The formal aspects of *Gore Hounds* and the landscape's animated and forceful appearance are resistant to easy, mindless consumption. The text reminds me that long-standing colonial histories of exploitation and violence have shaped understandings of place and impacted all of the living things that compose it. The western genre of landscape painting is revealing of this perspective, a view of material consumption that has defined the ethos of the United States.

Carlson's work focuses my attention on violence, a history of genocide and erasure of Indigenous people at the hands of colonists, but also the enduring violence embedded in many of the systems and institutions within which numerous people continue to live and work. Yet Carlson's *Gore Hounds* also diverges from the styles and perspectives found in nineteenth-century landscape painting, including the foundational works of the collection of "American" art at the Mead. These historical paintings, mainly by Anglo artists and including the painting by Cole mentioned above, are defined by a presentation of the land as an uninhabited resource that aligns with ideals of manifest destiny, an obsession with infinite expansion and individual land ownership as tied to prosperity. We've heard these stories.

Cultural cannibalism, in Carlson's hands, is an act centered in transformation, not replication or mimicry, offering a manipulation of landscape composed of fragments that resist access to the image while the words center attention on the violence of the act of consumption that is part of systems built on exploitation. As New York University professor Jens Andermann succinctly explains in *Entranced Earth: Art, Extractivism, and the End of Landscape*, "Landscape, in short, represents a key ideological apparatus of capitalism and colonialism that naturalizes what are in fact violent and uneven social and political (as well as, we should add, ecological) relations."[6] It is tricky to undo an invisible violence that is aestheticized and sold for pleasure and to resist this system or reveal its machinations without repeating it.

Carlson's work reminds me of the violence in historical paintings of North America that may be invisible to some. At one point, this violence was invisible to me. The reference to cannibalism makes me think of other instances of brutality through exploitation and consumption and ways that artists, writers, and scholars have used the metaphor of cannibalism to show broader webs of colonial and neocolonial practices, exerting it as resistance (sometimes mixed with contradiction).[7]

A few other artworks in *Boundless* link to themes of horror and exploitation. The work of photographer Jeremy Dennis (Shinnecock) confronts the colonial state's historical and present-day violence against Indigenous people and land in what is now the United States. Specifically, Dennis focuses on the Hamptons, where the Shinnecock Nation maintains a reservation. Dennis's photographs like *I Could Stand Here All Night* (2021), which is part of the series *Rise*, are informed by horror films. In Dennis's words, "*Rise* appropriates the aesthetic and concept of zombie apocalypse by replacing the gory zombie figure with the American Indian, whose simple presence causes terror."[8] Dennis stages non-Indigenous white volunteers as sometimes frozen and other times actively seeking to defend or escape the zombie(s) played by Dennis in the tableaux. Dennis contextualizes the series, which began in 2017, with reference to King Philip's War (1675–76), naming this historical battle of Native people against white colonists. The series asserts the agency of Indigenous people, while also recognizing the fear that some non-Native institutions and individuals have of this agency. While provocative, or because of the provocation, I absorb his critique.

I consider the fabricated nature of *I Could Stand Here All Night* (Figure 36) against the myths that are invented and recycled within so many seemingly (to some) benign landscapes. In this photograph by Dennis, the land and its Indigenous histories have been built over with homes and pools. The Hamptons are popularly defined by white wealth, something like the residence in Amagansett that served as the site for the image. Dennis's rising up from the water is a reminder that Native Americans are still present, and that Shinnecock people have remained in their homelands in the Hamptons. But does this imagery reinforce a notion of only a spectral presence through its reference to zombies? The encounter in this photograph is quiet. Are the individuals frozen by the roles they've each been assigned?

For his ongoing project *On This Site*, Dennis employs a different strategy. Composed of photographs, a book, and a website, the images document culturally important sites as records of Indigenous histories, continuous presence, and resistance. Dennis states that his "hope is to create curiosity for all audiences, as it [the project] creates a dialogue between Indigenous and non-Indigenous people on Long Island, and legitimizes the Long Island Indigenous population beyond their borders on reservations."[9] The photographs in each series have a different tone and style but are all invitations to consider the formal aspects of images and their subjects (be they a documentation of a present-day site or mashup of appropriated imagery and heightened stereotypes) and the layers sometimes hidden beneath the surface.

In *Boundless*, Carlson's and Dennis's works are organized within broader interconnected constellations of objects—books and visual art from the past and present—that center the art of Indigenous artists and writers as "American" art, on their own terms, while also creatively working beyond traditional constraints of this category. Erdrich builds from the words of Native authors, first. And through the framework that she constructs, she shapes a view of select works by artists from other cultures, including historical paintings by non-Native Euro-American artists. Erdrich selects paintings of nature that present views that are not defined by the magisterial gaze, with the exception of a couple of paintings, including one by Thomas Cole.

Thomas Cole's *Daniel Boone at His Cabin at Great Osage Lake* (1826) is an early work by the artist and purchase by Charles H. Morgan, the Mead's first director. Morgan intentionally began building the Mead's collection in the 1930s, preceding the opening of the Museum in 1950. This work is an invented scene that features the white settler Daniel Boone, alone in the wilderness.[10] Like other paintings of its moment, it was created in dialogue with literature and imagery circulated through print. Among the literary works produced at this time is James Fenimore Cooper's *The Last of the Mohicans* (1826). Art and literary works such as these fashioned stories that have endured as foundational parts of collections of "American" art and culture. They've been read as grand by some and emblematic of a culture defined by an obsession with expansion and erasure of North America's first peoples by others.

Brent Michael Davids's musical composition "The Last of James Fenimore Cooper" satirically responds to James Fenimore Cooper, and by extension to other legends emboldened in Cole's painting (Figure 35a and 35b). A recording is paired with the Cole painting in the first iteration of *Boundless*. Davids (Mohican/Munsee-Lenape) has noted that James Fenimore Cooper's account was inaccurate, stating that "Cooper's DEAD 'Mohicans,' have overshadowed the REAL 'Mohicans,' who remain quite alive!"[11] Brent Michael Davids fuses Cooper's story with a Mohican tale about a Snow Monster from the North, explaining "In my version, Cooper is a character in his own story and becomes transformed—his brainless deed forgiven. 'The Last of James Fenimore Cooper' is an act of forgiveness and transformation by someone who daily walks through the eclipse of his statue, blasting sunlight through the dark silhouette."[12]

Davids acknowledges historical violence and genocide, continued violence and oppression, falsehoods and misconceptions by Cooper as an individual, through the perpetuation of his story by many others, and as part of a much larger system. Davids's storytelling and music chart a new path for Cooper. So what could be in store for Daniel Boone? For Cole? How could we reimagine their stories as both an act of revision and opportunity for change? How could we all take a moment to consider possibilities for transformation by reassessing the stories of objects, historical figures, institutions, and our own roles as storytellers today? While *Boundless* tells its story through water, landscape paintings like Cole's and stories of the early colonial United States are rooted in land, in dirt. And the earth, I imagine, has many stories to tell. So I wonder what it could mean to dig through the layers of sediment, perhaps to taste earth as a corrective act, and to consider a link between our words and consumption, our responsibility to place and people.

My interpretation of the works by Carlson, Dennis, and Davids here is just one attempt to consider their approaches to confronting a colonial legacy without refashioning it. *Boundless* is a word that is about openness, not containment, and the project indeed is positioned as a call for ongoing work, and part of this ongoing work is rooted in stories and tied to the earth. Amy Lonetree (Ho-Chunk)—a scholar of Indigenous histories, and cultural and museum studies—calls for people working within museums to confront their institutions' colonial histories and the sometimes difficult stories of objects in their care.[13]

The Mead is located on Amherst College's campus in Amherst, Massachusetts, which is named after Sir Jeffery Amherst (1717–97). The Mead has portraits of the British general who notoriously and brutally proposed the spread of smallpox through gifts of contaminated blankets to Indigenous people. Among the Mead's portraits of Jeffery Amherst is one by the British painter Joshua Reynolds from 1765. It was purchased with Mead funds in 1967. Reynolds's skilled execution of the painting and the subject of the portrait, its representation of the city's namesake, make the Mead an unsurprising custodian of this work. But what do we do with it today? The painting, which was made as part of the commemoration of Amherst's exploits in Canada, includes boats made by Indigenous people that Erdrich explored during her research and considered highlighting in some way in the exhibition. Amherst and his company in fact are thought to have used Haudenosaunee boats and guides to cross the Saint Lawrence River. I appreciate Erdrich's attempt to center Indigenous presence in this painting. But in the end, the painting stayed in storage. It was moved to the sidelines to make space for other work by Indigenous artists and authors, emphasizing Native abundance. The violence of Reynolds's painting was kept from view, but we know it's there and that, like the landscapes, we need to consider what it means to maintain it in the collection and view it today. As a staff member at the Mead, I know we have the responsibility to tell more stories, including this one. Our work is not done.

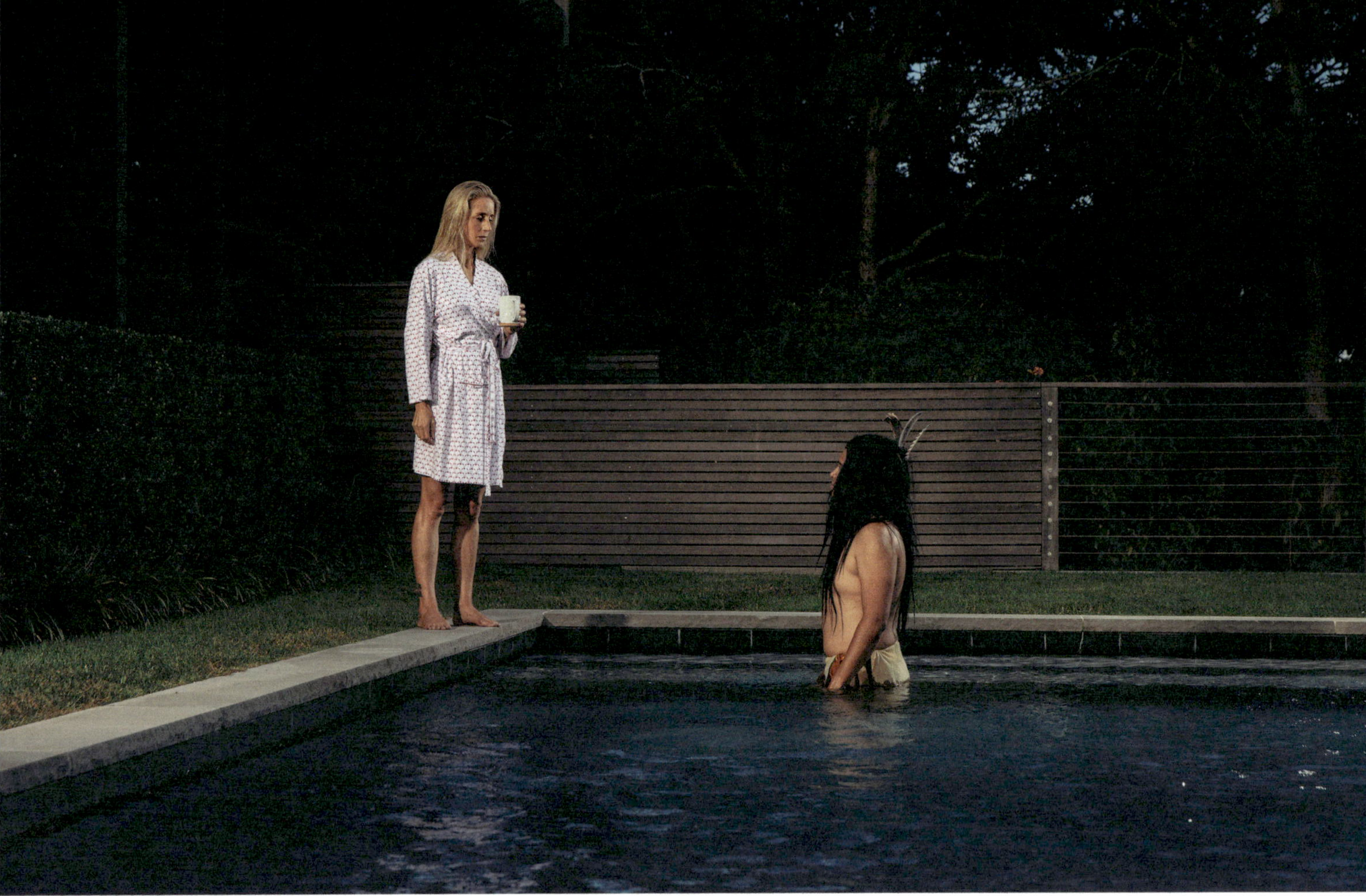

Figure 36: Jeremy Dennis (Shinnecock), *I Could Stand Here All Night*, from *Rise* series, 2021. Photograph on aluminum. Purchase with William W. Collins (Class of 1953) Print Fund. AC 2023.38.

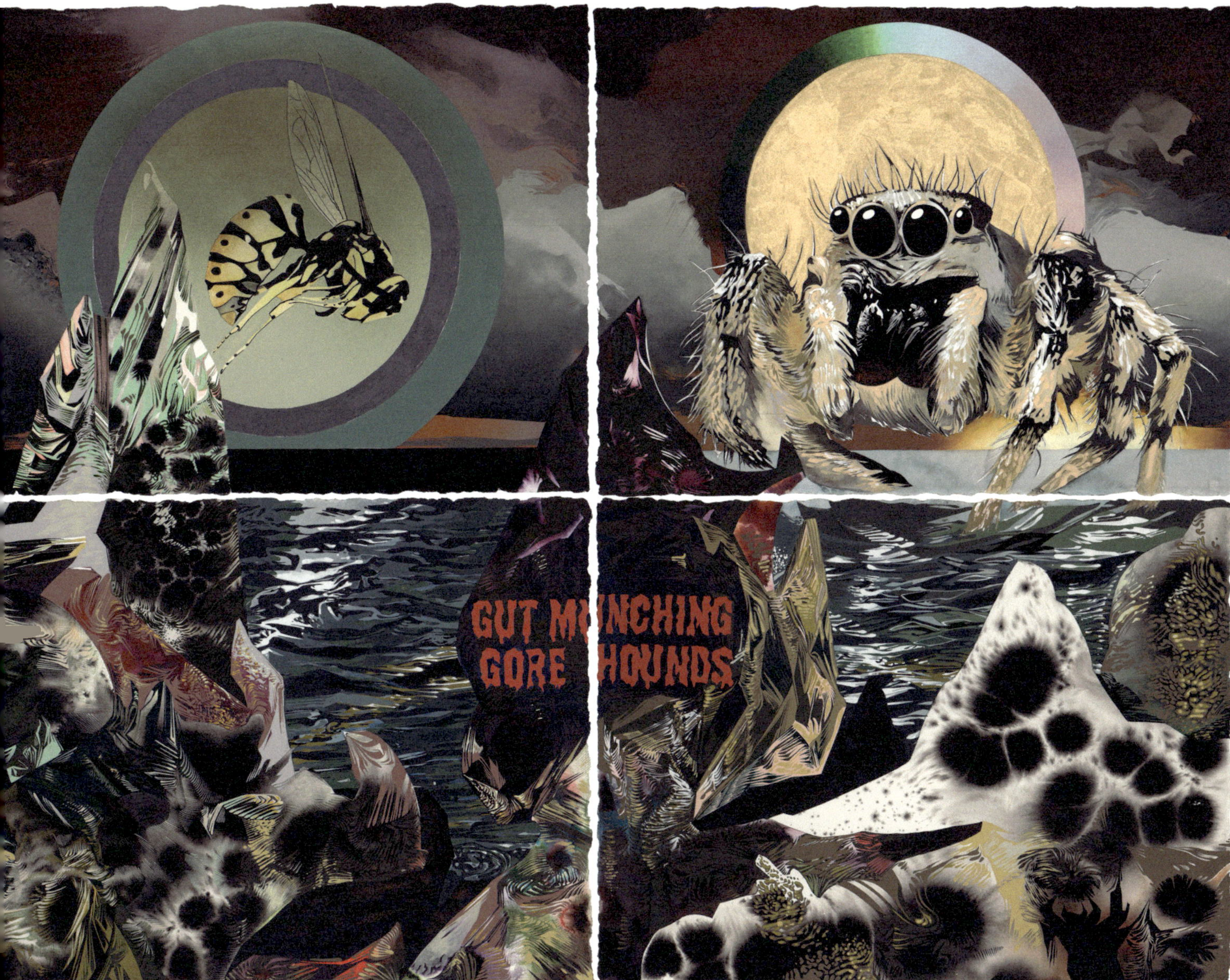

Figure 37: Andrea Carlson (Anishinaabe, descendant of the Grand Portage Band), *Gut Munching Gore Hounds*, 2010. Oil, acrylic, ink, color pencil, and graphite on four sheets of heavy-wove Arches Aquarelle paper. Overall: 45½″ × 61½″ (115.6 cm × 156.2 cm); each sheet: 22¾″ × 30½″ (57.8 cm × 77.5 cm). Mead Art Museum at Amherst College, museum purchase. AC 2022.05.a-d. © Andrea Carlson. Image credit: Petegorsky/Gipe.

NOTES

1 Heid E. Erdrich, "Variations True," poem, in *Little Big Bully* (Penguin Books, 2020). Andrea Carlson's *Exit* (2018) (Figure 36) is featured on the cover of *Little Big Bully*.

2 Candice Hopkins, "The Land Remembers," in *Water, Kinship, Belief*, ed. Candice Hopkins, Katie Lawson, and Tairone Bastien (Toronto: Art Metropole, 2022), 69.

3 Andrea Carlson, "An Artist Statement on VORE Works," March 27, 2017, https://www.mikinaak.com/blog/vore-works.

4 Carlson, "Artist Statement on VORE Works."

5 Andrea Carlson and Kris Kerzman, "Q & A: Andrea Carlson on 'VORE,'" *Plains Art Museum blog*, October 27, 2010, https://web.archive.org/web/20110519154958/https://plainsart.org/weblog/q-a-andrea-carlson-on-vore/.

6 Jens Andermann, *Entranced Earth: Art, Extractivism, and the End of Landscape* (Chicago: Northwestern University Press, 2023), 9.

7 Oswald de Andrade's "Manifesto Antropófago" (1928) used the metaphor of cannibalism to combat criticism that art from Brazil was derivative of European models and to assert power from an engagement with a kind of cultural cannibalism. Sayak Valencia's *Gore Capitalism* (2018) centers her exploration in Mexico, exploring the systemic impact of neoliberalism and its resulting hyper-consumption and hyper-masculinity from a transfeminist perspective.

8 Jeremy Dennis, "Rise," last modified March 14, 2023, https://www.jeremynative.com/portfolio/rise/. Jeremy Dennis named his series *On This Site* (https://nativelongisland.com/) after a project by Joel Sternfeld: "Between 1993 and 1996, Sternfeld photographed the locations of often notorious historical incidents, quiet explorations of America's intrinsic violence." Robert Sullivan, "A Landscape Shared by Native Americans and the One Per Cent," *The New Yorker*, February 17, 2023, https://www.newyorker.com/culture/photo-booth/a-landscape-shared-by-native-americans-and-the-one-per-cent.

9 Jeremy Dennis, "On This Site: Indigenous Long Island," last modified August 8, 2021, https://nativelongisland.com/about/. Jean M. O'Brien writes in *Firsting and Lasting: Writing Indians out of Existence in New England* about how the obsession with white lineage and claiming the land as "native" to settlers was manifested through a process of documenting the settler colonial first and erasing the possibility of Indigenous presence and futures occurred locally through texts, ceremonies, and visual art. See Jean M. O'Brien, *Firsting and Lasting: Writing Indians out of Existence in New England* (Minneapolis: University of Minnesota Press, 2010).

10 Catherine Morris, "Thomas Cole's Daniel Boone and His Cabin at Great Osage Lake: The 'Natural Man's' Sublime," PhD seminar paper, Florida State University, 2008.

11 Brent Michael Davids, "Introduction," in *The Last of James Fenimore Cooper*, performed by the Miró Quartet at the Caramoor International Music Festival, August 3, 2001.

12 Davids, "Introduction."

13 Amy Lonetree, *Decolonizing Museums: Representing Native America in National and Tribal Museums* (Chapel Hill: University of North Carolina Press, 2012).

A KILL HOLE IN A NEMADJI BOWL
Andrea Carlson

Andrea Carlson is an Anishinaabe artist and board member of the Center for Indigenous Futures. She is a lineal descendant from the Grand Portage Band of Ojibwe.

Long ago humans buried their dead with beautiful objects. They lived in the land that is now referred to as New Mexico. In the 1920s these graves were desecrated, looted, and bodies were hauled hundreds of miles away to the University of Minnesota. Understand this, the final resting place of 186 Mimbres people is in Bemidji, Minnesota.

A visual representation of 186 bodies is:
HUMAN HUMAN HUMAN HUMAN HUMAN HUMAN HUMAN HUMAN HUMAN
HUMAN HUMAN HUMAN HUMAN HUMAN HUMAN HUMAN HUMAN HUMAN
HUMAN HUMAN HUMAN HUMAN HUMAN HUMAN HUMAN HUMAN HUMAN
HUMAN HUMAN HUMAN HUMAN HUMAN HUMAN HUMAN HUMAN HUMAN
HUMAN HUMAN HUMAN HUMAN HUMAN HUMAN HUMAN HUMAN HUMAN
HUMAN HUMAN HUMAN HUMAN HUMAN HUMAN HUMAN HUMAN HUMAN
HUMAN HUMAN HUMAN HUMAN HUMAN HUMAN HUMAN HUMAN HUMAN
HUMAN HUMAN HUMAN HUMAN HUMAN HUMAN HUMAN HUMAN HUMAN
HUMAN HUMAN HUMAN HUMAN HUMAN HUMAN HUMAN HUMAN HUMAN
HUMAN HUMAN HUMAN HUMAN HUMAN HUMAN HUMAN HUMAN HUMAN
HUMAN HUMAN HUMAN HUMAN HUMAN HUMAN HUMAN HUMAN HUMAN
HUMAN HUMAN HUMAN HUMAN HUMAN HUMAN HUMAN HUMAN HUMAN
HUMAN HUMAN HUMAN HUMAN HUMAN HUMAN HUMAN HUMAN HUMAN
HUMAN HUMAN HUMAN HUMAN HUMAN HUMAN HUMAN HUMAN HUMAN
HUMAN HUMAN HUMAN HUMAN HUMAN HUMAN HUMAN HUMAN HUMAN
HUMAN HUMAN HUMAN HUMAN HUMAN HUMAN HUMAN HUMAN HUMAN
HUMAN HUMAN HUMAN HUMAN HUMAN HUMAN HUMAN HUMAN HUMAN
HUMAN HUMAN HUMAN HUMAN HUMAN HUMAN HUMAN HUMAN HUMAN
HUMAN HUMAN HUMAN HUMAN HUMAN HUMAN HUMAN HUMAN HUMAN
HUMAN HUMAN HUMAN HUMAN HUMAN HUMAN HUMAN HUMAN HUMAN
HUMAN HUMAN HUMAN HUMAN HUMAN HUMAN

Minnesota is a final resting place of 186 Mimbres people.

I drill a kill hole in a Nemadji bowl, one made by settlers.
I put it on the heads of those who have desired Mimbres grave belongings.
I suck out sickness and intend to fill the abscess with clay, but it slides through my fingers. I cannot cure it.

Desire is the poison that is its own cure.

Disclaimer: To preserve the meaning of the poet's lineation, this chapter is also available in its original, non-reflowable format as a PDF here: https://doi.org/10.3998/mpub.14513702.cmp.3.

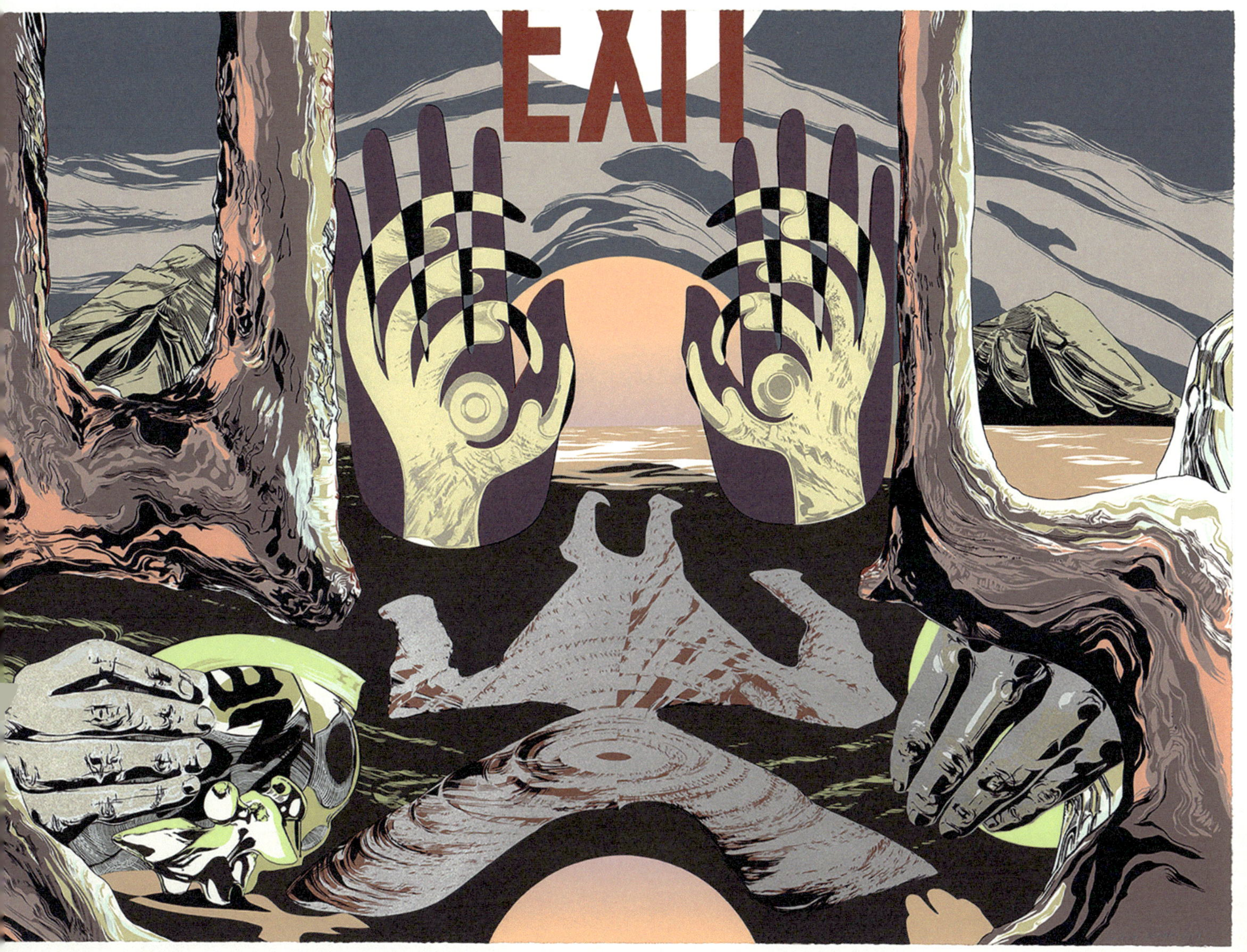

Figure 38: Andrea Carlson (Anishinaabe, descendant of the Grand Portage Band), *Exit*, 2018. Screenprint. Sheet: 34″ × 48″ (86.4 cm × 121.9 cm); frame: 33⅝″ × 47″. Mead Art Museum at Amherst College, purchase with Trinkett Clark Memorial Student Acquisition Fund. AC 2020.04. © Andrea Carlson. Image credit: Petegorsky/Gipe.

EXIT
Andrea Carlson

This piece by Andrea Carlson appeared in two other iterations: in the poetry collection *Little Big Bully* by Heid E. Erdrich; and on the Highpoint Center for Printmaking website. Reprint by permission of the author.

Based on one's vantage point or cultural expectations, the significance of a place can become lost. *The West* is a place of erasure and fantasy. It is, as Edouard Glissant notes, a colonial project. Odd descriptions of land such as the map-maker's "Americas" which are sometimes referred to as *new* land, or a *new* world, run concurrent to destroying and uprooting Indigenous place names and images. One example of this can be seen in the defacement of effigy mounds throughout what is now called Wisconsin. Hundreds of massive, shallow mounds depicting birds, lizards, a man, panthers, and turtles punctuate the landscape, but there had once been more of them. Despite the splendid joy and reverence that Native people feel when beholding the old mounds, settlers have destroyed many, dissecting them with roads, mines, or they have plowed them under.

Within Indigenous communities exists a deep-seated fear of losing cultural practices, languages, art forms, and land. Reasonably, we have developed a perpetual fear of exile. Indigenous land formations that are publicly accessible are vulnerable to destruction. The power of strength in numbers and the ability to multiply a single image into many renders the work diasporic. A print may be less susceptible to full destruction as it can exist in many places. That ability to exist in plurality is part of the thinking behind *Exit*'s references to Indigenous visual formations, such as Man Mound, mica hand and talon forms, bent tree trail markers, hands signing "exit" or "outside," and a bird stone (Figure 38). The imagery of this print also represents an attempt at a reparative presence for the space between the Twin Cities and Chicago, the lands of several Anishinaabe tribes, Dakota and Ho-Chunk people. This print is meant to be a protection sigil for the thoughts of those who travel Interstate 94, the road that cuts through mound country. Hopefully those who have seen this print, and by knowing its references, will carry the significance of that land respectfully in their minds. In this way, *Exit*—and its much larger cousin work, *RED EXIT,* a title that references a poem by Gordon Henry—is a print about absence and nonparticipation as a tactic and about propagating presence.

When *Exit* was selected to be the cover image of Heid E. Erdrich's *Little Big Bully*, I was elated, but cautious. This print, an intended protection sigil, was to be again propagated in printed form to a much larger audience. Reading the collected poetry, I felt implicated and tried to locate the bully in me, in my mind. Well after it was published, I sat with the words still swirling in my mind searching for the bully, and it was, no doubt, there. More recently I listened to the audio version of *Little Big Bully* and found relief because I felt I was sitting with my friend, and she was telling me about power, about language, about environments of hostility. She blanketed this collection of poems with my image, a traveling image, and as her words go into the minds of the readers my image is held in their hands too.

Miigwech

INTERTRIBAL FEAST

Heid E. Erdrich

There's a time at a powwow when the emcee will call for an "Intertribal," which invites Native Americans of any tribe to enter the arena and dance. It is a chance for those who do not dance for competition to show their cultural traditions and represent their tribes. It's an invitation and a welcome. We share in the beauty we can offer and then, often, we feed our guests.

Presenting Indigenous abundance became a powerful current in the *Boundless* project and, even in planning this exhibition, I felt its destination was a feast and a thanksgiving.

The inter- and intratribal art and text in *Boundless* highlights the kinship and collegiality shared between writers and visual artists from diverse Native American nations. Salish-Kootenai, Ojibwe/Anishinaabe, Luiseño, Chemehuevi, Creek, Potawatomi, and Diné artists and authors who illustrated their own and others' words shared space in a celebration of the bonds between Native American intellectual traditions. Works in Indigenous languages reminded visitors that part of what unites these artists from very different locations is English—a colonizing language that Native people share. Dictionaries and other works in Indigenous languages in *Boundless* remind us that, in the aftermath of assimilation our revitalization of Indigenous language and culture—especially our connections to animals, plants, and foods—sustains us.

Tribes from all directions were forced to live together when the United States cleared the lands of its original inhabitants so that white Americans could take it for free. Some were thrust together with unrelated Indigenous people in the mid-twentieth century when leaving our nations and starting over in urban areas was incentivized via government programs such as the Indian Relocation Act of 1956, which meant to empty our homelands. Literary works from the 1930s onward as well as cookbooks, books about Indigenous plants, and the food-related objects in *Boundless* reveal this period in history while also creating a sense of intertribal connection and, often, an invitation to feast.

Indigenous people often met hardships of devastating forced displacement and dislocation through camaraderie, solidarity, and creative expression. Now Indigenous people band together wherever we find ourselves—it is how we survive. With intertribal strength and solidarity, we create abundantly in literature, writing, music, dance and, always, through sharing Indigenous foods.

It is difficult for an Ojibwe woman to let guests go away without being fed—especially when invited into a space the way an exhibition invites visitors. Perhaps my research was drawing me toward a theme of intertribal solidarity as shown in books written and illustrated by Natives who were friends and colleagues. No doubt I arrived at the metaphor in sharing Indigenous foods because Amherst's collections contain both cookbooks by Indigenous authors and many domestic objects used to serve food. In the first iteration of *Boundless,* audio allowed visitors to learn about Indigenous foods, and recipes were printed on the walls in one gallery, and we offered visitors recipe cards to take with them, which was as close as we could get to a feast.

MOSS PUDDING
Zara CiscoeBrough (Nipmuc)

INGREDIENTS

Moss
Honey, maple syrup, or sugar
2 cups water
Egg
1 cup milk
¼–½ cup corn starch
¼ tsp vanilla
1 tsp yokeag or butter if unavailable

RECIPE

Pick moss from around trees.
Clean moss thoroughly. Wash many times to rid of foreign substances.
Then boil all ingredients with exception of milk and corn starch.
Crumble moss up, strain through cloth, then mix cornstarch and milk together over low heat.
Add strained moss and vanilla to cornstarch, let thicken, sprinkle yokeag on top. Serves four.

Northeastern Native American Foods (Nipmuc Elders Council, 2009)

APPLES
Gladys Widdiss (Wampanoag)

What I meant to tell you before.

When we were youngsters growing up, we ate anything and everything that grew, from the time it sprouted until the time it became food, whatever it was.

We ate swamp apples...it's a fruit that comes on the wild honeysuckle plant before the flower comes. We'd rummage through the woods to find these.

We'd eat green apples from the time they were as big as the tip on my finger until they were the size they should be, if there were any left."

Wampanoag Cookery, which includes "Apples," introduces its recipes by stating: "In all cultures, recipes are a form of oral tradition. The proper ways to prepare food are passed on from generation to generation. Ingredients may become "modernized," but the basic recipe is deeply rooted in cultural tradition. We are greatly indebted to the Wampanoag contributors to this cookbook for offering to share this aspect of their cultural heritage with all of us."[1]
The editors thank Cheryll Toney Holley, Chief of the Hassanamisco Nipmuc, editor and publisher of *Northeastern Native American Foods*, for permission to share this recipe.

NOTE

1 Boston Children's Museum, *Wampanoag Cookery* (Boston: American Science and Engineering, 1974), https://bcmstories.com/pdfs/JLWampanoag%20Cookbook.pdf.

THANKSGIVING(S)

Rachel Beth Sayet

Rachel Beth Sayet is a scholar who served as the Five Colleges Community Development Fellow, Native American and Indigenous Studies. She is Mohegan. This essay is excerpted and revised from "Wikôtamuwôk Wuci Ki tà Kihtahan (A Celebration of Land and Sea): Modern Indigenous Cuisine in New England" published on the web-based magazine *Dawnland Voices*, Issue 4, May 9, 2017.[1]

As a Mohegan tribal member, I grew up attending festivals and events that centered around Indigenous food, such as the Green Corn Festival, Succotash Time, and summer powwows throughout New England. Many of our traditional stories also relate to food. Tales of Moshup the giant and his wife, Granny Squannit, the leader of the Little People, emphasize land and sea. This is important because many tribes in New England live along the shoreline and therefore have the ability to hunt and fish. Granny is known as the keeper of the plants and medicine, while Moshup tales relate to the ocean. Moshup would wade out into the water and kill whales, which he would share with his people.

In my Mohegan community as well as throughout New England, many Algonquian peoples continue to keep these traditions alive. Today at Mohegan we honor Granny Squannit through an herb garden at our tribe's Tantaquidgeon Museum. We also have an educational garden where we teach children how to plant traditional crops such as corn, beans, squash, and Jerusalem artichokes. In years past, our tribal elders had a "Three Sisters Garden" at our elderly housing. This essay honors those ancient connections to land and sea by demonstrating the continuity of Indigenous cuisine in New England.

According to Mohegan Tribal Historian Melissa Tantaquidgeon Zobel, in New England, some tribes such as the Mohegan and Narragansett were lucky in that they were able to remain in their homeland due to being Christianized and "civilized" very early on.[2] Therefore, many of the ingredients that we as Native[3] people in New England utilize in our Indigenous cuisine are the same ones that our ancestors have been using for thousands of years.

The three sisters are corn, beans, and squash or pumpkin. The most vital of the three sisters was corn. Penobscot oral tradition states that after the first man and woman became husband and wife a long time ago, there came a famine. The woman asked her husband to take her life and draw her body around an open field. He was hesitant, but after talking with Glooskap, the great teacher, he did as she said. The man drew her body until the flesh was worn away, and in the middle of the field they buried her bones. When seven months had gone by and the husband returned to that place, he saw it filled with beautiful tall plants. The fruit of the plants tasted sweet and he called it Skarmunal.[4]

This corn creation story from the Penobscots of Maine emphasizes its importance to Algonquian people. Much more than just nourishment, corn symbolizes the very important Algonquian tradition of cooperation. In the story, people are starving, but the woman sacrifices herself, and her body turns into corn, which thereby rescues and sustains the people. This is exactly what corn did. It provided the proper nutrients for indigenous people to live healthy lives.

Corn originated in Mesoamerica, but later migrated up through the southwest.[5] According to Narragansett tradition, "the Crow brought them at first an Indian grain of corn in one ear, and an Indian bean in another, from the

Great God Kautantowit's field in the Southwest, from whence they hold come all their Corn and Beans."[6] Kautantowit is the name of the Great Spirit or Creator for many tribes in New England, and this is the direction that these communities pray to, and their graves face.[7]

Mohegan Tribal Elder Sharon Maynard notes that traditionally Native people would cook corn in ash, and the chemicals in the ash worked to enhance the niacin in the corn. Because the corn was so full of these nutrients, Natives did not become sick with pellagra, a severe illness caused by vitamin deficiency. However, African Americans and Europeans did not cook corn in the ash, and therefore they became ill.[8] Jacobs and Cox emphasized: "The alkaline in the ashes acts as a food supplement to balance the amino acids in which corn is deficient and makes it a well-balanced, life-sustaining food."[9] These ashes are created by burning "hardwood, bushes, or herbs until they turn to ash."[10] Many Native people still cook with ash today. It can also be used as a leavening agent or seasoning.[11] Beans are full of niacin, so they were eaten as a supplement to corn, in which case the ash was not necessary.[12]

The corn that is found in supermarkets today is a "hybridized version of sweet corn, but up until the 1920s, corn on the cob was 'green corn,' the immature ears of several varieties."[13] Many Native peoples make corn dishes, such as masa and hominy, but in New England, one of the most vital foods made from corn is known as yokeag in Mohegan or nokake in Wampanoag.[14] As Jayne Fawcett, former vice-chair of the Mohegan Tribal Council said, "The men and women who were steeped in the tradition...who were passing on the tradition...[were the ones] who knew the tradition of yokeag.'[15]

Yokeag is a very important traveling food in New England. Traditionally, yokeag was made by letting the corn dry out on the kernels all year, then picking the corn off the kernels from the previous year, parching them over an open flame, and then grinding the kernels with a mortar and pestle. Yokeag was traditionally eaten with some water as a meal and was very useful for hunters and warriors when going on a long journey. One of the more modern-day Mohegan traditions is that of eating yokeag sprinkled on top of ice cream for a sweet crunchy treat.

Corn is not only nourishment, but also has a spiritual component that intensified during the process of making yokeag with a mortar and pestle. Melissa Tantaquidgeon Zobel noted in her book *Medicine Trail: The Life and Lessons of Gladys Tantaquidgeon*, "Mohegans, in ancient times, guarded yokeag in containers with sacred designs, such as diamond medicine symbols."[16] The diamond shape is used for protection and good medicine. The pounding of yokeag is a tradition that has been passed on for hundreds of years from generation to generation of Mohegans, Wampanoags, Narragansetts, and other Indigenous peoples.

MODERN YOKEAG RECIPE

In 2013, I participated in cooking a modern version of yokeag with Mohegan Elder Sharon Maynard, who used to work as a commercial chef on a ferry, and is known throughout the tribe for her cooking.

For our modern yokeag recipe, we actually used Peruvian corn kernels, but it is preferable to use flint corn. First, we set the oven to 350°F (180°C), then roasted the kernels for about ten minutes and shook them around a few times while in the oven on a pan. The kernels began to pop a little bit because of the moisture in them. Next, we put the corn in the food processor, which is much quicker than the traditional approach of using a mortar and pestle (two minutes versus fifteen to twenty minutes). Finally, we poured it into a bowl and tada! Our yokeag was done.

Since that time, I have made yokeag many times, and mostly with traditional Mohegan flint corn (also called Narragansett white cap). For demos for our tribal youth, I used a griddle, and then ground the corn with a mortar and pestle to teach the children how much time and energy grinding corn would take in ancient times.

THANKSGIVING(S)

Thanksgiving is the most misunderstood holiday involving Wampanoag people and the first settlers. Indigenous people were celebrating Thanksgiving for hundreds of years before contact with Europeans. As stated by Jay Levy, Indigenous Colombian and Archaeology Field Specialist for the Mohegan tribe, "We always have had that relationship with all those living things."[17] In order to celebrate the gifts that they were given each season, Algonquian people had multiple thanksgivings, including Corn Thanksgiving, Maple Sugar Thanksgiving, Strawberry Thanksgiving, Green Bean Thanksgiving, and Cranberry Thanksgiving.[18] According to Loren Spears, executive director of Tomaquag Indian Museum (Narragansett) whose family used to run a Native-themed restaurant in Exeter, Rhode Island, called Dovecrest:

> We still do that....And it's still within the Narragansett community we do a good portion of them as well. So they are very much a part of the connection to our historical foodways and our food gathering ties, because then you gave thanks for gifts of the season. And so those gifts of the season become those things that you felt were most poignant that became the thing to celebrate, like in the case of the Strawberry Thanksgiving. In the Narragansett community it is also considered the gift of friendship, it is one of the first berries of the season that are ready to harvest in the wild.[19]

Many tribes in New England still cook traditional recipes with strawberries, such as strawberry drink and Narragansett Strawberry Bread.[20] Roger Williams, founder of Providence, Rhode Island, observed that "Indian women mashed them [strawberries] and mixed them with cornmeal to make a very fine strawberry bread."[21]

While many Natives celebrate Strawberry Thanksgiving, some do not celebrate the American Thanksgiving, because the story of "friendship" is not exactly true. The Wampanoag people who resided in the Plymouth region were actually not invited to feast. It was a three-day meeting to negotiate land, and therefore only Wampanoag warriors were in attendance, and no women or children.[22] Although the story is inaccurate, many Native people in the United States still celebrate the "Thanksgiving" harvest with their families, while others choose to attend a Thanksgiving protest held at Plymouth each year, known as the "National Day of Mourning."

Out of the many Thanksgivings that were held at Mohegan, the Green Corn Festival or Corn Thanksgiving was the most important: "We celebrate the gift of corn in our oral histories...and through living traditions such as the

Mohegan Wigwam Festival."[23] The Green Corn Festival was held for many years at Mohegan Church where "corn was celebrated because it is the sustainer of life and spirit."[24] When the Mohegan reservation was disbanded in the nineteenth century, Mohegan Medicine Woman Emma Baker worked to revitalize the Green Corn Festival (later called the "Wigwam").

Wiqômun means "welcome" in Mohegan, which is how the Wigwam Festival received its name. The late Mohegan Medicine Woman Gladys Tantaquidgeon recalls the early days of the Wigwam Festival:

> Tables were arranged inside…and many visitors appeared for the midday meal, clam chowder, oyster stew, succotash and the famous traveling food—yokeag, made of mortars of pepperidge wood. Yokeag was used by hunters and warriors. It was light to carry and nourishing. We have been told that a small quantity was placed in a deerskin sack to be placed at the waist of the warrior or hunter and with water served as a meal.[25]

Corn was always a "centerpiece" at the Wigwam Festival, and cornhusk dolls would be sold, as well as Mohegan succotash, a traditional Mohegan and Wampanoag soup made from corn and shell beans.

Today the Wigwam Festival, which takes place in August and is free and open to the public, features vendors from all over the Northeast, including Happy Hunting Grounds, an Iroquois vendor, and one of the most popular, Sly Fox Catering. Sherry Pocknett, the owner of Sly Fox, is the daughter of Earl Mills. Pocknett grew up working at the Flume restaurant and has been vending at powwows since she was twelve. Pocknett travels all around the New England powwow circuit, even making stops at small university powwows, such as Brown and Dartmouth. One of her yearly stops is the Mohegan Wigwam Festival. Pocknett's cuisine uses primarily ingredients from the Northeast, but also a sampling of Indigenous foods from all over the country. People line up for hours to receive such delicacies as venison with "three sisters rice" (wild rice with corn, beans, and squash), fried frog legs, smoked salmon salad with homemade cranberry vinaigrette, bison skewers, sassafras tea, smoked mussels, grilled quail, and of course, frybread. In addition to her catering business, Pocknett now runs her own restaurant in Charleston, Rhode Island called Sly Fox Den Too. In 2023 she won the James Beard Award for Best Chef in the Northeast. She is finally getting the recognition she deserves. Now one does not have to wait for powwow season to sample her spectacular Native cuisine. I recently interviewed Sherry about her big award for a Connecticut radio show called *Seasoned*.[26]

Algonquian people have always had many thanksgivings. They celebrated and continue to celebrate the bounties of the harvest all year round. Although many new ingredients, types of cookware, and methods of gathering and planting food have been incorporated in the past four hundred years since colonialism, the Indigenous people of New England still hold on to many of their traditional recipes. The stories and festivals that surround food have been passed on from generation to generation, and powwows and festivals are times when Algonquian people can still eat delicious food and celebrate the bounties of the harvest with their friends and family in this modern-day world.

Ni ya Yo
It is so.

ADDITIONAL RESOURCES

Aquinnah Cultural Center. "Wampanoag Way: An Aquinnah Cultural Trail." Pamphlet. Aquinnah, Mass.: Aquinnah Cultural Center, n.d.

De la Harpe, J. "A Dish Best Served Warm: Regional Food Traditions Live On at Powwows across the Nation ," *Indian Country Today*, 23, May 22, 2013. De la Harpe discusses some individual dishes in a series of articles available on the Indian Country Today website: https://ictnews.org/archive/best-indian-food-2013-smothered-muskrat-tail-off-teeth-showing.

Heckewelder, John Gottlieb Ernestus. *History, Manners, and Customs of the Indian Nations Who Once Inhabited Pennsylvania and the Neighboring States*. Berwyn Heights: Md.: Heritage Books, (1819, 1876) 2007.

Manning, Helen, and Jo-Ann Eccher. *Moshup's Footsteps: The Wampanoag Nation, Gay Head/Aquinnah; The People of First Light*. Aquinnah, Mass.: Blue Cloud Across the Moon, 2001.

Mills, Earl, and Betty Breen. *Cape Cod Wampanoag Cookbook: Wampanoag Indian Recipes Images* and *Lore*. Santa Fe: Clear Light, 2001.

Raine, Carolyn. *A Woodland Feast: Native American Foodways of the 17th* and *18th Centuries*. Huber Heights, Ohio: Penobscot Press, 1997.

Seasoned. "Exploring Indigenous Food with Members of the Mashantucket Pequot, Mohegan and Navajo Tribal Nations." Connecticut Public Radio, November 3, 2021. https://www.ctpublic.org/show/seasoned/2021-11-03/exploring-indigenous-food-with-members-of-the-mashantucket-pequot-mohegan-and-navajo-tribal-nations.

Tantaquidgeon, Gladys. "Notes on the Gay Head Indians of Massachusetts." *Indian Notes* 7, no. 1 (January 1930): 1–26. Museum of the American Indian, Heye Foundation. New York.

Weaver, William Woys. "Native American Gardening: The Three Sisters and More: Connect to an Ancient Heritage by Growing these Rare Vegetable Varieties Traced back to Native American Gardens." *Mother Earth News* 42 (February–March 2013).

NOTES

1 https://dawnlandvoices.org/rachel-sayet-issue-4/.

2 Melissa Jayne Fawcett, *The Lasting of the Mohegans: Part 1, The Story of the Wolf People* (Uncasville, Conn.: The Mohegan Tribe, 1995).

3 I will use the term *Native* (with a capital "N") to refer to the Indigenous peoples of the North American continent. Although current academic conventions employ a relatively modern term, *Native American*, the term that the Indigenous people of the North American continent most commonly use to refer to themselves is *Native*, because there was no "America" until after colonialism, according to Margaret M. Bruchac, "Earthshapers and Placemakers: Algonkian Indian Stories and the Landscape," in *Indigenous Archaeologies: Decolonizing Theory and Practice*, ed. Claire Smith and Hans Martin Wobst (London: Routledge, 2005), 52–74. When referring to Native people throughout the world, I will interchange between the words *Native* and *Indigenous*.

4 *As We Tell Our Stories: Living Traditions and the Algonkian Peoples of Indian New England,* exhibit at the American Indian Archeological Institute (now the Institute for American Indian Studies), Washington, Connecticut, 1990.

5 Betty Harper Fussell, *The Story of Corn* (Albuquerque: University of New Mexico Press, 1992).
6 Quoted in *As We Tell Our Stories*, AIAI (IAIS), 1990.
7 Roger Williams, *A Key into the Language of America* (Detroit: Wayne State University Press, 1973).
8 Sharon Maynard, personal communication, May 25, 2013.
9 Beverly Cox and Martin Jacobs, *Spirit of the Harvest: North American Indian Cooking* (New York: Stewart, Tabori & Chang, 2001), 239.
10 Cox and Jacobs, *Spirit of the Harvest*, 239.
11 D. Carson, personal communication, May 25, 2013.
12 Kathleen Fitzgerald and Keith Stavely, *America's Founding Food: The Story of New England Cooking* (Chapel Hill: University of North Carolina Press, 2015).
13 Cox and Jacobs, *Spirit of the Harvest*, 239.
14 Boston Children's Museum, *Many Thanksgivings: Teaching Thanksgiving Including the Wampanoag Perspective: A Guide for Educators* (Boston: Boston Children's Museum, 2002).
15 Melissa Jayne Fawcett, *Medicine Trail: The Life and Lessons of Gladys Tantaquidgeon* (Tucson: University of Arizona Press, 2000), 47.
16 Fawcett, *Medicine Trail*, 47.
17 Jay Levy, personal communication, April 25, 2013.
18 Loren Spears, personal communication, April 13, 2013.
19 Spears, personal communication, April 13, 2013.
20 Dale Carson, *New Native American Cooking* (New York: Random House, 1996).
21 Carson, *New Native American Cooking*, 63.
22 Boston Children's Museum, 2002.
23 *As We Tell Our Stories*, AIAI (IAIS), 1990.
24 Fawcett, *Lasting of the Mohegans*, 54.
25 Fawcett, *Lasting of the Mohegans*, 55.
26 *Seasoned*, "Chefs Sherry Pocknett and 'Diasporican' Author Illyanna Maisonet Make James Beard Award History," Connecticut Public Radio, August 17, 2023, https://www.ctpublic.org/show/seasoned/2023-08-17/chefs-sherry-pocknett-and-diasporican-author-illyanna-maisonet-make-james-beard-award-history.

YOKEAG
Zara CiscoeBrough (Nipmuc)

INGREDIENTS

Dried Corn Cobs
Nutmeg

RECIPE

Either sun dry or oven (175 degrees) dry corn cobs
Dry until moisture is gone. When drying in sun, turn over each day.
With mortar and pestle grind corn cobs very fine
Add dash of nutmeg
Mix thoroughly
Use as topping for tapioca, fruit, ice cream, puddings, etc., or as a substitute for nut topping

Northeastern Native American Foods (Nipmuc Elders Council, 2009): 36.

The editors thank Cheryll Toney Holley, Chief of the Hassanamisco Nipmuc, editor and publisher of *Northeastern Native American Foods*, for permission to share this recipe.

TOWN MEETING

Bonney Hartley

Bonney Hartley is a '25 MFA Creative Writing candidate at the Institute for American Indian Arts and an enrolled member of Stockbridge-Munsee Mohican Nation. Bonney lives and works within her tribe's ancestral territory in Williamstown, Massachusetts.

Brothers,

I, Mohican, enter the gym 250 years later for Town Meeting.[1] Shimmery lip-balmed mouths hush. Clipboard finger taps usher. Quick to remind: You do not live here, anymore. An obedient climb to the bleachers. Reflecting on how here I sit. A bag of cherries staining fingers red. On the lands of Tussunuck's field. ***I ache in the truth*** of that one final morning. When he straightened his shoulders, left the house and English plow behind. The one they made him go in debt to buy. Held Moshenemauk's hand. Knowing "brothers" would forever eat the fruits of their labor. Today's Town Meeting: This time under a basketball hoop. No peace pipe to be found. A cough drop and cuff links hold the moderator together. His bald forehead glistens. Gripping the podium bearing the town seal. Featuring Konkapot, hanging askew. The crooked town seal. Here, in the crooked town that sealed a Nation's fate. If I close my eyes, I can smell the earth. Tussunuck's cherry trees, maybe. Between the gaps of the exile bleachers, I let the pits that fall to the floor be an offering of sorts. ***I hope my life is an offering of sorts.*** The yea votes enlighten the room. It's hard to breathe, smile, and muster a thank you. Given the matter of the stain.

Listen to us

and the great good spirit will reward

your goodness

This is all I have to say.

NOTE

1 In American lore, colonial New England's Town Meetings are foundational to democracy. See also: performance art.

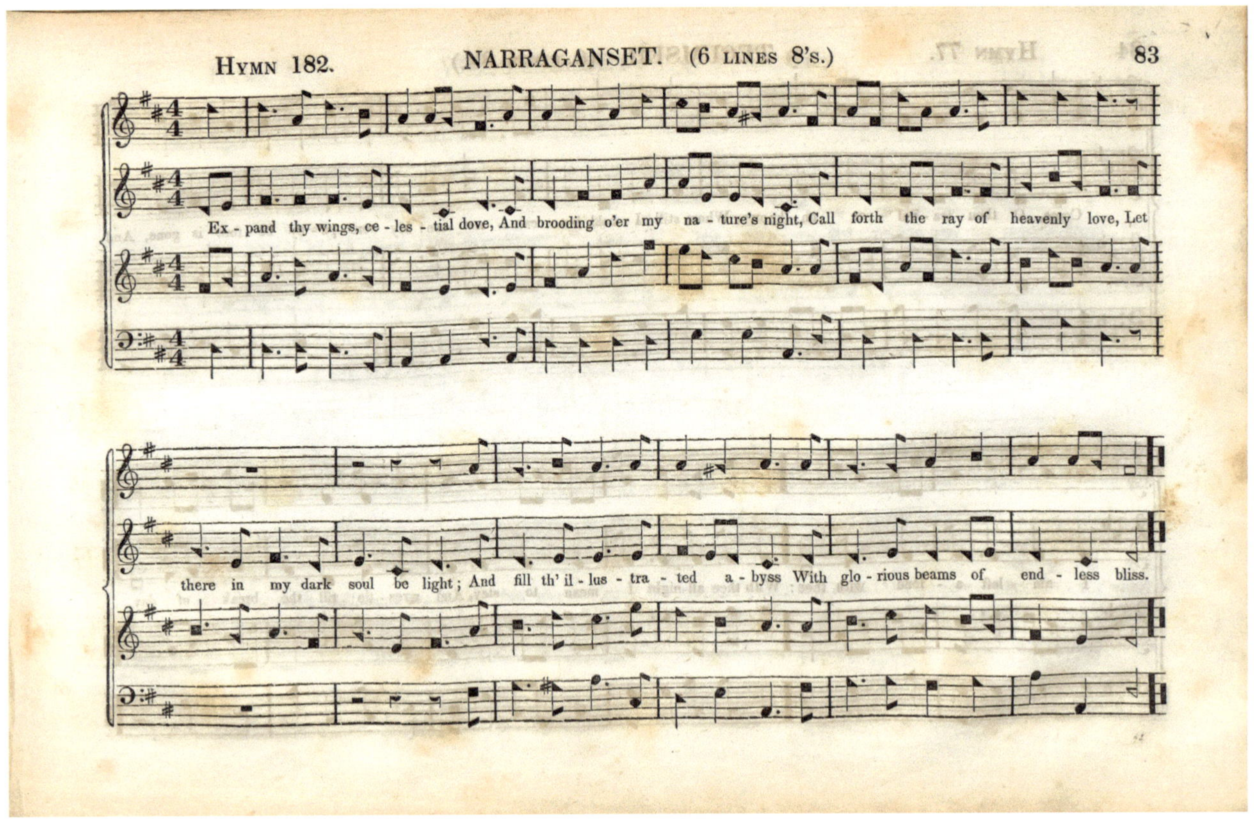

Figure 39: Thomas Commuck (Narragansett, 1804–55), *Indian Melodies.* Published by G. Lane & C.B. Tippett for the Methodist Episcopal Church, New York, 1845. Amherst College Archives and Special Collections. Younghee Kim-Wait (Class of 1982)/Pablo Eisenberg Collection of Native American Literature. M2117.C733 I53 1845.

Thomas Commuck was a Narragansett man trained as an ethnomusicologist, who honored individual Native American men and women as well as many Eastern tribes such as Mohican, Pawtucket, Brothertown, and other Indigenous culture groups with his hymns. These hymns use “shape note” notation.

5

FROM NEVER SETTLED TO BOUNDLESS

AFTERWORD: FROM NEVER SETTLED TO BOUNDLESS

Lisa A. Crossman and Emily Potter-Ndiaye

Lisa A. Crossman is the Mead Director of Curatorial Affairs. Emily Potter-Ndiaye is the Dwight and Kirsten Poler & Andrew W. Mellon Head of Education and Curator of Academic Programs.

Heid E. Erdrich has described her research process for *Boundless* as akin to the strategy of *dérive*, considering this method beyond the theory proposed by Guy Debord and through the words of Kenzie Allen, Oneida scholar and artist. Erdrich explains her "meandering method" in "A Water Way of Knowing," likening it to Allen's "*dérive* as movement in a landscape with no particular purpose except to follow the arising flow and draw from place to place or object to object."[1] She grounds her approach in Gerald Vizenor's theory of transmotion, the elements—notably water—and the Indigenous idea of relationality. In Erdrich's approach, I find connection as she alludes to a method and way of knowing rooted in curiosity, movement, and interconnection. In *Boundless*, Erdrich centers place, kinship, relationships, and the cultural production of Native American artists and authors at the Mead—a museum that has long celebrated its collection of "American" art without the intention of including works by Native American artists as part of it.

Upon starting work at the Mead (remotely!) in 2020, I learned from colleagues such as Emily Potter-Ndiaye about the hopes and efforts for greater truth telling at the Mead. We are sited in a college, named for a town, named for a man whose activity advocated for genocide against Native communities. I connected with colleagues at Frost Library and became aware of how they were actively expanding the Collection of Native American Literature that was acquired in 2013, while also building connections with Native communities, critically examining their practices, and collaborating with faculty and students to serve as a vital resource for Native and Indigenous studies curriculum across the region's academic institutions. In conversation, we created a proposal that would bring two collections together, the Collection of Native American Literature and the Mead's collection, with the support of Professor Kiara Vigil and a yet-to-be-found guest curator. The challenge and the opportunity was to work with and beyond each collection. As a placeholder, the project was called "Never Settled: American Art from Indigenous Perspectives"—a title I agonized over and resisted as the intention of the grant was more of an open offering than a fixed proposal. I share it now only to underscore the gap between the knowledge and experience that I brought to the project and the knowledge and experience embodied by *Boundless*, which was offered by Erdrich and the many artists, writers, scholars, students, museum and library professionals, and supporters, most of whom are Indigenous.

"Never Settled" was meant as a calling-out of the trope that pervades nineteenth-century landscape painting—a convention in which landscapes are presented as uninhabited wilderness, which supports erasure of Indigenous people and culture on the long-inhabited area of what is now the United States, including the Northeast. "Never Settled" was intended to allude to an unfixing of settler-colonial narratives, acknowledging and reacting against the insidious process of "firsting and lasting" that professor of history at the University of Minnesota Jean O'Brien (White Earth Ojibwe) writes of in *Firsting and Lasting: Writing Indians out of Existence in New England*. I realize now the extent to which the title pointed to a trope without undoing it. In an effort to revise a narrative, I inadvertently created a counternarrative whose structure still reinforced the story that we sought to retire.

Alternatively, *Boundless* is a title that suggests infinite possibilities. It is affirmative and powerful in its claim to, like water, endlessly meander. I invited Emily to join me in an exploration of some of the questions and directions that *Boundless* has opened for us at the Mead. As colleagues, both of us white women, leading the curatorial and education departments at the Mead throughout the *Boundless* project, we shared many conversations that speak both to our own personal experiences and hopes for our broader collaborations. The following pages capture a sample of these, which we hope are useful as a prompt to continue the dialogue.

—Lisa A. Crossman

BEYOND NARRATIVE/COUNTERNARRATIVE

We began work on *Boundless* with the hope and humility that the process would change us and the Mead in ways we couldn't yet know. We imagined from the beginning that *Boundless* would be a place for teaching and learning, for school groups, college classes, and faculty collaboration. It became so much more.

Boundless teaches museum educators and curators a model for reparative and restorative history and arts education that gets us beyond the oppositional approaches which start from a *desire* for decolonized curriculum and museum practices but end up returning like sand in a funnel to colonization/the colonizer/the violence as leader of the story.[2] But *Boundless* manifests a different kind of truth telling (which, as Amy Lonetree notes, is a vital step in reparative practice).[3] The abundance of materials and work by Indigenous artists, authors, and printers; the undeniable interconnectedness of all living beings, and of our past, present, and future communities; and the fallacy of long-standing boundaries or silos between all the ways, visual and textual, that knowledge and meaning is made, conveyed, and shared. Building from these affirmative realities made an exhibition, but also ensured that students—Native and non-Native, children and college students—would find meaning and connection without being reinscribed with reductionist stories about their own culture, or coming away with unintended feelings of imperial power and inevitability. The myriad Native communities and traditions referenced and represented by artists in *Boundless* reflect the impossibility of a single, linear, or totalizing narrative of the history of what is now the United States.

Without a single wall text or label saying so directly, *Boundless* manifested a world in which Indigenous knowledge flows through past, present, and future. Guidelines for gallery texts, including labels, are a microcosm of larger conversations about museum education and curatorial practice. The process of developing and editing texts for *Boundless* included a negotiation of expectations and assumptions about the function of these texts. Within conversations about the texts, we noted tension between our desire for a narrative arc or a clear, definitive statement to contain the boundlessness of *Boundless* and the knowledge that this desire was a trap. In reflecting on conversations about the texts now and their evolution, we realize the degree to which the texts became a site of collaboration and of working through how to express varying ways of knowing through many voices. Through the process of writing and revising, we believe that we all came to know the content in *Boundless* with more nuance and understanding than when we started. The gallery texts were not perfect. We revised and reprinted some of them based on continuing conversations with artists and writers. But the texts also faded into the background as the living and evolving dialogues evolved beyond them.

LEARNING TOGETHER

In hopes of embracing a process of learning together, and in partnership with our colleague, Olivia Feal (Manager of Experiential Learning and K–12 Programs), we started convening the Mead staff in reading groups (not a new practice, but new to our team). We started locally, reading Amherst college professor Lisa Brooks's book, *The Common Pot*, together. We shared passages, and made a collective artwork that connected the different threads of learning it sparked among our ten-person staff. We purchased other books for staff, including Heid E. Erdrich's collection of poems *Curator of Ephemera at the New Museum for Archaic Media* and *Visualities: Perspectives on Contemporary American Indian Film and Art*, edited by Denise K. Cummings.

Another idea that drove some of our work with students, and which *Boundless* enhanced and brought out to more areas of the Mead's work, is multidirectional, reciprocal, and community learning. We put together a large team of people, intergenerationally and with a range of experience and recognized their work. The group included fourteen people who contributed as advisory committee members, including local Indigenous library, archives, museum, and scholarly leaders, artists, and students, as well as a few committed non-Indigenous museum and archives professionals. Their names were listed on a large vinyl wall text in the main room of the exhibition, and many of these individuals, as well as curatorial intern Catherine Charnoky, contributed to this publication. In addition to these contributors, we oriented our annual summer internship around the *Boundless* exhibition, bringing in Amherst students Isabella Fuster-Crichfield, Max Valdez, and Samuel Nkengla to assist with research and labels. Jacquelyn Cabarrubia and Catherine Charnoky from Amherst College and Cameron Findlay from Smith College worked with Erdrich on research in both Archives and Special Collections and at the Mead as she worked remotely from Minneapolis, and curatorial intern Ziji Zhou also assisted.

EXPERIENTIAL LEARNING AND CURRICULUM WITH ABUNDANCE

For our museum educators, who included Potter-Ndiaye and Feal, as well as five student museum educators, the exhibition's fluidity and abundance insisted on post-oppositionalist pedagogies. As Erdrich envisioned, we wanted to first and foremost welcome and center Native students and visitors. We would also need to hold in tension the reality that many students grow up in the Northeast and beyond learning myths of Native erasure, and the inevitability and completion of colonization.[4] On a basic level the very premise of and artworks in the exhibition could be belief-altering, and require context and some breaking down of big ideas—of Indigenous survivance, continuance, and futurity, of interrelationships of land and water, of movements for decolonization. *And* it would be entirely antithetical to Erdrich's *dérive* to develop a linear, didactic experience for our children, college, and community group classes in order to attempt to manage and prepare for those ambitious learning objectives. *As well*, when we plan to engage a class of, say, fifth graders, or first-year college students in an hour-long museum session, we do need to build a container for that experience, to help them learn and scaffold what they experience onto their existing knowledge and enduring questionings. In other words, while the exhibition flows like water and has no beginning or end, a class visit requires that we start somewhere!

Potter-Ndiaye and Feal had ongoing conversations in the months leading up to the exhibition opening to surface the moments in the exhibition that we wanted to use to ground our various educational groups—K–12 and college—in *Boundless*. Our process was also concurrent to and interrelated to the development of a web-based curriculum for *Boundless*, which included Genevieve Simermeyer (Osage; curriculum developer) who brought incredible leadership while working closely with Feal to develop a framework of four big ideas with essential questions to put some structure around teaching with *Boundless* artworks and materials in an online curriculum developed for students and teachers in Massachusetts public schools. These four themes—place, continuance, kinship, and creativity—animated the way Potter-Ndiaye invited college groups to approach the exhibition as well as Feal and the student museum educators who lead our K–12 groups.

Because of the differences and sometimes cultural silos between our respective teaching loads, we noticed and appreciated how *Boundless* invited and even required us to coordinate our teaching across age groups, and to be in better relation with each other as colleagues. In all these ways and more, *Boundless* helped us to approach the kind of highly integrative, embodied, experiential, and reparative culture we seek to build and live in.

Perhaps the most experiential learning project it convened was a course collaboration with Professor Kiara Vigil (Dakota) and her fall 2023 course at Amherst College: Indigenous Art and Books: A Boundless Approach to Image and Text. Vigil, a partner on the *Boundless* project from the start, and her eleven students met regularly with Potter-Ndiaye in *Boundless* to read the exhibition alongside their core texts: Amy Lonetree, *Decolonizing Museum Practice*; Susan Dion, *Braided Learning*; and Philip Deloria, *Becoming Mary Sully*. They also worked closely with Brandon Castle (who was project coordinator for Mapping Native Intellectual Networks of the Northeast, and is now Native American and Indigenous Studies Librarian at the University of Massachusetts Amherst) to curate a small exhibition of texts in the library from the same Native American Literature Collection that was a collaborator on *Boundless*. With an open door between theory and practice, they critically engaged with *Boundless* through some of Lonetree's tenets of a decolonial museum practice—truth telling, healing from generational trauma from colonization, and education. Students also met with Erdrich to share and receive feedback on their projects. Working in pairs and small groups, they developed additional resources to add to the conversations *Boundless* already stirs, which live online as part of the web curriculum, well past when the exhibition came down.

RETURNING TO AGREEMENTS

An inescapable part of exhibition development is administration. We began *Boundless* wanting to build processes that were relational and non-extractive, and to carry those forward well after *Boundless* would close. We hoped to embrace the changes that the project opens up not just in the galleries but across the entire museum, and part of this work involves policies and protocols: loan agreements, contracts and compensation for commissions, artist fees, timelines, budgets, grant guidelines, and interwoven into all of these elements, our responsibility to the artists and communities with whom we work.

Throughout *Boundless*, we felt the tension between institutional and grant-mandated timelines and overloaded commitments, bare-bones budgets, and the need to create more space and time for each part of the project. *Boundless* developed during a period of staff turnover and leadership transitions. As these steps led to a desire to contract, the mandate of *Boundless* was to spread and open. And we did. As we sit here now and reflect on the ways that we stretched, we consider a few areas of change and ways to sustainably move forward.

Boundless was a collection-based show that was oriented around the purchasing of work by Native artists and doing so through relationship building and conversations with the artists and Erdrich, and in relation to the Collection of Native American Literature, place, and the Mead's existing collections. As the project progressed we realized the need to include artist loans to a larger extent than imagined to honor the vision of the project and the importance of centering Native artists based in the Northeast. Sometimes purchases weren't possible because of the Mead's limits (such as storage space or budget) and sometimes artists wanted to participate in the exhibition but did not want their work to be purchased for the collection. A range of unique circumstances surfaced that required adjustments; we hope to apply these learnings to collections and exhibitions policies and practices in the future.

During *Boundless* we formalized a structure for artist fees, using WAGE (Working Artists and the Greater Economy) guidelines as a touchstone.[5] There are still parameters that deserve continued consideration, negotiating individual artist needs with institutional limits and a goal of equity. We held an artist residency because it was requested by an artist and felt the discomfort of holding space and trying to "administer" the process without controlling it. The process was not without missteps. The Mead held its first open hours for Indigenous community members, and we aspire to continue not only with this practice but also more generally being responsive to ways that we are asked to hold space.

One part of the *Boundless* process to note and that we'll continue to work on as we move forward is that "the idea of returning to agreements is foundational...."[6] Contracts and policies require reworking, and in the bustle of moving through the to-do list, we must come back to the fact that they are between people.

FROM NEVER SETTLED TO UNSETTLING

Threshold concepts are ones that, once we know them, fundamentally shift our thinking, going so far as to undo at times other fast held concepts and beliefs. Through our work on *Boundless,* we noticed a number of thresholds—how leading with relationships (over other sometimes driving forces in museum work, like static protocols, rapid timelines, and a focus on owning artworks) sets the stage for a more loving, and celebratory exhibition; how to move beyond the binary of a narrative/counternarrative and truly imagine other worlds and possibilities; what it looks like for a settler museum to try to prioritize and center Indigenous audience members and students in the stories and curricula we present. But we are also aware of how these thresholds were most available to a core group of staff—those in education and curatorial affairs who worked most closely with Erdrich, the participating artists, and the advisory committee and student staff. As we enter a more reflective space in the project, we need better ways of carrying the process currently embodied in a few staff members into lasting and shared shifts in museum processes, policies, and pedagogies toward integrative, relationship-first ways of working. It is important to keep being in good relation with one another and all of the friends and collaborators on this project, even as we enter into new and other projects. We should continue to revise and review our policies that make it possible and desirable for Native and other racialized artists to show work at the Mead. We will continue work to integrate the pedagogical approach and staffing models across college and all other groups. We should keep learning, together, as a staff and as a feature of working at the Mead. Perhaps "Never Settled" was never meant to be the title of this project, but of the Mead's next phase—to unsettle the various material, discursive, and relational traditions in this 75-year-old campus art museum that are fictions of colonization, of harmful categories, hierarchies, and binaries.[7] We hope this next phase will be supported by a belief in the boundless path we are on and the significance of even imperfect attempts to change.

NOTES

1 See page 23 of Erdrich's "A Water Way of Knowing," in which Erdrich paraphrases Allen and describes her approach in greater detail.

2 We've also come to understand models beyond narrative/counternarrative through AnaLouise Keating's work on post-oppositionalism, "an alternative approach to social justice work," which encompasses traits as "belief in people's interconnectedness with all that exists, acceptance of paradox and contradiction, and the desire to be radically inclusive—to seek and create complex commonalities and broad-based alliances for social change." AnaLouise Keating, "Foreword," in *Teaching with Tenderness: Toward an Embodied Practice*, Becky Thompson (Champaign: University of Illinois Press, 2017), ix.

3 Amy Lonetree, *Decolonizing Museums: Representing Native America in National and Tribal Museums* (Chapel Hill: University of North Carolina Press, 2012).

4 Kathleen Brown-Perez, passed on in conversations and classes by Kiara Vigil.

5 For reference, the WAGE fee calculator can be found here: https://wageforwork.com/fee-calculator#top.

6 Ange Loft, "Indigenous Context and Concepts for Toronto (Excerpts): The Dish with One Spoon," in *Water, Kinship, Belief*, ed. Candice Hopkins, Katie Lawson, and Tairone Bastien (Toronto: Art Metropole, 2022), https://torontobiennial.org/indigenous-context/.

7 Noah Romero, closing words of *Boundless* exhibit tour.

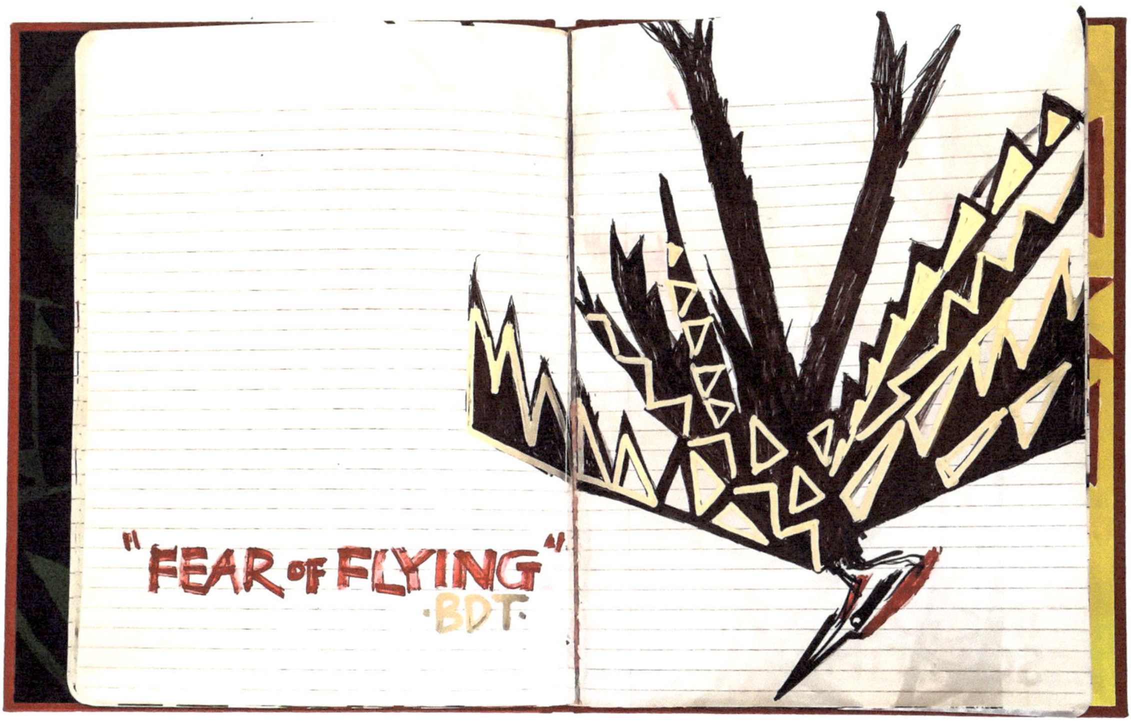

Figure 40: Brian D. Tripp (Karuk), *Like Fire*, 2018. Hand painting, ink, cloth case. Amherst College Archives and Special Collections, Collection of Native American Literature. N7433.4.T77 L5 2018.

DIRECTORS' NOTE

Martin L. Garnar, Director of the Frost Library, and Siddhartha V. Shah, the Mead's John Wieland 1958 Director

Boundless has offered the Mead Art Museum and the Amherst College Library a special opportunity to reimagine our respective collections and to advance scholarship through collaboration and in partnership. This project does more than just engage with literature and art side by side. Rather, both the exhibition and this publication demonstrate an integration of art and literature in a way that advances the fields of Native American and Indigenous studies and American studies at Amherst College, across the Five Colleges, and, we hope, far beyond. A collaboration like this extending across various departments, mediums, cultures, and histories can pose unique challenges while also opening up new ways of knowing and learning. The process of bringing *Boundless* to life has shown us how we can benefit from bringing our collections together, and what is possible when siloed institutions like libraries and museums seek integration for ourselves and the public we serve. We recognize that we—a campus museum and an academic library—are stronger together, and that we can bridge a nebulous divide between the literary and visual arts to enhance the learning experience for all.

It has become the practice of many institutions to include land acknowledgments at the start of events. While these statements list the peoples who have been displaced through colonization, many do not include a call for action beyond mindfulness, and most are not paired with concrete steps toward repair. Through *Boundless*, our intention is to build and maintain relationships with the Indigenous communities represented through the exhibition. We are learning about the centrality of relationships in this work and see this exhibition and publication as early steps on our journey toward community. Our goal is to cultivate a sense of belonging on the Amherst campus, including for our Indigenous collaborators and community members.

A project of this size and scope could not have been possible without the work of many hands, including our team members from the museum and library, students and professors, the artists, the many partners on Amherst College's campus, and from the Five Colleges and surrounding communities. We offer our sincere thanks to them, for their transformative input in and deep intellectual engagement with *Boundless*. And our deepest gratitude to guest curator and contributor, Heid E. Erdrich (Ojibwe), for her inspiring leadership and integrity, and for creating this project that will surely resonate and resound for years to come.

Martin L. Garnar
Director of the Frost Library

Siddhartha V. Shah
John Wieland 1958 Director, Mead Art Museum

Contributor Biographies

Kohar Avakian is a Nipmuc, Black, and Armenian multimedia artist, visual storyteller, and scholar from Worcester, Massachusetts. She holds a BA in history (modified with Native American Studies) from Dartmouth College and is currently pursuing her PhD in American studies at Yale. As a descendant of genocide survivors still awaiting reparations, she has experienced the unparalleled power of learning about other peoples' histories through their own eyes. Adding vibrancy to her life as a graduate student, oral history and visual art provide her an outlet to explore the intersection of race, recognition, reparations, kinship, and ancestral presence. Her words have been featured in *Vice News*, *Armenian Weekly, The Armenian-Mirror Spectator, Haytoug Talks,* and more. Her essay "An Inter/Racial Love History" is featured in the anthology *We Are All Armenian: Voices from the Diaspora* (University of Texas Press, 2023). She also cohosts *Name It!*, a podcast with her best friend and fellow PhD candidate, Iman AbdoulKarim, where they break down big ideas and help name what it means to live at the intersections, one case study at a time.

Andrea Carlson is a visual artist who maintains a studio practice in northern Minnesota and Chicago, Illinois. She is Anishinaabe and a lineal descendant of the Grand Portage Band. Carlson works primarily on paper, creating painted and drawn surfaces with many media. Her work addresses land and institutional spaces, decolonization narratives, and assimilation metaphors in film. Her work has been acquired by institutions such as the Whitney Museum of American Art, the Walker Art Center, the Museum of Contemporary Art in Chicago, the Denver Art Museum, the Minneapolis Institute of Art, and the National Gallery of Canada. Carlson was a recipient of a 2008 McKnight Fellowship, a 2017 Joan Mitchell Foundation Painters and Sculptors award, a 2021 Chicago Artadia Award, and a 2022 United States Artists Fellowship. Carlson is a cofounder of the Center for Native Futures in Chicago.

Brandon Castle is Native American and Indigenous Studies Librarian at the University of Massachusetts Amherst. He was the project coordinator for a two-year grant, "Mapping Native Intellectual Networks of the Northeast," which aims to increase accessibility to the Amherst College Collection of Native American Literature and integrate Indigenous methodologies into the stewardship of the collection. Brandon is interested in the intersections of identity, cultural revitalization, cultural heritage institutions, and working with and for Indigenous communities. Brandon is a graduate of the University of Washington Museology Graduate Program and is currently pursuing a library science degree at San Jose State University. Brandon is an enrolled member of the Ketchikan Indian Community and is a descendant of the Tsimshian Peoples.

Abigail Chabitnoy is the author of *In the Current Where Drowning Is Beautiful* (Wesleyan, 2022); *How to Dress a Fish* (Wesleyan, 2019), shortlisted for the 2020 International Griffin Prize for Poetry and winner of the 2020 Colorado Book Award; and the linocut illustrated chapbook *Converging Lines of Light* (Flower Press, 2021). She currently teaches at the Institute of American Indian Arts low-residency MFA program and is an assistant professor at UMass Amherst. Abigail is a member of the Tangirnaq Native Village in Kodiak. Find her at salmonfisherpoet.com.

Catherine Charnoky, a senior environmental studies major at Amherst College, hails from Ithaca, New York and is an enrolled member of the Citizen Potawatomi Nation. Catherine's curiosity and love of trying new things, even if she is not good at them, inspired a love for surfing and rock climbing while studying abroad in New Zealand. Alongside her academic pursuits, Catherine is involved in the Native and Indigenous Student Association, works at the Beneski Museum, and sings in the TI acapella group.

Lisa A. Crossman is Director of Curatorial Affairs at the Mead Art Museum, Amherst College. Since joining the Mead, Lisa's projects have centered collaborations with artists, students, faculty, and guest curators. Prior to this position, she was curator at the Fitchburg Art Museum and worked with the Cultural Agents Initiative at Harvard University. Lisa holds a PhD from Tulane University, specializing in the history of modern and contemporary art of Latin America with a focus on themes relating to nature and ecology. In her curatorial practice she explores art as part of interdisciplinary conversations, with current research focusing on labor.

Philip J. Deloria (Dakota descent) is the Leverett Saltonstall Professor of History at Harvard University, and the author of *Playing Indian*, *Indians in Unexpected Places*, and *Becoming Mary Sully: Toward an American Indian Abstract*. Deloria received a PhD in American studies from Yale University and has taught at the University of Colorado and the University of Michigan. He has been a long-serving trustee of the Smithsonian Institution's National Museum of the American Indian, president of the American Studies Association and the Organization of American Historians, and is an elected member of the American Philosophical Society and the American Academy of Arts and Sciences.

Heid E. Erdrich is a writer, interdisciplinary artist, educator, and curator. She is the author of several poetry collections—including the forthcoming chapbook *Verb Animate* and *Little Big Bully* (2020), winner of the 2022 Rebekah Johnson Bobbitt National Prize for Poetry from the Library of Congress. Erdrich has curated dozens of Native American art exhibits in Minnesota and was a community curator of literary arts for Hearts of Our People, the traveling exhibition of Native women's art from Mia (Minneapolis Institute of Art). She was guest curator for the Mead Art Museum at Amherst College from 2020 to 2024. Erdrich is Ojibwe and an enrolled member of the Turtle Mountain Band of Chippewa.

Eric Gansworth, S·ha-weñ na-saeˀ, (Onondaga, Eel Clan) is a writer and visual artist from Tuscarora Nation. He has been widely published and exhibited. Lowery Writer-in-Residence at Canisius University, he has also been an NEH Distinguished Visiting Professor at Colgate University. His work has received a Printz Honor, was longlisted for the National Book Award, and has received an American Indian Library Association Youth Literature Award, PEN Oakland Award, and American Book Award. *Apple (Skin to the Core)* was chosen for *Time*'s 10 Best YA and Children's Books for 2020.

Martin Garnar, PhD, is director of the Amherst College Library and editor of the tenth edition of the *Intellectual Freedom Manual*. His professional activities and speaking schedule reflect a profound inability to say no. A native New Yorker, Martin lives in western Massachusetts with his husband Mark and their impossibly cute miniature dachshunds.

Bonney Hartley is a founding member of Mohican Writers Circle, whose poetry has been published in the group's journals, with additional work forthcoming by Tupelo Press. An enrolled citizen of Stockbridge-Munsee Mohican Nation (Wisconsin), she serves the community's repatriation efforts in its homelands and is based in Williamstown, Massachusetts. She holds a master's degree in international relations from the University of Cape Town, South Africa and is currently pursuing an MFA creative writing degree for poetry at the Institute of American Indian Arts in Santa Fe.

Sierra Henries (Chaubunagungamaug Nipmuc), pyrography and birch bark artist, has been drawing and experimenting with many different materials and visual media since she was young, but she has always been especially inspired by designs, colors, and shapes in the natural world. Her Nipmuc heritage and her family's involvement with the Native community has shaped her desire to express Eastern Woodlands traditional art forms in her own unique way. Through a combination of both these loves, she eventually became interested in working with birch bark, a material that is utilized by many Indigenous peoples around the world.

Frank Buffalo Hyde studied at the Santa Fe Fine Arts Institute and the Institute of American Indian Arts. He creates from what he calls "the collective unconsciousness of the 21st century," drawing on popular culture and landscape in his paintings. He grew up in New York and is a member of the Onondaga Nation. Hyde is also Nez Perce.

Mike Kelly has been the Head of the Archives and Special Collections at Amherst College since 2009. In 2016, he was awarded the Reese Fellowship for American Bibliography and the History of the Book in the Americas by the Bibliographical Society of America for his work on the bibliography of Samson Occom, a member of the Mohegan tribe of Connecticut. In the summer of 2018, Mike cotaught the course "A History of Native American Books and Indigenous Sovereignty" in Amherst for Rare Book School. He served as the co-chair of the Steering Committee on a Racial History of Amherst College (2020–23).

Jason R. Montgomery is a Chicano/Indigenous Californian activist, writer, painter, and playwright from El Centro, California. In 2016 he cofounded the arts activism collective Attack Bear Press and in 2020 he founded 50 Arrow Gallery. Along with Alexandra Woolner, Jason is one of the 2021–23 Easthampton Poets Laureate.

Emily Potter-Ndiaye is the Dwight & Kirsten Poler and Andrew W. Mellon Head of Education and Curator of Academic Programs at the Mead Art Museum at Amherst College. Prior to Amherst College, Emily led education programs and teams as director of education at Brooklyn Historical Society and as an educator at New York Historical Society, the Contemporary Jewish Museum of San Francisco, and in schools. Her formal education includes an undergraduate degree in history, with a focus on dance from Macalester College and a master's degree in museum studies from New York University. In her work as a museum educator, she aims to bring people together across boundaries by telling better, fuller stories about ourselves and each other.

Rachel Beth Sayet or **Ákitusut (She Who Reads)** is a member of the Mohegan nation. Raised with the spirits of her ancestors, she grew up learning traditional stories, teachings, and participating in tribal events. Rachel has always been passionate about and proud of her Mohegan heritage and identity as well as an avid learner about other cultures, Indigenous and beyond. Rachel has a BS in restaurant management from Cornell University and an MA in anthropology and museum studies from Harvard University. Through her training and passions in history, food, and culture, she now gives guest lectures, presentations, and cooking demos throughout New England to students of all ages. Rachel is currently teaching the course "Native American Women" at the University of Massachusetts Boston.

Siddhartha V. Shah is the John Wieland 1958 Director of Mead Art Museum at Amherst College, where he oversees a variety of initiatives aimed at deepening community engagement both on and off campus. Shah's academic and curatorial projects have been featured in publications ranging from the *Times of India* and *Psychology Today* to

The New Yorker and *The Wall Street Journal*. He received a BA in art history from Johns Hopkins University, an MA in East–West psychology from the California Institute of Integral Studies, and a PhD in art history and archaeology from Columbia University.

Kimberly Toney is a member of the Hassanamisco Band of Nipmuc and the inaugural coordinating curator of Native American and Indigenous collections at the John Hay Library at Brown University and the John Carter Brown Library in Providence, Rhode Island. Previous to her work at Brown, Kim was Head of Readers' Services and Director of Indigenous Initiatives at the American Antiquarian Society. Additionally, Kim regularly consults with cultural heritage institutions in the Northeast related to Nipmuc history and presence, foregrounding equitable access to libraries and archives, community engagement, and connecting Indigenous knowledges and practices to all scholarly endeavors.

Kiara M. Vigil is currently Dean of New Students and associate professor of American Studies at Amherst College. She has served as a council member for the Native American and Indigenous Studies Association and currently edits the journal *SAIL* (*Studies in American Indian Literatures*). She has a PhD in American culture from the University of Michigan, and her research and teaching is grounded in Native American and Indigenous studies. Her first book, *Indigenous Intellectuals: Sovereignty, Citizenship, and the American Imagination, 1890–1930*, was published by Cambridge University Press in 2015. She has published several articles and essays in peer-reviewed journals and books, one of which, "Who was Henry Standing Bear? Remembering Lakota Activism from the Early Twentieth Century," won the Frederick C. Luebke Award for Outstanding Regional Scholarship from the *Great Plains Quarterly*. Her new book, *Natives in Transit: Indian Entertainment, Urban Life, and Activism*, is a cultural history of Native performance and activist networks from the mid-twentieth century. Kiara is also working with other Dakota linguistic experts and cultural knowledge keepers on a Dakota-language translation and scholarly project centered on the rare newspaper *Iapi Oaye*, which has funding support from the Mellon Foundation and the National Endowment for the Humanities.

Brittney Peauwe Wunnepog Walley is a citizen of the Nipmuc Tribe. During her childhood, her father, Bradley Big Tree Walley, served their tribe as a pauwau (medicine person) along with one of her uncles, Henry Sly Fox Walley. This connection created a path for Brittney to find meaningful ways to serve her community. Her pieces are created with methods as old as time immemorial. Weaving enables her to honor her ancestors while uplifting present and future generations. Brittney hopes to continue teaching about, and sharing the beauty of, Northeastern Woodland art. She is grateful for her teacher, her community that supports her, and those willing to learn alongside her.

Boundless Reading List

Apess, William. *Eulogy on King Philip: As Pronounced at the Odeon, in Federal Street, Boston*. Boston: published by the author, 1836. Amherst College Archives and Special Collections, part of the original Younghee Kim-Wait (Class of 1982)/Pablo Eisenberg Collection of Native American Literature, E83.67 .A64 1836. https://acdc.amherst.edu/view/NativeLiterature/E83-67_A64_1836.

Apess, William. *Indian Nullification of the Unconstitutional Laws of Massachusetts Relative to the Marshpee Tribe: or, The Pretended Riot Explained*. Boston: Jonathan Howe, 1835. Amherst College Archives and Special Collections, part of the original Younghee Kim-Wait (Class of 1982)/Pablo Eisenberg Collection of Native American Literature, E99.M4 A6 1835. https://acdc.amherst.edu/view/NativeLiterature/E99-M4_A6_1835.

Atsitty, Tacey M. *Rain Scald: Poems.* Albuquerque: University of New Mexico Press, 2018.

Brooks, Joanna, ed. *The Collected Writings of Samson Occom, Mohegan: Leadership and Literature in Eighteenth-Century Native America*. New York: Oxford University Press, 2006.

Brooks, Lisa. *Our Beloved Kin: A New History of King Philip's War*. London: Yale University Press, 2018.

Brooks, Lisa. *The Common Pot: The Recovery of Native Space in the Northeast*. Minneapolis: University of Minnesota Press, 2008.

Chacon, Raven. *For Zitkála-Šá*. Toronto: Art Metropole, 2022.

Chen, Jess X., and Demian DinéYazhi'. *Solastalgia: A Queer Eco-Feminist Poetry Tour*. Albuquerque: printed by the author, 2016.

Coombs, Linda. *Colonization and the Wampanoag Story.* New York: Crown Books for Young Readers, 2023.

Cuffe, Paul. *Narrative of the Life and Adventures of Paul Cuffe, A Pequot Indian: During Thirty Years Spent at Sea, and in Travelling in Foreign Lands*. Vernon, N.Y.: Horace N. Bill, 1839. Amherst College Archives and Special Collections, G463.C8465 1839. https://acdc.amherst.edu/view/NativeLiterature/G463_C8465_1839-c2.

Cummings, Denise K., ed. *Visualities: Perspectives on Contemporary American Indian Film and Art*. East Lansing: Michigan State University Press, 2011.

Curtis, Natalie, ed. *The Indians' Book: An Offering by the American Indians of Indian Lore, Musical and Narrative, to Form a Record of the Songs and Legends of Their Race.* New York: Harper and Brothers, 1907. Reprint, New York: Bonanza Books, 1987.

Deloria, Ella Cara. *Waterlily*. Lincoln: University of Nebraska Press, 1988. Biographical sketch of the author by Agnes Picotte, afterword by Raymond J. DeMallie. Amherst College Archives and Special Collections, PS3554.E44445 W3 1988.

Deloria, Philip J. *Becoming Mary Sully: Toward an American Indian Abstract*. Seattle: University of Washington Press, 2019.

Deloria, Philip J. *Indians in Unexpected Places*. Lawrence: University Press of Kansas, 2004. Amherst College Archives and Special Collections, E98.S67 D46 2004.

Deloria, Vine, Jr. *Of Utmost Good Faith.* San Francisco: Straight Arrow Books, 1971. Amherst College Archives and Special Collections, E93 .D38 1971.

Deloria, Vine, Jr. *We Talk, You Listen: New Tribes, New Turf.* New York: Macmillan, 1970. Amherst College Archives and Special Collections, E184.A1 D33 1970.

Dennis, Jeremy. *On This Site.* Printed by the author, 2017.

Drake, Kinsale. *Hummingbird Heart*. Art by Alice Mao. Tuba City, Ariz.: Abalone Mountain Press, 2022.

Erdrich, Heid E. *Curator of Ephemera at the New Museum for Archaic Media*. East Lansing: Michigan State University Press, 2017.

Erdrich, Heid E. *Little Big Bully.* New York: Penguin Books, 2020.

Fawcett, Melissa Jayne, and Joseph Bruchac. *Makiawisug: The Gift of the Little People*. Illustrated by David Wagner. United States: Little People Publications, 1997.

First American Art Magazine. https://firstamericanartmagazine.com/.

Fiveash, Julie. *Why Can't You: A Comic About Multiracial Identity*. Printed by the author, 2016. Amherst College Archives and Special Collections, PN6727.F595 W59 2016.

Flahive, Jean, and Donald Soctomah. *The Canoe Maker/El Constructor de Canoas*. Illustrated by Mari Dieumegard. Thomaston: Maine Authors Publishing, 2019.

Frank, Della, and Roberta D. Joe. *Storm Pattern: Poems from Two Navajo Women*. Illustration by David Chethlahe Paladin. Tsaile, Ariz.: Navajo Community College Press, 1993. Amherst College Archives and Special Collections, PS591.I55 F73 1993.

Gould, D. Rae, Holly Herbster, Heather Law Pezzarossi, and Stephen A. Mrozowski. *Historical Archaeology and Indigenous Collaboration: Discovering Histories That Have Futures.* Gainesville: University Press of Florida, 2020.

Greendeer, Danielle, Anthony Perry, and Alexis Bunten. *Keepunumuk: Weeâchumun's Thanksgiving Story*. Illustrated by Garry Meeches Sr. Watertown, Mass.: Charlesbridge, 2022.

Greenlaw, Suzanne, and Gabriel Frey. *The First Blade of Sweetgrass: A Native American Story*. Illustrated by Nancy Baker. Thomaston, Maine: Tilbury House, 2021.

Harjo, Joy. *Remember*. Illustrated by Michaela Goade. New York: Random House, 2023.

Hopinka, Sky. *Around the Edge of Encircling Lake*. Milwaukee: Green Gallery Press, 2018.

Hopinka, Sky. *Perfidia*. New York: Wendy's Subway; Bard CCS, 2020.

Hopinka, Sky. *Sky Hopinka: Downward, Upward, Around and Around the Spinning Whorl.* Exhibition catalog from the "Great Poor Farm Experiment." Minawa, Wisc.: Poor Farm Press, 2021.

Hopkins, Candice, Katie Lawson, and Tairone Bastien, eds. *Water, Kinship, Belief: Toronto Biennial of Art 2019–2022*. Toronto: Art Metropole and Toronto Biennial of Art, 2022.

Johnson, E. Pauline (Tekahionwake). *Flint and Feather: Collected Verse*. Toronto: Musson Book Co., 1913. Amherst College Archives and Special Collections, part of the original Younghee Kim-Wait (Class of 1982)/Pablo Eisenberg Collection of Native American Literature, PR9199.2.J64 F5 1913. https://acdc.amherst.edu/view/NativeLiterature/PR9199-2-J64_F5_1913.

Jung, Chanti, Julie Fiveash, Sierra Edd, and Amber McCrary. *Portals of Indigenous Futurism: A Zine Anthology of Indigenous Futurism*. Tuba City, Ariz.: Abalone Mountain Press, 2021.

Lonetree, Amy. *Decolonizing Museums: Representing Native America in National and Tribal Museums*. Chapel Hill: University of North Carolina Press, 2012.

Mann, Larry Spotted Crow. *Drumming and Dreaming*. Massachusetts: CrowStorm Publishing, 2017.

Mann, Larry Spotted Crow. *The Mourning Road to Thanksgiving*. Massachusetts: CrowStorm Publishing, 2016.

Mann, Larry Spotted Crow. *Tales from the Whispering Basket*. Edited by Donna Caruso. Boston: Published by the author, 2011.

Matthews, Sandra, David Brule, and Suzanne Gardinier. *Occupying Massachusetts: Layers of History on Indigenous Land*. Staunton, Va.: George F. Thompson Publishing, 2022.

Neptune, Jennifer, Kathleen Mundell, Barry Dana, and Jeremy Frey, eds. *Wíwənikan...The Beauty We Carry*. Foreword by Theresa Secord. Waterville, Maine: Colby College Museum of Art, 2019.

Newell, Chris. *If You Lived During the Plimoth Thanksgiving*. Illustrated by Winona Nelson. New York: Scholastic Press, 2021.

O'Brien, Jean M. *Firsting and Lasting: Writing Indians out of Existence in New England.* Minneapolis: University of Minnesota Press, 2010.

Occom, Samson. *A Sermon Preached at the Execution of Moses Paul, an Indian, Who Was Executed at New-Haven, on the 2d of September 1772, for the Murder of Mr. Moses Cook, Late of Waterbury, on the 7th of December 1771*. New London, Conn.: T. Green, 1772. Amherst College Archives and Special Collections, E98.M6 O16 1772d. https://acdc.amherst.edu/view/NativeLiterature/E98-M6_O16_1772d.

Peirce, Ebenezer W. *Indian History, Biography and Genealogy: Pertaining to the Good Sachem Massasoit of the Wampanoag Tribe, and His Descendants*. North Abington, Mass.: Zerviah Gould Mitchell, 1878. Amherst College Archives and Special Collections, E78.N5 P45 1878. https://acdc.amherst.edu/view/NativeLiterature/E78-N5_P45_1878.

Peyer, Bernd C., ed. *American Indian Nonfiction: An Anthology of Writings, 1760s–1930s*. Norman: University of Oklahoma Press, 2007.

Phillips, Patsy, Manuela Well-Off-Man, Suzanne Newman Fricke, et al. *Indigenous Futurisms: Transcending Past/Present/Future*. Santa Fe, N.M.: IAIA Museum of Contemporary Indian Arts, 2020. Amherst College Archives and Special Collections, ASCBL.0939.

Posey, Alexander Lawrence. *The Poems of Alexander Lawrence Posey*. Collected and arranged by Mrs. Minnie H. Posey. Topeka, Kans.: Crane Printers, 1910. Amherst College Archives and Special Collections, PS2649.P55 A6 1910.

Pokagon, Simon. *O-gî-mäw-kwě Mit-i-gwä-kî*. Hartford, Mich.: C. H. Engle, 1899. Amherst College Archives and Special Collections, part of the original Younghee Kim-Wait (Class of 1982)/Pablo Eisenberg Collection of Native American Literature, E99.P8 P65 1899 c.2. https://acdc.amherst.edu/view/NativeLiterature/E99-P8_P65_1899.

Priest, Rena, ed. *The Larger Voice: Celebrating Native Arts and Cultures Foundation Literature Fellows*. Portland, Ore.: Native Arts and Cultures Foundation, 2022

Sanchez, Joseph M. *Fritz Scholder: An Intimate Look*. Santa Fe, N.M.: Institute of American Indian Arts Museum, 2008. Amherst College Archives and Special Collections, ASCBL.0929.

Scholder, Fritz. *Flirting with Possessions*. Tucson: Nazraeli Press, 1997. Amherst College Archives and Special Collections, ND237. S4335 A4 1997.

Senier, Siobhan, ed. *Dawnland Voices: An Anthology of Indigenous Writing from New England*. Lincoln: University of Nebraska Press, 2014.

Sockabasin, Allen. *Thanks to the Animals*. Illustrated by Rebekah Raye. Gardiner, Maine: Tilbury House, 2005.

Sorell, Traci. *We Are Grateful: Otsaliheliga*. Illustrated by Frané Lessac. Watertown, Mass.: Charlesbridge, 2018.

Swamp, Chief Jake. *Giving Thanks: A Native American Good Morning Message*. Illustrated by Erwin Printup, Jr. New York: Lee and Low Books, 1995.

Toney, Kimberly. *From English to Algonquian: Early New England Translations*. Online exhibition created in 2016, Worcester, Mass.: American Antiquarian Society. https://collections.americanantiquarian.org/EnglishtoAlgonquian/.

Vigil, Kiara M. *Indigenous Intellectuals: Sovereignty, Citizenship, and the American Imagination, 1880–1930*. New York: Cambridge University Press, 2015.

Vizenor, Gerald Robert. "George Morrison: Anishinaabe Expressionist Artist." *American Indian Quarterly* 30, no. 3/4 (Summer–Fall 2006): 646–660. http://www.jstor.org/stable/4139034.

Vizenor, Gerald Robert. *Literary Chance: Essays on Native American Survivance*. València: Universitad de València, 2007. Biblioteca Javier Coy d'estudis nord-americans 50. Amherst College Archives and Special Collections, PS3572.I9 L58 2007.

Vizenor, Gerald Robert. "Moby Dick and Transmotion: Natural Motion and Literary Scenes of Survivance." *Sky-Hawk: Journal of the Melville Society of Japan*, n.s., 2 (29): 2014. Amherst College Archives and Special Collections, PS2384.M62 V59 2014.

White Hawk, Sandy. *A Child of the Indian Race: A Story of Return*. St. Paul: Minnesota Historical Society Press, 2022.

Wilson, Diane. *Ella Cara Deloria: Dakota Language Protector*. Illustrated by Tashia Hart. Minneapolis: Wise Ink Creative Publishing, 2020.

Zitkala-Ša (Gertrude Bonnin). *American Indian Stories*. Washington, D.C.: Hayworth Publishing House, 1921. Amherst College Archives and Special Collections, part of the Original Younghee Kim-Wait (Class of 1982)/Pablo Eisenberg Collection of Native American Literature, E99.Y25 Z57 1921. https://acdc.amherst.edu/view/NativeLiterature/E99-Y25_Z57_1921.

Checklist, Part I

August 29, 2023–January 7, 2024

AMHERST COLLEGE ARCHIVES AND SPECIAL COLLECTIONS, COLLECTION OF NATIVE AMERICAN LITERATURE

Mae Wadley Abbott
Choctaw-Chickasaw
Born Oklahoma

Acee Blue Eagle, illustrator
Creek-Pawnee
Born Wichita Reservation, Oklahoma, 1907–59

Oklahoma Indian Cook Book: The Best Indian Recipes from the Best Indian State, Published by Mae Abbott, printed by Acorn Printing Co., Tulsa, Oklahoma, 1956

File TX715 .A22 1956

All Tribes Community Church
North America, Baptist Church in Oklahoma

Feasting with All Tribes & Friends: A Collection of Recipes, Published by All Tribes Community Church, Tulsa, Oklahoma; printed by Morris Press, Kearney, Nebraska, 2000

E98.F7 F43 2000

William Apess
Pequot/Mashpee
Born Massachusetts, 1798–1839

Eulogy on King Philip: As Pronounced at the Odeon, in Federal Street, Boston, Published by the author, 1836

Younghee Kim-Wait (Class of 1982)/Pablo Eisenberg Collection of Native American Literature, Vault E83.67.A64 1836

William Apess
Pequot/Mashpee
Born Massachusetts, 1798–1839

Indian Nullification of the Unconstitutional Laws of Massachusetts Relative to The Marshpee Tribe: or The Pretended Riot Explained, Press of Jonathan Howe, Boston, 1835

Younghee Kim-Wait (Class of 1982)/Pablo Eisenberg Collection of Native American Literature, E99.M4 A6 1835

Andrew Blackbird (Makadebinesi)
Odawa
Born Michigan, 1814–1908

Margaret Blackbird Boyd, binding and illustrations
Odawa
Born Michigan, 1817–92

History of the Ottawa and Chippewa Indians of Michigan: A Grammar of their Language/Personal and Family History, The Ypsilantian Job Printing House, Ypsilanti, Michigan, 1887

E99.O9 B6 1887 c.2

Acee Blue Eagle
Creek/Pawnee
Born Wichita Reservation, Oklahoma, 1907–59

Mae Abbott, publisher
Choctaw-Chickasaw
Born Oklahoma

Echogee: The Little Blue Deer, Palmco Investment Corp., 1971

Younghee Kim-Wait (Class of 1982)/Pablo Eisenberg Collection of Native American Literature, xFile PS3552.L78 E34 1971

Acee Blue Eagle
Creek/Pawnee
Born Wichita Reservation Oklahoma, 1907–59

Oklahoma Indian Painting-Poetry, Acorn Publishing Co., Tulsa, Oklahoma, 1959

Younghee Kim-Wait (Class of 1982)/Pablo Eisenberg Collection of Native American Literature, ND238.A4 O4 1959

Nonabah Gorman Bryan
Diné
New Mexico, 1887–1942

Charles Keetsie Shirley, illustrator
Diné
Born Arizona and lived in New Mexico, 1906–70

Navajo Native Dyes: Their Preparation and Use, Bureau of Indian Affairs, Branch of Education, Washington, D.C., 1940

Younghee Kim-Wait (Class of 1982)/Pablo Eisenberg Collection of Native American Literature, File E99.N3 N29 1940

Diane Burns
Chemehuevi/Anishinabe
Born Kansas and lived in New York, New York, 1956–2006

Riding the One-Eyed Ford, Contact II Publications, New York, 1981

Younghee Kim-Wait (Class of 1982)/Pablo Eisenberg Collection of Native American Literature, File PS3552.U73 R5 1981

Calumet and Cross Heritage Society
Brothertown Indian (Eetamquittoowauconnuck) Heritage Society, Nonprofit, American

The Brothertown Indians: Seven Tribes, Seven Generations/2022 Historical Calendar, Created for Calumet and Cross, A Heritage Society, 2022

File E99.B7 C35 2021

Rev. Philip Canestrelli, Society of Jesus
Lived St. Ignatius Mission, Montana, 1839–1918

A Catechism of Christian Doctrine: Prepared and Enjoined by Order of the Third Plenary Council of Baltimore; Translated into Flat-head by a Father of the Society of Jesus, Woodstock College, Woodstock, Maryland, 1891

File PM2264 .C3 1891

Raven Chacon
Diné
Born 1977, Fort Defiance, Navajo Nation, Arizona and Lives in New Mexico and New York

For Zitkála-Šá, Art Metropole, Toronto, 2022

xFile E99.Y25 Z59 2022

Thomas Commuck
Narragansett
Born Rhode Island; lived in Wisconsin and New York, 1804–55

Indian Melodies, Published by G. Lane and C.B. Tippett, for the Methodist Episcopal Church, New York, 1845

Younghee Kim-Wait (Class of 1982)/Pablo Eisenberg Collection of Native American Literature, M2117.C733 I53 1845

Paul Cuffe, Jr.

Wampanoag and African descent
Born and lived in Massachusetts, 1795–1839

Narrative of the Life and Adventures of Paul Cuffe, A Pequot Indian: During Thirty Years Spent at Sea, and in Travelling in Foreign Lands, Printed by Horace N. Bill, Vernon, New York, 1839

Younghee Kim-Wait (Class of 1982)/Pablo Eisenberg Collection of Native American Literature, Vault G463 .C8465 1839

Natalie Curtis Burlin
United States, 1875–1921

Angel De Cora (Henook-Makhewe-Kelenaka), illustrator
Ho-Chunk
Born Nebraska and lived Virginia, Massachusetts, Pennsylvania, 1871–1919

The Indians' Book: An Offering by the American Indians of Indian Lore, Musical and Narrative, to Form a Record of the Songs and Legends of Their Race, Harper and Brothers, New York, 1935

E98.F6146 1935

David Cusick
Tuscarora
Born and lived New York, 1780–1831

David Cusick's Sketches of Ancient History of the Six Nations, Turner & McCollum, Lockport, New York, 1848
Third edition with illustrations

Younghee Kim-Wait (Class of 1982)/Pablo Eisenberg Collection of Native American Literature, Vault E99.I7 C87 1848

Sharon Day
Ojibwe
Born 1951 and lives in Minnesota

Pat Panagoulias

Jaune Quick-to-See Smith, illustrator

Salish-Kootenai
Born 1940, St. Ignatius, Flathead Reservation, Montana and active in New Mexico

Drink the Winds, Let the Waters Flow Free, Johnson Institute, Minneapolis, 1983

File E98.L7 D3 1983

Rosemarie Asiniiyobii DeBungie
Anishinaabe

Andrea Carlson, illustrator
Anishinaabe, descendant of the Grand Portage Band
Born 1979 and lives in Minnesota

Wiijikiiwending, Mineappolis, Wiigwaas Press, 2014

File PM845 .W44 2014

Charlotte De Clue
Osage
Born United States, 1946

Jaune Quick-to-See Smith, illustrator
Salish-Kootenai
Born 1940, St. Ignatius, Flathead Reservation, Montana and active in New Mexico

Without Warning: Poems, Strawberry Press, New York, 1985

Younghee Kim-Wait (Class of 1982)/Pablo Eisenberg Collection of Native American Literature, File PS3554.E235 W5 1985

Angel De Cora (Henook-Makhewee-Kelenaka)
Ho-Chunk
Born Nebraska and lived Virginia, Massachusetts, Pennsylvania, 1871–1919

"Gray Wolf's Daughter," *Harper's Monthly Magazine* 99, no. 594 (November 1899): 860–862

File E99.W7 H46 1899

Ella Cara Deloria
Yankton Dakota
Born South Dakota, 1889–1971

Mary Sully, illustrator of cover design
Yankton Dakota
Born South Dakota, 1896–1963

Speaking of Indians, Friendship Press, New York, 1944

Younghee Kim-Wait (Class of 1982)/Pablo Eisenberg Collection of Native American Literature, E99.T34 D45 1944

Philip J. Deloria
Dakota
Born 1959 and lives Massachusetts

Becoming Mary Sully: Toward an American Indian Abstract, University of Washington Press, 2019

Museum exhibition copy

Vine Deloria Jr.
Standing Rock Sioux
Born South Dakota, 1933–2005

Custer Died for Your Sins: An Indian Manifesto, Macmillan Publishers, New York, 1969

Younghee Kim-Wait (Class of 1982)/Pablo Eisenberg Collection of Native American Literature, E93 .D36 1969 c.1

Published by John Eliot. Translated by Job Nesuton (Massachusett), Joel Iacoomes (Wampanoag), and Caleb Cheeshateaumuck (Wampanoag). Printed by Samuel Green, Marmaduke Johnson, and Wawaus/James the Printer (Nipmuc)

Fragment of *Mamusse Wunneetupanatamwe Up-Biblum God*, Cambridge, Mass., 1663

Vault BS345.A2E41663

Louise Erdrich
Ojibwe (Turtle Mountain Band)
Born 1954 and lives in Minnesota

The Bingo Palace, Perennial, New York, 2001

PS3555.R42 B5 2001

Louise Erdrich
Ojibwe (Turtle Mountain Band)
Born 1954 and lives in Minnesota

The Last Report on the Miracles at Little No Horse, HarperCollins, New York, 2001

PS3555.R42 L37 2001

Louise Erdrich
Ojibwe (Turtle Mountain Band)
Born 1954 and lives in Minnesota

Love Medicine, Perennial, New York, 2001

PS3555.R42 L6 2001

Louise Erdrich
Ojibwe (Turtle Mountain Band)
Born 1954 and lives in Minnesota

The Beet Queen, Perennial, New York, 2001

PS3555.R42 B4 2001

Melissa Jane Fawcett (Melissa Tantaquidgeon Zobel)
Mohegan

Born 1960 and lives in Connecticut

Medicine Trail: The Life and Lessons of Gladys Tantaquidgeon, University of Arizona Press, 2000

Gift of Melissa Tantaquidgeon Zobel, E99.M83 T364 2000

James Garvie (Tatanka Kinina)
Yankton
United States, 1862–1952

Jennie W. Cox
United States

Eunice Kitto
United States

Abraham Lincoln toni kin qa Aesop tawoyake kin (Life of Abraham Lincoln and Aesop's Fables), Published by A. L. Riggs and printed by Indian pupils of Santee Normal Training School, Nebraska, 1893
Book in Dakota language, Santee dialect

File PM1024.G37 1893

Harriett Crippen Brown Gumbs
Shinnecock/Montaukett
Born Shinnecock Reservation, Long Island, New York, 1921–2020

We Hang in the Balance, Published by the author, 1956

Younghee Kim-Wait (Class of 1982)/Pablo Eisenberg Collection of Native American Literature, File E99.S38 B7 1956

Joy Harjo
Mvskoke-Creek
Born 1951 and lives in Tulsa, Oklahoma, United States

In Mad Love and War, Wesleyan University Press, Middletown, Connecticut, 1990

Younghee Kim-Wait (Class of 1982)/Pablo Eisenberg Collection of Native American Literature, PS3558.A62423 I6 1990

Asa Hitchcock, translator
Born Cortland County, New York, 1800–1849

John Preaching in the Wilderness; The Star in the East; The Ten Commandments, Pendleton's Lithography, Boston, 1836

xx File PM784.H58 S37 1836

Elizabeth James-Perry
Aquinnah Wampanoag
Born 1973 and lives in Massachusetts

MASHQ from the *Decolonized Bear Map* series, 2021
Watercolor and graphite on paper

Courtesy of the artist, now part of the collection of Frost Library's Archives and Special Collections.

Elizabeth James-Perry
Aquinnah Wampanoag
Born 1973 and lives in Massachusetts

Wampumspeak, 2023
Beaded wampum belt

Vault E98.C8 J36 2022

Rex Lee Jim
Diné
Born 1962, United States

Saad/Mazii Dinéłtsoi Áyiilaa, Published by Princeton Collections of Western Americana, Princeton, New Jersey, 1995

Younghee Kim-Wait (Class of 1982)/Pablo Eisenberg Collection of Native American Literature, File PM2009.J5 S3 1995

Rex Lee Jim, editor
Diné

Born 1962, United States

Woodrow Wilson Crumbo, illustrator
Potawatomi
United States, 1912–89

Dancing Voices: Wisdom of the American Indian, Peter Pauper Press, White Plains, New York, 1994

E98.P5 D36 1994

Lydia A. Jocelyn
United States, 1836–1912

Nathaniel J. Cuffee
Montaukett/Narragansett
United States, 1854–1912

Lords of the Soil: A Romance of Indian Life Among the Early English Settlers, C.M. Clark Publishing Co., Boston, Mass., 1905

Gift of Heid E. Erdrich, PS2859.S455 L6 1905

E. Pauline Johnson (Tekahionwake)
Mohawk
Canada, 1861–1913

Flint and Feather, Musson Book Company, Toronto, Canada, 1912

Younghee Kim-Wait (Class of 1982)/Pablo Eisenberg Collection of Native American Literature, PR9199.2.J64 F5 1912

E. Pauline Johnson (Tekahionwake)
Mohawk
Canada, 1861–1913

The White Wampum, Published simultaneously by John Lane, London; The Copp Clark Co., Toronto; Lamson, Wolffe & Co., Boston, 1895
Book with Tomahawk illustrations

Younghee Kim-Wait (Class of 1982)/Pablo Eisenberg Collection of Native American Literature, PR9199.2.J64 W55 1895

Francis La Flesche
Omaha/Ponca and French descent, Omaha, Nebraska, 1857–1932

Angel De Cora (Henook-Makhewe-Kelenaka), illustrator
Ho-Chunk
Born Nebraska and lived in Virginia, Massachusetts, Pennsylvania, 1871–1919

The Middle Five: Indian Boys at School, Small, Maynard & Company, 1900

Younghee Kim-Wait (Class of 1982)/Pablo Eisenberg Collection of Native American Literature, E99.04 L165 1900

Joseph Laurent
Wôbanakiak
Canada, 1839–1917

New Familiar Abenakis and English Dialogues: The First Ever Published on the Grammatical System, Printed by Leger Brousseau, Quebec, 1884

PM551.L3 1884 c.3

Helen Manning
Aquinnah Wampanoag
Born Gay Head, Massachusetts and lived in Washington D.C. and Massachusetts, 1919–2008

Jo-Ann Eccher
Born 1954, United States

Moshup's Footsteps: The Wampanoag Nation, Gay Head/Aquinnah; The People of First Light, Blue Cloud Across the Moon Publishing Company, Aquinnah, Massachusetts, 2001

Gift of the Aquinnah Cultural Center, File E99.W2 M35 2001

Robert McGill Loughridge
United States, 1809–1900

David McKellop Hodge

Creek and European descent, United States, 1841–1921

English and Muskokee Dictionary: Collected from Various Sources, Westminster Press, Philadelphia, 1914

PM991.Z5 L7 1914

N. Scott Momaday, editor and contributor
Kiowa
Born Lawton, Oklahoma, 1934–2024

Aleksandr Vaschenko, editor
Russia, 1933–98

"I͡A svi͡azan dobrom s zemleĭ": iz sovremennoĭ literatury indeĭt͡sev SShA: sbornik (I Am Connected with the Earth by Goodness: from Modern Literature of the American Indians), Published by Raduga (Rainbow), Moscow, 1983

Purchased from Gerald Vizenor (Chippewa, White Earth Reservation), PS525.R8 I2 1983

Samson Occom
Mohegan
Connecticut and New York, 1723–92

A Sermon: Preached at the Execution of Moses Paul, Printed and sold by Timothy Green, New London, Connecticut, 1772

Vault E98.M6 O16 1772a

Samson Occom
Mohegan
Connecticut and New York, 1723–92

Pregeth ar ddihenyddiad Moses Paul, Caernarfon, Wales, 1772
Book in Welsh language

Vault E98.M6 O16188 1827

Oronhyatekha (Peter Martin)
Mohawk

Canada, 1841–1907

"The Mohawk Language," *Canadian Journal of Industry, Science and Art*, new series no. 57 (May 1865): 182–194, Printed for the Canadian Institute by Lovell and Gibson, Toronto, 1865

Younghee Kim-Wait (Class of 1982)/Pablo Eisenberg Collection of Native American Literature, File PM1881.O76 1865

Owahyah
Canada

Birch Bark Legends of Niagara/Founded on Traditions Among the Iroquois, or Six Nations/A Story of the Lunar-Bow/or Origin of the Totem of the Wolf, Journal Printing Co., St. Catharines, Ontario, 1884

Younghee Kim-Wait (Class of 1982)/Pablo Eisenberg Collection of Native American Literature, File E99.I7 O93 1884

Père Pacifique de St. Anne de Ristigouche Church
Born France and lived in Canada, 1863–1917

Alasotmapegiatimgeoel: paroissien Micmac noté = Singing book in Micmac,
prepared by Père Pacifique, Québec, 1923

File PM1794 .A43 1923

Peter Pitseolak
Inuit
Canada, 1902–73

Ttitugágit Peter Pitseoláp (Drawings by Peter Pitseolak), Kinngait Press, Cape Dorset (now Kinngait, Nunavut, Canada), 1975

xFile E99.E7 T56 1975

Arthur Caswell Parker
Seneca and Scottish-English descent
Lived in New York, 1881–1955

Indian Episodes of New York State: A Drama-Story of the Empire State, Rochester Museum of Arts and Sciences, Rochester, N.Y., 1935

Younghee Kim-Wait (Class of 1982)/Pablo Eisenberg Collection of Native American Literature, E78.N7 P36 1935

Paula Peters
Mashpee Wampanoag
Massachusetts

Mashpee Nine: A Story of Cultural Justice, SmokeSygnals, Mashpee, Mass., 2016

Gift of Paula Peters, E99.M4 P48 2016

Simon Pokagon
Potawatomi
United States, 1830–99

Ogimawke Mitigwaki (Queen of the Woods), Published by C. H. Engle, Hartford, Michigan, 1899

Younghee Kim-Wait (Class of 1982)/Pablo Eisenberg Collection of Native American Literature, E99.P8 P65 1899 c.1

Louis Riel
Métis
Canada and United States, 1844–85

Poésies religieuses et politiques/par Louis "David" Riel, Published by the Riel family, Montreal, 1886
Archival reproductions from library copy

Younghee Kim-Wait (Class of 1982)/Pablo Eisenberg Collection of Native American Literature, PQ3919.R5 P6 1886eb

---

William Schenck Robertson
United States, 1820–81

David Winslett
United States, ca.1820–62

Mvskoke nakcokv eskerretv esvhokkolat: Creek second reader, American Tract Society, New York, 1871

PM991.Z4 R63 1871

Fritz Scholder
Luiseño
Born Breckenridge, Minnesota; active in Santa Fe, New Mexico, 1937–2005

Lithograph in *Random Thoughts and Memories*, Published by ARC Press, Scottsdale, Arizona and printed by The Stinehour Press, Lunenberg, Vermont, 1979

PS3569.C52533 R3 1979

Fritz Scholder
Luiseño
Born Breckenridge, Minnesota; active in Santa Fe, New Mexico, 1937–2005

Afternoon Nap, Published by Nazraeli Press, Munich, Germany, 1991
Illustrations folded in boards

Purchase from Heid E. Erdrich, N6537.S358 A4 1991

R. P. Sebastien
Canada

Omer Clergue
Canada

Chant national des Micmacs, Calgary, Alberta, Canada, circa 1910

File PM1794 .C43

Siobhan Senier, editor
Born 1965, United States

Dawnland Voices: An Anthology of Indigenous Writing from New England, University of Nebraska Press, 2014

PS508.I5 D38 2014

Gladys Tantaquidgeon
Mohegan
Connecticut, 1899–2005

Harold Tantaquidgeon
Mohegan
Connecticut, 1904–89

Tantaquidgeon Indian Museum in the Heart of Mohegan Country, Published by The Mohegan Tribe, Uncasville, Connecticut, circa 1970s

Gift of Heid Erdrich, E99.M83 T45

Unidentified author
Alutiiq Yup'ik

Neq'rkat: The Wild Foods Cookbook, Alutiiq Museum and Archaeological Repository, Kodiak, Alaska, 2014
Wild foods cookbook in English

File E99.E7 N457 2014

Unidentified artist
United States

Growing Corn Festival Poster, New York, New Haven, and Hartford Railroad Company, 1940

xx File E78.C7 I63 1940

Unidentified author
North America, Diné

Learning English (Bilagáana Bizaad Bíhoo'Aah), Published by Navajo Mission's Press, Farmington, New Mexico, 1960s

File PM2006 .L43

Unidentified author
Canada

Unidentified Indigenous translator or translators
Canada

Indian Child's Book: A Primer in English and Cree Languages, Unidentified publisher, 1880s
Book in English and Cree languages

PM986 .I5

Unidentified author(s)
Gitxsan of 'Ksan

Hilary Stewart, illustrator
Canada, born Saint Lucia, 1924–80

Gathering What the Great Nature Provided: Food Traditions of the Gitskan, University of Washington Press, 1980
Recipe book

Purchased from Joseph Bruchac, E99.K55 P46 1980

Unidentified author
Haudenosaunee

Ganondagan Iroquois White Corn Recipes/Friends of Ganondagan, New York, Published by Friends of Ganondagan, Victor, New York, 2015, File TX809.M2 G3 2015

Unidentified Indigenous artist
North America

Birch Bark Blank Notebook, ca.1910

E98.B53 B57 1910

Eugene Vetromile
Italy, 1819–81

Indian Good Book (Alnambay uli awikhigan) for the Benefit of the Penobscot, Passamaquoddy, St. John's, Micmac, and Other Tribes of the Abnaki Indians, Published by E. Dunigan and Brother, New York, 1857

Collection of Native American Literature, PM551.Z77 V44 1857

Eugene Vetromile
Italy, 1819–81

Of Vetromile's Noble Bible: Such As Happened Great-Truths (Vetromile wewessi ubibian) for the Benefit of the Penobscot, Passamaquoddy, St. John's, Micmac, and Other Tribes of the Abnaki Indians, Published by Rennie, Shea, and Lindsay, New York, 1860

PM551.Z77 V48 1860

Gerald Robert Vizenor
Anishinabe
Born 1934, United States

Jaune Quick-to-See Smith, illustrator
Salish-Kootenai
Born 1940, St. Ignatius, Flathead Reservation, Montana and active in New Mexico

Earthdivers: Tribal Narratives on Mixed Descent, University of Minnesota Press, 1981

Purchased from Gerald Vizenor, PS3572.I9 E2 1981

Ted Curtis Williams
Tuscarora
United States, 1930–2005

The Reservation, Syracuse University Press, 1976

Younghee Kim-Wait (Class of 1982)/Pablo Eisenberg Collection of Native American Literature, E99.T9 W54 1976

Elizabeth Woody
Diné/Warm Springs-Wasco-Yakama
Born 1959, United States

Jaune Quick-to-See Smith, illustrator
Salish-Kootenai

Born 1940, St. Ignatius, Flathead Reservation, Montana and active in New Mexico

Hand into Stone: Poems, Contact II Publications, New York City, 1988

Younghee Kim-Wait (Class of 1982)/Pablo Eisenberg Collection of Native American Literature, PS3573.O6455 H3 1988

Zitkála-Šá (Gertrude Simmons Bonin)
Yankton Dakota 1876–1938

Angel De Cora (Henook-Makhewee-Kelenaka), illustrations
Ho-Chunk
Born Nebraska and lived Virginia, Massachusetts, Pennsylvania, 1871–1919

Old Indian Legends, The Athenæum Press, Boston, 1901

Younghee Kim-Wait (Class of 1982)/Pablo Eisenberg Collection of Native American Literature, E98.F6 Z58 1901 c.1

Zitkála-Šá (Gertrude Simmons Bonin)
Yankton Dakota
United States, 1876–1938

Jane P. Hafen
Taos Pueblo
Born 1955, United States

Dreams and Thunder: Stories, Poems, and the Sun Dance Opera, University of Nebraska Press, 2001

PS3549.I89 D74 2001

Melissa (Jayne Fawcett) Tantaquidgeon Zobel
Mohegan
Born 1960, United States

The Secret Guide: Mohegan Sun, Published by Mohegan Tribal Offices, Uncasville, Connecticut, 2008

Gift of Melissa Tantaquidgeon Zobel, File E99.M83 S43 2008

Melissa (Jayne Fawcett) Tantaquidgeon Zobel
Mohegan
Born 1960, United States

The Lasting of the Mohegans: Part 1, The Story of the Wolf People, Published by The Mohegan Tribe, Uncasville, Connecticut, 1995

Gift of Melissa Tantaquidgeon Zobel, File E99.M83 F35 1995

MEAD ART MUSEUM

Justin Beatty
Ojibwe, Garden River First Nations
Born 1972, New York and lives in Massachusetts

No Colonizing, 2021; printed 2023
Digital print on metal

Courtesy of the artist, now part of the Mead Art Museum's collections, AC 2024.13

Justin Beatty
Ojibwe, Garden River First Nations
Born 1972, New York and lives in Massachusetts

No Colonizing, Anytime, 2021; printed 2023
Digital print on metal

Courtesy of the artist

George Wesley Bellows
Born Columbus, Ohio, 1882–1925

Fern Woods, 1913
Oil on board

Gift of Albert Sylvester (Class of 1956), Susan Hopwood, Amy Katoh, and Duncan Sylvester in memory of their parents, Elizabeth E. and Albert L. Sylvester (Class of 1924), AC 1986.124

Frank Weston Benson
Born Salem, Massachusetts, 1862–1951

River Drivers, 1914
Etching

Gift of Mrs. Joseph W. Fribley, AC 1958.173

Acee Blue Eagle
Creek/Pawnee
Born on the Wichita Reservation Oklahoma, 1907–59

Four Teacups (Hen-Toh - Wyandot; Geronimo - Apache; Ruling his Son - Pawnee; Bacon Rind - Osage) and Two Plates, ca.1950

Transfer printing on porcelain made in Japan

Museum purchase, AC 2022.35-38, 2023.04-5

Eric Busch
United States, 1946–2022

Oxbow from Below, 2022
Acrylic on canvas

Gift of Stephen A Rozwenc, AC 2014.89

Andrea Carlson
Anishinaabe, descendant of the Grand Portage Band
Born 1979 and lives in Minnesota

Exit, 2018

Screenprint

Purchase with the Trinkett Clark Memorial Student Acquisition Fund, AC 2020.04

Andrea Carlson
Anishinaabe, descendant of the Grand Portage Band
Born 1979 and lives in Minnesota

Gut Munching Gore Hounds, 2010
Oil, acrylic, ink, color pencil, and graphite on four sheets of heavy wove Arches Aquarelle paper

Museum Purchase, AC 2022.05.a-d

Joseph Goodhue Chandler
Born South Hadley, Massachusetts, 1813–84

The Moon as Seen February 2, 1882, at Baldwinville, Massachusetts, 1882
Oil on canvas

Gift of Mary A. C. Ware, AC P.C.1890.4

William Merritt Chase
Born Williamsburg (now Nineveh), Indiana; lived in Europe and New York, New York, 1849–1916

Landscape, ca.1890s
Oil on board

Bequest of William R. Mead (Class of 1867), AC P.1936.15

Larry Clark
Born 1943, Tulsa, Oklahoma

Untitled from the portfolio *Tulsa*, 1971, printed 1980
Gelatin silver print

Gift of Steven M. Jacobson (Class of 1953), AC 1994.4.49

Edmund C. Coates
Born England and lived in United States, 1816–71

The Connecticut River from Mount Holyoke, 1855
Oil on canvas

Museum purchase, AC 1955.674

Thomas Cole
Born England and lived in the United States, 1801–48

Daniel Boone at His Cabin at Great Osage Lake, 1826
Oil on canvas

Museum purchase, AC P.1939.7

Joseph Cornell
Born New York, 1903–72

Untitled (Hôtel de l'Étoile: Grand Hotel Fontaine), 1953–55
Mixed media

Gift of the C and B Foundation, AC 1976.65

Jeremy Dennis
Shinnecock
Born 1990 and lives in Southampton, New York

Ayeuonganit Wampum Ayimꝏup – Here, Wampum Was Made, from *On This Site* series, 2016
Archival inkjet print on matte paper

Purchase with William W. Collins (Class of 1953) Print Fund, AC 2023.37

Jeremy Dennis
Shinnecock
Born 1990 and lives in Southampton, New York

I Could Stand Here All Night, from *Rise* series, 2021
Photograph on aluminum

Purchase with William W. Collins (Class of 1953) Print Fund, AC 2023.38

Eric L. Gansworth
Onondaga
Born 1965 and raised in Tuscarora Nation, New York; lives in Buffalo, New York

A long time ago on a turtle's back, not far away..., 2023
Gouache, archival ink on Arches watercolor paper

Museum and Archives & Special Collections Purchase

Edward Hicks
Born Attleborough (now Langhorne), Pennsylvania, 1780–1849

Peaceable Kingdom, ca.1822–25
Oil on canvas

Gift of Stephen Carlton Clark, AC 1951.384

Frank Buffalo Hyde
Onondaga/Niimiipuu (Nez Perce), Beaver Clan
Born 1974, Santa Fe, New Mexico; grew up in New York, Onondaga Reservation; lives in Minnesota

I Got Rambling on My Mind, 2021–22
Acrylic on canvas

Museum purchase with Wise Fund for Fine Arts, AC 2022.08

Frank Buffalo Hyde
Onondaga/Niimiipuu (Nez Perce), Beaver Clan
Born 1974, Santa Fe, New Mexico; grew up in New York, Onondaga Reservation; lives in Minnesota

Pezervation Pony, 2022
Acrylic on canvas

Museum purchase with Wise Fund for Fine Arts, AC 2022.23

Robert Indiana
Born New Castle, Indiana, 1928–2018

Demuth American Dream, No. 5, 1980
Silkscreen

Gift of Jane P. Singer, AC 1985.69.a–e

John La Farge
Born New York City, New York, 1835–1910

Water Lily, 1872
Oil on panel

Museum purchase, 1947.123

Inuit artist, likely Povungnituk or Inukjuak community, Canada

Untitled, n.d.
Soapstone

Mead Art Museum at Amherst Collection. Found in Collection

Courtney M. Leonard
Shinnecock
Born 1980, Long Island, New York and lives in Minnesota

Collider Study #1, from *BREACH: Logbook 21*, 2021
Mixed-media, clay, acrylic on canvas

Museum purchase with Wise Fund for Fine Arts, 2022.22

Evelyn Lewis
Diné, 1921–91

Storm Pattern Blanket, ca.1950–70
Blanket in handspun wool, black and grey dye, aniline red dye

Gift of Sanborn Partridge (Class of 1936), AC 1991.12

Maggie Lincoln
Diné
United States, 1939

Ganado Rug, ca.1955
Dyed wool in black, gray, white, and red

Gift of Sanborn Partridge (Class of 1936), AC 1991.15

Richard Meach
English

Cake Server, 1768–69
Silver

Gift of Herbert L. Pratt, AC 1945.203

Joel Meyerowitz
Born 1938, New York, New York; lives in London, United Kingdom and New York

New Mexico (Indians in Street), 1972
Gelatin silver print

Gift of Stanley and Diane Person, AC 2000.441.10

Joshua Reynolds
Born Plympton, Devon, England
United Kingdom, 1723–92

Sir Jeffery Amherst, 1765
Oil on canvas

Museum purchase, AC 1967.85

Cara Romero
Chemehuevi
Born 1977, Inglewood, California; raised between Chemehuevi Reservation and Houston, Texas; lives between Santa Fe, New Mexico and Chemehuevi Reservation

Eufaula Girls, 2015
Photograph, pigment print mounted on plexiglass

Museum purchase, AC 2022.07

Cara Romero
Chemehuevi
Born 1977, Inglewood, California; raised between Chemehuevi Reservation and Houston, Texas; lives between Santa Fe, New Mexico and Chemehuevi Reservation

No Wall, 2019
Photograph, pigment print mounted on plexiglass

Museum purchase, AC 2022.06

Olga Vladimirovna Rozanova
Born Melenki, Vladimir Oblast, Russia, 1886–1918

Poem by Aleksei Kruchenykh from the portfolio *War*, 1915, published 1916
Linoleum cut printed in green on paper

Gift of Thomas P. Whitney (Class of 1937), AC
2001.56.15

Boston & Sandwich Glass Company
Founded in Sandwich, Massachusetts,
active 1826–88

Whale Oil Lamp, ca.1835
Glass

Gift of Preston R. Bassett (Class of 1913), AC 1973.41

Fritz Scholder
Luiseño
Born Breckenridge, Minnesota; active in Santa Fe, New Mexico, 1937–2005

Navajo Fetish, n.d.
Acrylic on board

Gift of Richard H. Templeton (Class of 1931), AC 1980.19

Fritz Scholder
Luiseño
Born Breckenridge, Minnesota; active in Santa Fe, New Mexico, 1937–2005

New Mexico Image, 1969
Pen and ink drawing

Gift of Richard H. Templeton (Class of 1931), AC 1981.127.b

Fritz Scholder
Luiseño
Born Breckenridge, Minnesota; active in Santa Fe, New Mexico, 1937–2005

Untitled, 1972
Lithograph

Gift of Richard H. Templeton (Class of 1931), AC 1981.126

Theresa Secord
Penobscot
Born 1958 and lives in Maine

Penobscot Sewing Basket, 2023
Ash and braided sweetgrass, cedar bark, velvet photograph

Museum purchase with William K. Allison (Class of 1920) Memorial Fund, AC 2023.03

John Sloan
Born Lock Haven, Pennsylvania, 1871–1951

Dolly Reading, 1914
Oil on canvas

Bequeath of Dr. Sanford B. Sternlieb (Class of 1946), AC 2019.22

John Sloan
Born Lock Haven, Pennsylvania, 1871–1951

She's Got the Point, 1913
Charcoal drawing

Museum purchase, AC 1954.45

Jaune Quick-to-See Smith
Salish-Kootenai
Born 1940, St. Ignatius, Flathead Reservation, Montana and active in New Mexico

Waiting for Rain, 2012
Lithograph

Museum purchase with William K. Allison (Class of 1920) Memorial Fund, AC 2022.04

Jaune Quick-to-See Smith

Salish-Kootenai
Born 1940, St. Ignatius, Flathead Reservation, Montana and active in New Mexico

Charlo #7, 1985
Pastel on paper

Museum purchase with Charles H. Morgan Fine Arts Fund, AC 2022.26

Frank Stella
Born 1936, Malden, Massachusetts

Of Whales in Paint, in Teeth, &c., 1990
Acrylic on aluminum

Gift of Steven M. Jacobson (Class of 1953), AC 1994.8

Thomas Sully
Born Horncastle, Lincolnshire, England and lived in the United States, 1783–1872

Self-Portrait, 1809
Oil on canvas

Bequest of Herbert L. Pratt (Class of 1895), AC 1945.147

Unidentified artist
Mexico, Puebla

Apothecary Jar, late 19th century
Glazed earthenware

Gift of the children of Dwight W. Morrow (Class of 1895) and Elizabeth C. Morrow, AC 1955.523.b

---

Unidentified artist
China

Cricket Cage, 19th century
Carved gourd, ivory cover

Gift of George D. Pratt, AC M.1930.5

Unidentified artist
Dutch

Delft Box, n.d.
Porcelain and silver

Gift of Miss Susan D. Bliss, AC 1958.88

Unidentified artist
Mexico, Uruapan, Michoacán

Gourd Bowl (Tecomate), late 19th century
Lacquered gourd

Gift of the children of Dwight W. Morrow (Class of 1895) and Elizabeth C. Morrow, AC 1955.637

Indigenous artist
Mexico, Uruapan, Michoacán

Gourd Bowl with Lid (Jicara), late 19th century
Lacquered gourd

Gift of the children of Dwight W. Morrow (Class of 1895) and Elizabeth C. Morrow, AC 1955.634

Unidentified artist
France

Ivory and Brass Whistle, ca.18th century
Engraved ivory with metal key loop

Gift of Miss Susan D. Bliss, AC 1958.113

Indigenous artist
Inuit

Ivory Bracelet, n.d.
Ivory

Gift of the children of Dwight W. Morrow (Class of 1895) and Elizabeth C. Morrow, AC 1955.548

Unidentified artist
Mesopotamian (Babylonian), Third Dynasty of Ur

Model Nail with Cuneiform Inscription, ca.2400 BCE
Baked clay

Gift of Calvin K. Arter, AC 1961.60

Unidentified artist
China

Pewter Preserve Box, 19th c.
Pewter

Gift of Mrs. Richard A. Robinson III, AC 1955.196.a,b

Indigenous artist
Pre-Columbian, Peru

Small Carved Ear of Maize, 1000–1500 CE
Carved stone

Museum purchase, President Charles Cole Collection, AC 1975.25

Unidentified artist
British, produced in the factory of Thomas Whieldon (1719–95)

Teapot, ca.1765
Glazed earthenware

Gift of Mrs. Winifred Arms (wife of Robert Arms, Class of 1927), AC 1984.128

Unidentified artist

Thomas Sully, ca.1845
Daguerreotype

Gift of William Macbeth Gallery, AC 1990.18

Pieter Gerritsz van Roestraten (attributed to)
Born Haarlem, North Holland, 1630–98

Still Life, ca.17th century
Oil on canvas

Museum purchase, AC 1976.12

Ai Weiwei
Born 1975, Beijing, China and lives in Portugal

Sunflower Seeds, 2020
Print on mask, made in Berlin, Germany

Museum purchase with Charles H. Morgan Fine Arts Fund, AC 2020.07.5

Dyani White Hawk
Sicangu Lakota, German and Welsh ancestry
Born 1976, Madison, Wisconsin and lives in Minneapolis, Minnesota

Wačháŋtognaka (Nurture) from the *Takes Care of Them* suite, 2019
Screenprint with metal foil

Museum purchase with Trinkett Clark Memorial Student Acquisition Fund, AC 2020.05

Dyani White Hawk
Sicangu Lakota, German and Welsh ancestry,
Born 1976, Madison, Wisconsin and lives in Minneapolis, Minnesota

Nakíčižiŋ (Protect) from the *Takes Care of Them* suite, 2019
Screenprint with metal foil

Museum purchase with Trinkett Clark Memorial Student Acquisition Fund, AC 2020.06

Marion Post Wolcott
Born Montclair, New Jersey, 1910–90

Making Biscuits, Cornhusking Day, Tallyho, North Carolina, 1939
Gelatin silver print

Bequest of Richard Templeton (Class of 1931), AC 1989.15

LOANS

Tacey M. Atsitty
Diné
Born 1977, Utah

Rain Scald, University of New Mexico Press, 2018

Museum exhibition copy

Justin Beatty
Ojibwe, Garden River First Nations
Born 1972, New York and lives in Massachusetts

We Are Still Here, 2020; printed 2023
Digital print on canvas

Courtesy of the artist

Natalie Curtis Burlin
Born New York, New York 1875–1921

Angel De Cora (Henook-Makhewe-Kelenaka), illustrator
Ho-Chunk
Born Nebraska and lived Virginia, Massachusetts, Pennsylvania, 1871–1919

The Indians' Book: An Offering by the American Indians of Indian Lore, Musical and Narrative, to Form a Record of the Songs and Legends of Their Race, 1907, Reprinted by Bonanza Books, New York, 1987

Courtesy of Heid E. Erdrich

Brent Michael Davids
Mohican/Munsee-Lenape
Born 1959, Madison, Wisconsin

The Last of James Fenimore Cooper, 2001

Courtesy of the artist

Vine Deloria Jr.
Standing Rock Sioux
Born Martin, South Dakota, near the Pine Ridge Indian Reservation, 1933–2005

C.G. Jung and the Sioux Traditions: Dreams, Visions, Nature, and the Primitive, Fulcrum Publishing, Wheat Ridge, CO, 2022

Courtesy of Heid E. Erdrich

Jeremy Dennis
Shinnecock
Born 1990 and lives in Southampton, New York

Circassian Shipwreck, from *On This Site* series, 2016
Archival inkjet print on matte paper

Courtesy of the artist

Jeremy Dennis
Shinnecock
Born 1990 and lives in Southampton, New York

On This Site, 2017

Courtesy of Lisa Crossman

Heid E. Erdrich
Ojibwe (Turtle Mountain Band)
Born 1963 and lives in Minnesota

Eric L. Gansworth, illustrator
Onondaga

Born 1965 and raised in Tuscarora Nation, New York; lives in Buffalo, New York

Native Poets, June 2018, Poetry Foundation, Poetry Magazine, 2018

Courtesy of Heid E. Erdrich

Eric L. Gansworth
Onondaga
Born 1965 and raised in Tuscarora Nation, New York; lives in Buffalo, New York

Half-Life of Cardiopulmonary Function, Syracuse University Press, 2008

Courtesy of Lisa Crossman

James Greenfield, attributed to
American, active 1775–77

Powder Horn: Nathaniel Sunsimon, February 24, 1777
Armament horn, maple wood, iron, brown stain

Courtesy of Historic Deerfield, William H. Guthman Collection of American Engraved Powder Horns of Historic Deerfield Museum, HD 2005.20.60

Sierra Henries
Chaubunagungamaug Nipmuc
Born 1987, Providence, Rhode Island; lives in Maine

Pathways, 2023
Pyrography on birch bark, shell, synthetic sinew

Courtesy of the artist

Sky Hopinka
Ho-Chunk, descendent of Pechanga Luiseño
Born Ferndale, Washington, 1984; lives in New York

Here you are before the trees, 2020
HD video, stereo, color, 3-channel, synchronous loop

Courtesy of the artist and Broadway Gallery

Elizabeth James-Perry
Aquinnah Wampanoag
Born 1973 and lives in Massachusetts

At Waters Edge, 2022
Necklace in wampum, milkweed plant, logwood dye, glass trade beads, sterling silver

Courtesy of the artist

Jonathan James-Perry
Aquinnah Wampanoag
Born 1976, Massachusetts; lives in Rhode Island

Paddle 1 — Where We Come From, 2023
White ash, stain of black walnut and red ochre

Courtesy of the artist

Jonathan James-Perry
Aquinnah Wampanoag
Born 1976, Massachusetts and lives in Rhode Island

Paddle 2 — Where We Are, 2023
White ash

Courtesy of the artist

Courtney M. Leonard
Shinnecock
Born 1980, Long Island, New York and lives in Minnesota

BREACH #2, from *BREACH: Logbook 21*, 2016–21
Ceramic on wood pallet

Courtesy of Mount Holyoke College Art Museum, Purchased with the Jean C. Harris Art Acquisition Fund, MH 2021.12

Sandra Matthews, photography
American
Born 1951 and lives in Massachusetts

David Brule, texts
Nehantic and Huron/Wendat descent
Born 1946 and lives in Massachusetts

Suzanne Gardinier, texts
American, born 1961

Occupying Massachusetts: Layers of History on Indigenous Land, Published by George F. Thompson Publishing in association with the Center for the Study of Place, Staunton, Virginia, 2022

Museum exhibition copy

Bernd C. Peyer
Born 1946, Austria, Switzerland

American Indian Nonfiction: An Anthology of Writings, 1760s–1930s, University of Oklahoma Press, 2007

Courtesy of Heid E. Erdrich

Mary Sully
Yankton Dakota
Born on the Standing Rock Reservation, United States, 1896–1963

Dog with Blue Blanket, ca.1940s–1950s
Drawing

Courtesy of the Mary Sully Foundation

Mary Sully
Yankton Dakota
Born on the Standing Rock Reservation, United States, 1896–1963

Dog with Headdress, ca.1940s–1950s
Drawing

Courtesy of the Mary Sully Foundation

Mary Sully
Yankton Dakota
Born on the Standing Rock Reservation, United States, 1896–1963

John Philip Sousa, n.d.
Triptych, colored pencil and ink on paper

Courtesy of the Mary Sully Foundation

Unidentified artist
United States

Hepsibeth Bowman/Crosman Hemenway, ca. 1840s
Oil on canvas

Courtesy of the Collection of Worcester Historical Museum, Gift of Frederick F. Hopkins

---

Brittney Peauwe Wunnepog Walley
Nipmuc
Born 1991 and lives in Massachusetts

Different Footprints (continued), 2023
Hemp fiber cordage

Courtesy of the artist

Brittney Peauwe Wunnepog Walley
Nipmuc
Born 1991 and lives in Massachusetts

3-Tier Statement Earrings, 2022
Hemp fiber cordage earrings

Courtesy of the artist

Marie Watt
Born 1967, Seattle, Washington and lives in Portland, Oregon

Companion Species (Fortress), 2017
Reclaimed wool blankets, thread, embroidery floss

Courtesy of the Smith College Museum of Art, Museum purchase with the Dorothy C. Millery (Class of 1925) Fund, SC 2018.6

Checklist, Part II

February 27–July 7, 2024

AMHERST COLLEGE ARCHIVES AND SPECIAL COLLECTIONS, COLLECTION OF NATIVE AMERICAN LITERATURE

William Apess, author and publisher
Pequot/Mashpee
Born Massachusetts, 1798–1839

A Son of the Forest: the Experience of William Apes, a Native of the Forest, New York, 1831

Younghee Kim-Wait (Class of 1982)/Pablo Eisenberg Collection of Native American Literature, E90.A5 A5 1831 c.1

William Apess, author and publisher
Pequot/Mashpee
Born Massachusetts, 1798–1839

A Son of the Forest: the Experience of William Apes, a Native of the Forest,
New York, 1831

Gift of Peter Webb (Class of 1974)
E90.A5 A5 1831 c.4

William Apess, author and publisher
Pequot/Mashpee
Born Massachusetts, 1798–1839

A Son of the Forest: the Experience of William Apes, a Native of the Forest: Comprising a Notice of the Pequod Tribe of Indians, New York, 1829

Younghee Kim-Wait (Class of 1982)/Pablo Eisenberg Collection of Native American Literature, E90.A5 A5 1829 c.

Noël Bennett
Born 1939, United States

Tiana Bighorse
Diné (Navajo)
Born Coconino, Arizona, 1917–2003

Robert Jacobson, illustrator

Working with the Wool: How to Weave a Navajo Rug, 7th printing, Flagstaff, Arizona, Northland Press, 1977

Younghee Kim-Wait (Class of 1982)/Pablo Eisenberg Collection of Native American Literature, E99.N3 B49

Abbé Charles-Étienne Brasseur de Bourbourg
Born Bourbourg, France, 1814–74

Gramatica de la lengua quiche = Grammaire de la langue quichée
Paris: Arthus Bertrand, 1862

Amherst College Archives and Special Collections
Collection of Native American Literature
PM4231 .B7 1862

Cherokee Syllabary Type
Swamp Press in 2018

Thomas Commuck
Narragansett
Born Rhode Island; lived in Wisconsin and New York, 1804–55

Indian Melodies, Published by G. Lane and C.B. Tippett, for the Methodist Episcopal Church, New York, 1845
Reproductions

Younghee Kim-Wait (Class of 1982)/Pablo Eisenberg Collection of Native American Literature, M2117.C733 I53 1845

Convergencia Grafica MALLA with the Justseeds Artists' Cooperative

La autonomía es la vida, la sumisión es la muerte, 2014
Silkscreened box with 19 silkscreen and woodcut images with a hand-printed scarf

Published by Ejército Zapatista de Liberación Nacional (EZLN), Escuela de Cultura Popular Mártires del 68, Mexico City, Mexico

xxN7433.35.M4 A98 2014

Nathaniel J. Cuffee
Montaukett/Narragansett
United States, 1854–1912

Lydia A. Jocelyn
United States, 1836–1912

Lords of the Soil; A Romance of Indian Life Among the Early English Settlers, C.M. Clark Publishing Co., Boston, Mass., 1905

PS2859.S455 L6 1905

Paul Cuffe, Jr.
Wampanoag and African descent
Born Bristol, Massachusetts, 1795–1839
Reproduction

Narrative of the Life and Adventures of Paul Cuffe, A Pequot Indian: During Thirty Years Spent at Sea, and in Travelling in Foreign Lands, Printed by Horace N. Bill, Vernon, New York, 1839

Younghee Kim-Wait (Class of 1982)/Pablo Eisenberg Collection of Native American Literature, Vault G463.C8465 1839

Carol A. Dana
Penobscot
United States

Margo Lukens
United States

Conor M. Quinn
United States

"Still They Remember Me" = "Eskwa·tte nəmihkawitəhaməkok kohsəssənawak,"
Amherst, Mass., University of Massachusetts Press, 2021

E99.P5 D36 2021

Demian DinéYazhi', artist
Diné
Born Gallup 1983, New Mexico and live in Portland, Oregon

This land: is not your land was not your land will never be your land
R.I.S.E. (Radical Indigenous Survivance & Empowerment), Portland, OR, 2020

xxFile G3300 1797 .D56 2020

Jess X. Chen, author
Chinese-American
Born 1992; and lives between New York, New York and Seattle, Washington

Demian DinéYazhi', author, publisher
Diné
Born Gallup 1983, New Mexico and live in Portland, Oregon

Solastalgia: A Queer Eco-Feminist Poetry Tour, Albuquerque, New Mexico, 2016
File PS3604.I474 S64 2016

The Española Hospital Auxiliary Cookbook Committee

Española Valley Cookbook: Recipes from Three Cultures Spanish, Anglo, Indian
Española, New Mexico, 1975

File E99.P9 E76 1975

Frank G. Speck
Born Brooklyn, New York, 1881–1950

Fidelia Fielding
Mohegan
Born Montville, Connecticut, 1827–1908

Native Tribes and Dialects of Connecticut: A Mohegan-Pequot Diary,
published in the 43rd Annual Report of the Bureau of American Ethnology (Smithsonian Institution), 1926

Younghee Kim-Wait (Class of 1982)/Pablo Eisenberg Collection of Native American Literature, xE51.U55 43rd (1925–26)

Della Frank, author
Diné

Roberta D. Joe, author
Diné

David Chethlahe Paladin, illustrator
Diné
1926–84

Storm Pattern: Poems from Two Navajo Women

Tsaile, Arizona: Navajo Community College Press 1993

PS591.I55 F73 1993

Nonabah Gorman Bryan
Diné (Navajo)
Born San Juan County, New Mexico, 1887–1942

Charles Keetsie Shirley, illustrator
Diné (Navajo)
Born Apache, Arizona, 1906–70

Navajo Native Dyes: Their Preparation and Use, Bureau of Indian Affairs, Branch of Education, Washington, D.C., 1940

Younghee Kim-Wait (Class of 1982)/Pablo Eisenberg Collection of Native American Literature, File E99.N3 N29 1940

Asa Hitchcock, translator
Born Cortland County, New York, 1800–1849

John Preaching in the Wilderness; The Star in the East; The Ten Commandments, Pendleton's Lithography, Boston, 1836

Collection of Native American Literature
xx File PM784.H58 S37 1836

Ebenezer W. Peirce, author
Born Assonet, Massachusetts, 1822–1902

Zerviah Gould Mitchell, publisher
Wampanoag
Born Abington, Massachusetts, 1807–98

Indian History, Biography and Genealogy: Pertaining to the Good Sachem Massasoit of the Wampanoag Tribe, and His Descendants; with an appendix
North Abington, Mass., 1878

Younghee Kim-Wait (Class of 1982)/Pablo Eisenberg Collection of Native American Literature, E78.N5 P45 1878

Carol M. Kimball, editor
United States, 1916–2010

Mary Virginia Goodman, columnist
Mohegan, 1897–1988

Noank Notes: Newspaper Columns of Mary Virginia Goodman, Groton, CT: Groton Public Library and Information Center, 1990

Gift of Melissa Tantaquidgeon Zobel
F104.N79 G66 1990

Elizabeth James-Perry
Aquinnah Wampanoag
Born 1973 and lives in Massachusetts

Wampumpeak, Apponeganset (Dartmouth), Massachusetts, 2022
Wampum, milkweed fiber, copper dye

Vault E98.C8 J36 2022

Laura J. Murray, editor
Born 1965
United States

Joseph Johnson, author
Mohegan
Born Connecticut, 1751–76

To Do Good to My Indian Brethren: The Writings of Joseph Johnson, Jr. 1751–1776, Amherst, Mass University of Massachusetts Press, 1998

Gift of Neal Salisbury, E99.M83 J657 1998

Amber McCrary, editor, publisher
Diné (Navajo)
Originally from Shonto, Arizona; raised in Flagstaff, Arizona

Sierra Edd, artist
Diné (Navajo)
Raised in Durango, Colorado

Plants & Animals of Diné Bikéyah Coloring Book, Abalone Mountain Press, Occupied Akimel O'odham land (Phoenix, Arizona), 2021

File E99.N3 P54 2021 c.1

Traci Sorrel
Cherokee
Born 1972 and raised in the Cherokee Nation, Oklahoma; lives in Oklahoma and Southern California

Frané Lessac (illustrator)
Born 1954, Jersey City, New Jersey; lived in Caribbean Island of Montserrat, United Kingdom, and later moved to Australia

We Are Still Here! Native American Truths Everyone Should Know, Charlesbridge, Watertown, Massachusetts, 2021

E77.4 .S625 2021

Gladys Tantaquidgeon
Mohegan
Born Mohegan Hill, Uncasville, Connecticut, 1899–2005

Folk Medicine of the Delaware and Related Algonkian Indians, Pennsylvania Historical and Museum Commission, Harrisburg, Pennsylvania, 1972

Younghee Kim-Wait (Class of 1982)/Pablo Eisenberg, Collection of Native American Literature, E99.D2 T2 1972

Tekaronianekon (Jake Swamp) orator
Wolf Clan Mohawk
1940–2010

Kahionhes (John Fadden), illustrator
Turtle Clan Mohawk
Born Massena, New York, 1938–2022

John Stokes, translator, English edition
Born 1952

Kanawahienton (David Benedict), translator, English and Mohawk
Turtle Clan Mohawk

Rokwaho (Dan Thompson) Mohawk version
Wolf Clan Mohawk
Born 1953

Thanksgiving Address: Greetings to the Natural World Ohén:ton Karihwatéhkwen: words before all else,
Six Nations Indian Museum, Onchiota, New York, and The Tracking Project, Corrales, New Mexico. English 1993, French 2004, Hawaiian 2010, Italian 2013, Japanese undetermined.

E99.I7 T582

Brian D. Tripp
Karuk
Born Eureka, California, 1945–2022

22 Million Beers Powered by the Sun, 2023 (published posthumously)
(book design by Marshall Weber, binding by Sophia Kramer)
Acrylic, collage, ink, marker pen, pencil, toner print

xN7433.4.T77 T84 2023

Brian D. Tripp
Karuk
Born Eureka, California, 1945–2022

The Best Things in Life Aren't Free, 2021
Acrylic, foil, ink, marker pen, photography, stones

xN7433.4.T77 B47 2021

Brian D. Tripp
Karuk
Born Eureka, California, 1945–2022

You Should See My House, 2022
Ink, marker, pen

N7433.4.T77 Y68

Brian D. Tripp
Karuk
Born Eureka, California, 1945–2022

It's in the Book, 2021
Collage, hand-painting, ink, cloth case

N7433.4.T77 I88 2021

Brian D. Tripp
Karuk
Born Eureka, California, 1945–2022

Talking His Talk, 2022
(updated by artist)
Hand-sewn, Acrylic, paint, colored pencil, ink, marker pen, pencil plexiglass

File N7433.4.T77 T34 2022

Brian D. Tripp
Karuk
Born Eureka, California, 1945–2022

Like Fire, 2018
Hand painting, ink, cloth case

N7433.4.T77 L5 2018

Published by John Eliot. Translated by Job Nesuton (Massachusett), Joel Iacoomes (Wampanoag), and Caleb Cheeshateaumuck (Wampanoag). Printed by Samuel Green, Marmaduke Johnson, and Wawaus/James the Printer (Nipmuc)
Massachusetts

Fragment of Mamusse Wunneetupanatamwe Up-Biblum God, Cambridge, Mass., 1663

Vault BS345.A2 E4 1663

MEAD ART MUSEUM

Kaya Agari
Kurâ people
Born 1986, Cuiabá, in the Brazilian state of Mato Grosso, Brazil

Grafismo masculino—Pintura de Kahuli—Gafanhoto, 2021
Acrylic on canvas

The Scott H. Nagle (Class of 1985) Fund for Contemporary Art Acquisitions
2023.40

Kaya Agari
Kurâ people
Born 1986, Cuiabá, in the Brazilian state of Mato Grosso, Brazil

Grafismo feminino—Menxú, 2021
Acrylic on canvas

The Scott H. Nagle (Class of 1985) Fund for Contemporary Art Acquisitions
2023.39

Justin Beatty
Ojibwe, Garden River First Nations
Born, 1972 New York and lives in Massachusetts

No Colonizing, 2021; printed 2023
Digital print on metal

Courtesy of the artist, now part of the Mead Art Museum's collection, AC 2024.13

Justin Beatty
Ojibwe, Garden River First Nations
Born 1972, New York and lives in Massachusetts

No Colonizing, Anytime, 2021; printed 2023
Digital print on metal

Courtesy of the artist, now part of the collection of the Mead Art Museum's collection, AC 2024.14

Albert Bierstadt
Born Rhine Province, Prussia; lived in the United States and Prussia, 1830–1902

Boston Harbor at Night, ca.1850
Oil on canvas

Bequest of Judge Daniel Beecher (Class of 1907) and Mrs. Daniel (Genevieve Thompson) Beecher, 1955.123

Acee Blue Eagle
Creek/Pawnee
Born on the Wichita Reservation Oklahoma, 1907–59

Dinner Plate: Sequoyah – Cherokee, ca.1950
Tea Cup: Geronimo – Apache, ca.1950

Transfer printing on porcelain made in Japan

Museum purchase
2023.04
2022.37

Andrea Carlson
Anishinaabe, descendant of the Grand Portage Band
Born 1979 and lives in Minnesota

Gut Munching Gore Hounds, 2010
Oil, acrylic, ink, color pencil, and graphite on 4 sheets of heavy wove Arches Aquarelle paper

Museum Purchase, AC 2022.05.a–d

Enrique Chagoya
Born 1953, Mexico City, Mexico; lives in Mexico and United States

Illegal Alien's Guide to Somewhere Over the Rainbow, 2010
Color lithograph with chine collé on hand-made Amate paper

Purchase, Trinkett Clark Memorial Student Acquisition Fund
2019.01

Jeremy Dennis
Shinnecock
Born 1990 and lives in Southampton, New York

I Could Stand Here All Night, from *Rise* series, 2021
Photograph on aluminum

Purchase with William W. Collins (Class of 1953) Print Fund, AC 2023.38

Frank Buffalo Hyde
Onondaga/Niimiipuu (Nez Perce), Beaver Clan
Born 1974, Santa Fe, New Mexico; grew up in New York, Onondaga Reservation; lives in Minnesota

I Got Rambling on My Mind, 2021–22
Acrylic on canvas

Museum purchase with Wise Fund for Fine Arts
2022.08

Elizabeth James-Perry
Aquinnah Wampanoag
Born 1973 and lives in Massachusetts
Resilience, 2022
Quahog shell wampum beads, milkweed fiber, silver

Purchase with William K. Allison (Class of 1920) Memorial Fund
2022.39

Courtney M. Leonard
Shinnecock
Born 1980, Long Island, New York and lives in Minnesota

Collider Study #1, from *BREACH: Logbook 21*, 2021
Mixed-media, clay, acrylic on canvas

Museum purchase with Wise Fund for Fine Arts
2022.22

Evelyn Lewis
Diné
United States, 20th century

Storm Pattern Blanket, ca.1950–70
Handspun wool; black and gray dye; aniline red dye

Gift of Sanborn Partridge (Class of 1936); Mead Art Museum at Amherst College
1991.12

Maggie Lincoln
Diné
Born 1939, United States

Ganado Rug, ca.1955
Wool; black, gray, white, and red dye

Gift of Sanborn Partridge (Class of 1936); Mead Art Museum at Amherst College
1991.15

Boston & Sandwich Glass Company
Founded in Sandwich, Massachusetts, active 1826–88

Whale Oil Lamp, ca.1835
Glass

Gift of Preston R. Bassett (Class of 1913)
1973.41

Theresa Secord
Penobscot
Born 1958 and lives in Maine

Penobscot Sewing Basket, 2023
Ash and braided sweetgrass, cedar bark, velvet photograph

Museum purchase with William K. Allison (Class of 1920) Memorial Fund
2023.03

Naine Terena
Terena people
Born 1980, Curitiba, Brazil

I am a Tree 1, image 2022, printed 2023
Archival inkjet print on matte paper

The Scott H. Nagle (Class of 1985) Fund for Contemporary Art Acquisitions
2023.43

Naine Terena
Terena people
Born 1980, Curitiba, Brazil

I am a Tree 1, image 2022, printed 2023

Archival inkjet print on matte paper

The Scott H. Nagle (Class of 1985) Fund for Contemporary Art Acquisitions
2023.44

Indigenous artist
Pre-Columbian, Peru

Small Carved Ear of Maize, 1000–1500 CE
Carved stone

Museum purchase, President Charles Cole Collection
1975.25

Unidentified artist
Mesopotamia (Babylonia), Third Dynasty of Ur

Model Nail with Cuneiform Inscription, ca.2400 BCE
Baked clay

Gift of Calvin K. Arter
1961.60

Unidentified artist(s)
Mesopotamia, Assyrian Period

Relief of winged, human-headed Apkallu [Genie] from the Palace of Ashurnasirpal II, 883–859 BCE
Alabaster

Relief representing King Ashurnasirpal II from Room H in the Palace of Ashurnasirpal II, 883–859 BCE
Alabaster

Relief of winged, human-headed Apkallu [Genie] from the Palace of Ashurnasirpal II, 883–859 BCE
Alabaster

Gift of Henry John Lobdell (Class of 1849)
S.1855.4, 2, 6

Judy Napangardi Watson
Walpiri people
Born Mount Doreen Station, Northern Territory, Australia, ca.1925–2016

Yunkaranyi Jukurrpa [Honey Ant Dreaming], ca.1994
Acrylic on canvas

Gift of Diane Wright, P'87 G'22
2023.54

Maggie Napangardi Watson
Walpiri people
Born Yuendumu in the Tanami Desert, Northern Territory, Australia, ca.1920–2004

Ngalyipi Jukurrpa [Snake Vine Dreaming], ca.1992
Acrylic on canvas

Gift of Diane Wright, P'87 G'22
2023.52

LOANS

Kohar Avakian
Nipmuc, Black, Armenian
Born 1995, Worcester, Massachusetts and lives in Connecticut

U.S. Deaths Near an Incalculable Loss, 2022
Digital collage

Courtesy of the artist

Kohar Avakian
Nipmuc, Black, Armenian
Born 1995, Worcester, Massachusetts and lives in Connecticut

Land Acknowledgment: Hammonasset, 2022
Photograph

Courtesy of the artist

Justin Beatty
Ojibwe, Garden River First Nations
Born 1972, New York and lives in Massachusetts

We Are Still Here, 2020; printed 2023
Digital print on canvas

Courtesy of the artist

Raven Chacon
Diné
Born 1977, Fort Defiance, Navajo Nation, Arizona and lives in New Mexico and New York

For Zitkála-Šá, Art Metropole, Toronto, 2022
Museum exhibition copy

Jeremy Dennis
Shinnecock
Born 1990 and lives in Southampton, New York

On This Site: Native Long Island, 2023
Second edition

Museum exhibition copy

Sierra Henries
Chaubunagungamaug Nipmuc
Born 1987, Providence, Rhode Island and lives in Maine

Pathways, 2023
Pyrography on birch bark, shell, synthetic sinew

Courtesy of the artist

Elizabeth James-Perry
Aquinnah Wampanoag
Born 1973 and lives in Massachusetts

Wild Rice, 2012
Soft Fiber Round basket, patterned twine technique; Organic Hand-spun hemp, black walnut dye

Courtesy of the artist

Elizabeth James-Perry
Aquinnah Wampanoag
Born 1973 and lives in Massachusetts

At Waters Edge, 2022
Necklace in wampum, milkweed plant,
logwood dye, glass trade beads, sterling silver

Courtesy of the artist

Jonathan James-Perry
Aquinnah Wampanoag
Born 1976, Massachusetts and lives in Rhode Island

Paddle 1—Where We Come From, 2023
White ash, stain of black walnut and red ochre

Courtesy of the artist

Jonathan James-Perry
Aquinnah Wampanoag
Born 1976, Massachusetts and lives in Rhode Island

Paddle 2—Where We Are, 2023
White ash

Courtesy of the artist

George Morrison
Ojibwe, Grand Portage Band
Born on the Grand Portage Indian Reservation, Minnesota, 1919–2000

Untitled, 1962
Oil on canvas

Courtesy of the University Museum of Contemporary Art at UMass Amherst, Gift of Mr. and Mrs. Leonard Bocour, UM 1964.14

Brittney Peauwe Wunnepog Walley
Nipmuc
Born 1991 and lives in Massachusetts

Different Footprints (continued), 2023
Hemp fiber cordage

Courtesy of the artist

Unidentified artist
United States

Hepsibeth Bowman/Crosman Hemenway, ca. 1840s
Oil on canvas

Courtesy of the Collection of Worcester Historical Museum, Gift of Frederick F. Hopkins